Research Methods in Information Technology and Information Systems

Research Methods in Information Technology and Information Systems aims to equip researchers with the knowledge needed for navigating the complex dynamics of research methods specifically tailored to the Information Systems domain.

The influence of digital technologies, innovation, and novel processes, coupled with the exponential growth of data, has reshaped the way researchers approach their inquiries and investigations in this field. In this digital era, the traditional boundaries of research methodologies are constantly being redefined, necessitating an exploration of innovative research in IS. This book explores how digital transformation is revolutionizing the research landscape, offering a comprehensive examination of the evolving methodologies and techniques that researchers must adapt to produce high-quality research in the IS field. From data collection and analysis to experimental design and qualitative inquiry, each chapter provides invaluable insights into the unique challenges and opportunities faced by researchers in IS and will prove useful for both students using quantitative and qualitative research in the digital sphere and researchers alike.

Designed to equip students with the skills needed to develop, execute, and analyze research projects, this book serves as an indispensable resource in academic settings. However, its practical insights and thorough coverage of contemporary research techniques also make it a valuable tool for IT practitioners seeking to enhance their knowledge base and refine their investigative skills. Additionally, educators will find this book to be a beneficial reference for staying updated with the latest research methodologies and trends in IT, facilitating their own professional development and improving their teaching practices.

Karim Feroz is an Assistant Professor of MIS at the J. Whitney Bunting College of Business & Technology, Georgia College and State University in the United States. He is a research scientist with expertise in information systems, digital transformation, information security, and data analytics.

Kembley Lingelbach is an Associate Professor in the Department of Information Technology at Middle Georgia State University, USA. She is an accomplished academic and cybersecurity expert with a wealth of experience spanning over three decades.

Research Methods in Information Technology and Information Systems

Karim Feroz and Kembley Lingelbach

Routledge
Taylor & Francis Group
LONDON AND NEW YORK

Designed cover image: Getty Images

First published 2026
by Routledge
4 Park Square, Milton Park, Abingdon, Oxon OX14 4RN

and by Routledge
605 Third Avenue, New York, NY 10158

Routledge is an imprint of the Taylor & Francis Group, an informa business

British Library Cataloguing-in-Publication Data
A catalogue record for this book is available from the British Library

ISBN: 978-1-032-89958-9 (hbk)
ISBN: 978-1-032-89957-2 (pbk)
ISBN: 978-1-003-54552-1 (ebk)

DOI: 10.4324/9781003545521

Typeset in Optima
by KnowledgeWorks Global Ltd.

Contents

Preface

Today is the age of digital transformation. In an era such as this, marked by rapid technological advancement, the landscape of research in information technology and information systems has evolved profoundly. As scholars and practitioners, we are witnessing a growing demand for methodological rigor, adaptability, and innovation in how research is conducted, analyzed, and disseminated in these domains. This book, *Research Methods in Information Technology and Information Systems*, is a response to that demand. It is a comprehensive resource designed to guide current and aspiring researchers through the diverse and dynamic world of IT and IS research methodologies.

We wrote this book because we've been there ourselves as students and novice researchers, facing a complex and often confusing world of research methods in IT and IS where technological change is constant and the rules seem to evolve just as quickly. Over the years, as professors, researchers, and professionals in the field, we've seen firsthand how challenging it can be for students and early-career scholars to navigate this landscape. Our motivation was simple: to create a practical, accessible, and up-to-date guide that speaks directly to the needs of those just starting their research journey or looking to strengthen it.

The digital age has reshaped how we ask questions, collect data, and interpret results. Emerging technologies like AI, cloud computing, mobile apps, and analytics aren't just subjects of research, and they're transforming the research process itself. We felt there was a real need for a book that reflects this reality. One that doesn't just list methods, but connects them to real-world challenges in IT and IS. One that helps students understand not only what to do, but why, when, and how to do it. And most importantly, one that bridges theory with practice.

The book is divided into two main sections. The first section (Chapters 1–6), authored by Dr. Karim Feroz, focuses on quantitative research methods. It begins by situating research within the broader context of digital transformation, highlighting how emerging technologies are reshaping both the objects of study and the tools used for inquiry. The six chapters in this section systematically cover the foundations and advanced techniques of quantitative research: from designing surveys and conducting longitudinal studies to analyzing complex datasets and navigating the publication process. With special emphasis on tools, strategies, and contemporary challenges, this section provides a robust foundation for conducting impactful quantitative research in IT and IS.

The second section (Chapters 7–12), authored by Dr. Kem Lingelbach, explores qualitative research methods and their growing significance in the study of socio-technical systems. Through six richly detailed chapters, it addresses a wide range of qualitative approaches, including grounded theory, interview studies, content analysis, and focus groups, while also exploring the influence of digital technologies on research practices. This section emphasizes the philosophical underpinnings of qualitative research, offers guidance on data collection and analysis, and discusses strategies for publishing qualitative work in high-impact journals. It also considers emerging frontiers such as digital ethnography, AI-enabled qualitative analysis, and virtual reality applications in research.

Throughout the book, you'll find practice labs designed to help you apply what you've learned. These labs aren't just academic exercises; they're hands-on scenarios that bring the material to life. Whether you're designing a survey, analyzing case study data, or choosing a method for your thesis, these labs will help you build confidence and develop practical research skills. We've written this book with you, the graduate student, the novice researcher, the curious learner, in mind. Our goal is to make research feel less intimidating and more empowering. Research doesn't have to be overwhelming. With the right tools, guidance, and mindset, it can be a rewarding and even exciting part of your academic and professional growth.

We extend our sincere gratitude to our colleagues, students, and professional communities whose insights, feedback, and encouragement have shaped the development of this book. We also acknowledge the growing community of interdisciplinary researchers who continuously push the boundaries of what IT and IS research can achieve in a digital world.

Dr. Karim Feroz
Dr. Kem Lingelbach
June 2025

Section I

Quantitative Research in Information Technology and IS

1 Research Methods and Digital Transformation

Chapter Objectives

After reading this chapter, readers should understand:

- What Is Research
- Research Topic
- Overview of Traditional Research Method
- The Evolving Landscape of Research Methods
- Digital Transformation
- Challenges and Opportunities Presented by Digital Transformation for Research
- Need for Adaptation and Innovation in Research Methodologies
- Digital Data Collection Methods

What Is Research?

Whether you are an academic, a student, or an office worker, you must have used the word "research" at some point in your life. Research literally means to "search again," derived from the Latin re- (again) and cercare (to search). We randomly use phrases like "I did my research on this coffee" and "I am going to do my research on this school" to indicate our intention to gather data and information. In daily life, we have different ways of gathering and processing data and converting it into useful information. In a more academic setting, it is a systematic process to discover, interpret, or revise facts, events, or theories (Aspers & Corte, 2019; Otani, 2017).

Broadly speaking, research is done for a variety of reasons including:

- ***Knowledge Expansion:*** Often academics engage in research to investigate and comprehend unexplored phenomena by addressing questions

DOI: 10.4324/9781003545521-2

about the mechanisms and reasons behind how things operate. This is either because of their own curiosity or the drive to expand their knowledge.

- ***Problem-Solving:*** Researchers conduct studies for developing solutions to specific issues or enhance existing methods and systems for better efficiency and effectiveness. Research can help organizations develop specific solutions for dealing with customer services, operations, and other functions within the organizations.
- ***Innovation and Advancement:*** Research is often driven by the need to develop new technologies, products, or processes that improve the quality of life and push industries toward innovation and growth.
- ***Informed Decision-Making:*** Research plays a crucial role in informed decision-making by providing data-driven insights that guide choices in areas like policy-making, business strategy, and information technology (IT) policies. By collecting and analyzing data, research helps ensure decisions are based on evidence rather than guesswork.
- ***Validation or Disproof:*** Research is essential for verifying the accuracy of hypotheses, theories, and previous findings, ensuring their reliability and validity. Through systematic investigation and analysis, research helps confirm or refine existing knowledge, strengthening the foundation for future discoveries.
- ***Personal or Professional Growth:*** Research enables individuals to gain expertise, achieve academic goals, and make meaningful contributions to their field. It fosters deeper understanding, encourages critical thinking, and drives innovation, ultimately shaping the future of knowledge and practice.

In academia, research is primarily undertaken to expand knowledge, drive innovation, and support societal progress. Scholars entering PhD programs have unprecedented opportunities for knowledge creation. Academics engage to develop evidence-based practices across diverse disciplines, including science, technology, the humanities, and social sciences. Academics also pursue applied research to tackle global challenges, enhance educational methods, and shape public policy. Research enriches academic curricula by incorporating the latest discoveries into teaching, fostering critical thinking and problem-solving skills among students. For faculty, research is a core professional responsibility, enabling them to deepen their expertise, collaborate with peers, and advance their fields of study. Ultimately, academic research fuels progress by creating a knowledge base that empowers societies to innovate, adapt, and thrive.

In terms of conducting academic research, we present the simplified research in Figure 1.1. As shown in the figure, the research process begins by identifying a problem, recognizing a gap in knowledge, or posing

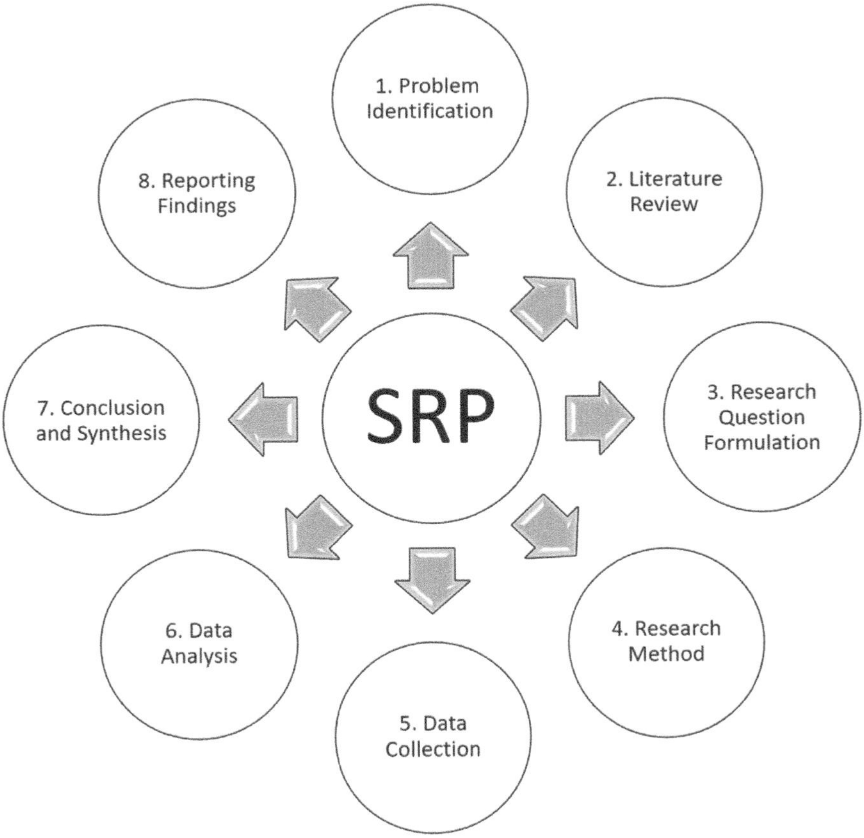

Figure 1.1 The Simplified Research Process (SRP)

Source: Authors.

a question that needs answering. Next, a review of existing literature helps explore what has already been studied on the topic. Based on this, a research question or hypothesis is formulated to define the investigation's focus. The researcher then selects an appropriate method, such as surveys, experiments, or interviews, to collect data. Once the data is gathered, it is analyzed to identify patterns, trends, or insights. Conclusions are then drawn by interpreting the results in relation to the research question. Finally, the findings are reported through presentations, publications, or reports to contribute to the broader knowledge base. Table 1.1 provides definitions of each step, tools that can be used, techniques that be applied to achieve the objectives in the process.

Table 1.1 Simplified Research Process

Stage	*Definition*	*Key Tools*	*Common Activities*
Identifying Research Problem	This stage involves recognizing a specific issue, gap, or area of interest that warrants investigation. It often stems from observations, trends in industry or academia, or unsolved problems in current technologies or systems. The goal is to define a clear and meaningful research focus.	Academic databases (e.g., Google Scholar, IEEE Xplore, ACM Digital Library), brainstorming tools, research forums	SWOT analysis, problem tree analysis, exploratory interviews, environmental scanning
Literature Review	This step involves systematically reviewing existing research to understand what has already been studied, identify theoretical frameworks, and reveal knowledge gaps. A strong literature review provides a foundation for your study and ensures originality.	Reference managers (e.g., Zotero, Mendeley, EndNote), databases (Google Scholar, Scopus), digital libraries (Springer, ScienceDirect)	Systematic review, bibliometric analysis, thematic coding, meta-analysis
Research Question Formulation	Developing a focused and researchable question that clearly defines the aim and scope of the study. A well-formulated research question guides the entire research design and should be specific, measurable, and aligned with the identified problem.	Concept mapping tools (e.g., MindMeister), research design guides, logical frameworks	SMART criteria, 5W1H technique (Who, What, When, Where, Why, How), hypothesis framing, sub-question generation
Research Method Selection	Selecting the appropriate methodological approach – quantitative, qualitative, or mixed methods – based on the nature of the research question, data availability, and the goals of the study. This step includes defining variables, sampling methods, and tools for data gathering.	Research design frameworks, methodology textbooks, tools like Qualtrics (for surveys), SPSS (for planning statistical methods)	Experimental design, survey design, case study, ethnography, action research

(Continued)

Table 1.1 (Continued)

Stage	*Definition*	*Key Tools*	*Common Activities*
Data Collection	Gathering empirical evidence or observations relevant to the research question using the selected method. This can include numerical data, textual data, behavioral logs, or system-level metrics. Data should be valid, reliable, and ethically obtained.	Data collection platforms (e.g., SurveyMonkey, Google Forms), APIs, web scraping tools (e.g., Scrapy), interview tools (e.g., Otter.ai)	Online surveys, structured interviews, focus groups, transaction log analysis, sensor/IoT data collection
Data Analysis	This stage involves organizing, processing, and interpreting the collected data to extract patterns, trends, or relationships. The choice of analysis technique depends on the type of data (qualitative vs. quantitative) and the research objectives.	Statistical tools (SPSS, R, Python libraries such as Pandas, NumPy), data visualization platforms (Tableau, Power BI)	Descriptive statistics, inferential analysis (e.g., t-tests, regression), clustering, sentiment analysis, coding & thematic analysis
Conclusion and Synthesis	Drawing meaningful conclusions by interpreting the analysis results in light of the original research question and objectives. This stage includes identifying implications, confirming or refuting hypotheses, and integrating findings with existing literature.	Word processors (MS Word, Google Docs), visualization tools, concept mapping software	Comparative analysis, synthesis matrices, validation against theory, reflective analysis
Reporting Findings	Communicating the results in an accessible and structured format, whether through academic writing, presentations, or visual formats. This step ensures the dissemination of knowledge to relevant stakeholders, including researchers, practitioners, or decision-makers.	Document tools (LaTeX, MS Word), presentation software (PowerPoint, Prezi, Canva), referencing tools	Academic paper writing, poster presentations, executive summaries, research blogs, journal publication preparation

The Fundamental Step in Academic Research – Topic Selection

Selecting a research topic is a fundamental step in academic research, as it establishes the foundation for the entire study. A well-defined, relevant, and feasible topic ensures that the research remains focused, meaningful, and manageable. An effective topic should align with the researcher's interests, address a gap in existing literature, and offer new insights to the field. Additionally, considering data availability, research feasibility, and the scope of analysis is essential. A carefully chosen topic not only enhances the quality of the research but also sustains the researcher's engagement and motivation throughout the process.

Being in the academia, I can tell you that research isn't just a task, it's a passion-driven pursuit that captivates those who engage in it. True researchers don't see their work as a chore or obligation; they are naturally drawn to their subject, eager to dive deep into literature, analyze data for hours, and uncover new insights. The excitement of discovery fuels them, and they can discuss their findings with enthusiasm for hours on end. The common stereotype of researchers as isolated intellectuals buried in dry, tedious work couldn't be further from the truth. In reality, research is an all-consuming journey, much like an intricate puzzle or an engrossing game where every breakthrough unlocks new challenges and rewards. It doesn't adhere to a strict schedule; it seeps into everyday life, igniting curiosity at the most unexpected moments. Understanding this deep connection between passion and research can help you uncover the topics that truly inspire you. What subjects naturally hold your attention? What articles, blogs, or news stories do you instinctively gravitate toward? When you have free time, what do you find yourself reading, watching, or discussing with friends? Do you get excited about technological advancements, fashion trends, psychological theories, space exploration, or financial markets? Sometimes, the key to finding your research interest lies in paying closer attention to your daily habits. Take a step back and observe – what topics make you lose track of time? What questions keep lingering in your mind? By reflecting on these patterns, you can identify the areas that genuinely spark your curiosity, setting the foundation for meaningful and engaging research.

Here, we detail some tips and guidelines to help you identify your research area and select a research topic.

Figure Out Your Interests

As mentioned before, research is all about passion. The reason I said "figure out" rather than follow your interest is that it takes some research to find your research interests. Start by thinking about what genuinely excites you. Research is a long journey, so choosing a topic that aligns with your academic background, professional experience, or personal curiosity will keep you motivated. Ask yourself: What topics do I enjoy reading about? What problems do I find intriguing? What issues do I feel passionate about solving? If you are just entering the academia, this may be one of the most important decisions of your life regarding what research area you follow. While it is common for researchers to conduct research in different areas, the topic you choose at the beginning of your academic journey stays with you for the rest of your career.

Look into Existing Research

In academic terms we call this a literature review. While you don't have to do a formal literature review to settle on a research topic, it is best to take the time to explore existing studies in your field. There are many ways you can go about doing this. For instance, you can start with reading journal articles, conference papers, and industry reports to identify gaps, unanswered questions, or emerging trends. This will help you refine your focus and ensure that your research contributes something new to the conversation.

Talk to Your Peers, Professors, and Experts

Before I identified my PhD topic at KAIST, I did a lot of consultation and talked with people around to get a better understanding of my research area – digital transformation (DT). In the beginning, it was very difficult to specify a topic but I eventually did – after a lot of talking and looking around. I can't stress the importance of this enough. Don't hesitate to discuss your ideas with professors, colleagues, or mentors. They can offer valuable feedback, suggest resources, and help you refine your research question. Even a casual conversation can spark new ideas or highlight aspects you may not have considered.

Choose a Real-World Issue

This makes things easier for scholars interested in applied research. Novice researchers can start small and consider selecting a topic that has practical significance. Research that addresses current societal, technological, or business challenges tends to have a greater impact. Consider questions like, how does this topic relate to real-world problems? Could my findings benefit a particular industry or community? Contributions to theoretical research can be complemented by research into real-world issues.

Practicality of Your Topic

In the beginning phases of considering a topic, a lot of great but impractical ideas will surround your mind. Ask yourself whether your topic is too ambitious and if it is doable. While ambitious research is great, feasibility is key. Ensure that you have access to enough data, credible sources, and the right research methods to carry out your study effectively. Avoid topics that are too broad, too complex, or lack sufficient resources.

Narrow It Down

I can't stress this enough! Narrow it down, narrow it down, narrow it down! This is one thing that novice researchers struggle with. It's common to start with a broad subject, but refining it into a specific research question or hypothesis is crucial. A focused topic will lead to a clearer, more structured study. If your topic feels too vague, try breaking it down into smaller, more specific aspects. To refine your research topic, defining your population of interest is crucial. Suppose you're studying the quality of education in U.S. universities – you must clarify what "quality" means. Does it refer to student outcomes, faculty effectiveness, curriculum design, or student satisfaction? Identifying your target group – students, professors, administrators, or employers – helps eliminate ambiguity. Narrowing further, you might focus on students' perspectives, specifically first-generation college students, in public universities.

Stay Up to Date

If you go to Google Scholar, you will see this phrase "Stand of the shoulders of the giants." In the context of academic research, this means reviewing previous studies, understanding key theories, and using established methodologies to develop new insights. Google Scholar uses this phrase to highlight how research builds upon prior work, encouraging scholars to cite influential studies and contribute to the ongoing academic conversation. That is why it is important to stay updated by regularly engaging with recent publications, industry news, and academic conferences. These sources provide valuable insights into emerging trends, technological advancements, and evolving discussions within your field. By following the latest research, you can identify gaps in existing knowledge and discover new areas of exploration. Sometimes, the most exciting research opportunities arise from newly developing fields, interdisciplinary studies, or topics that have yet to be thoroughly investigated. Keeping a pulse on current developments not only ensures the relevance of your research but also positions you at the forefront of innovation in your discipline. An excellent example of "standing on the shoulders of giants" in research is the evolution of artificial intelligence (AI) in healthcare. If you were researching AI-driven diagnostics today, you wouldn't start from scratch. Instead, you would build upon foundational studies, such as those on machine learning models for medical imaging or predictive analytics for patient care.

Find the Research Gaps

Identifying gaps in existing knowledge is a key step in developing a strong research topic, but it can be challenging, especially for new researchers. When you're just starting out, it may be difficult to recognize what has already been extensively studied versus what remains underexplored. This is where conducting a thorough literature review, engaging with recent publications, and seeking guidance from experienced researchers can be invaluable. As you gain more experience in your field, your ability to spot research gaps improves. You develop a deeper understanding of recurring themes, unresolved questions, and emerging debates. Over time, patterns become clearer, and you can more easily identify areas where additional investigation could contribute valuable insights. A strong research topic not only fills a gap in knowledge but also pushes the conversation forward by offering new perspectives, refining existing theories, or applying methodologies in innovative ways. Staying curious, continuously reading, and critically analyzing existing studies will help you develop the skill of identifying meaningful research opportunities.

Test Your Idea/Research Practicality

Before fully committing to a research topic, take the time to formulate a preliminary research question and critically evaluate it to make sure it is something that is feasible given your time and resources. Ask yourself: Is it clear? Is it researchable? Is it significant? A well-defined research question should be specific, free from ambiguity, and directly address a gap in existing literature. For PhD/doctoral students, this step is especially crucial. Choosing the wrong topic can lead to wasted time, resources, and frustration. A poorly defined research question can result in difficulties securing data, flawed methodologies, or a lack of meaningful contribution to the field. Since PhD research is a long-term commitment, mistakes in topic selection can be costly, potentially delaying graduation or requiring major revisions later. To avoid these pitfalls, PhD students should test their ideas early and seek feedback from their advisors, mentors, or peers. Advisors can provide valuable insights, helping to refine the topic, assess feasibility, and ensure alignment with academic and industry expectations. By carefully evaluating and confirming the research idea, students can build a solid foundation for their dissertation, making the research journey smoother and more productive.

Overview of Traditional Research Methods

Once you know your topic and have identified your research area, the next step is to determine how to approach your research question. Selecting the right research method is crucial, as it shapes how you collect, analyze, and interpret data. Traditional research methods are broadly categorized into quantitative, qualitative, and mixed methods, each serving different purposes depending on the nature of your study.

Quantitative Research Method

The first half of this book primarily focuses on quantitative research, a methodology that emphasizes the collection and analysis of numerical data to identify patterns, relationships, and measurable outcomes. Quantitative research is widely employed across various academic disciplines, particularly in scientific and social science studies, where objective, replicable, and generalizable results are crucial. This approach is valued for its ability to quantify variables, test hypotheses, and produce results that can be analyzed statistically. One of the most common methods in quantitative research is surveys, where researchers collect structured data from a large group of respondents. Surveys are particularly useful in fields like IT, computer science, psychology, sociology, and market research, where researchers may aim to understand behaviors, attitudes, or opinions on a specific subject. Another key approach is experiments, often used in natural sciences, psychology, and education. Experiments allow researchers to manipulate independent variables and observe their effects on dependent variables, providing causal relationships between them. For example, a biologist may conduct a lab experiment to measure how different environmental conditions affect plant growth, or a psychologist might examine the impact of different teaching methods on student performance.

In the information systems, IT, and computer science fields, the use of quantitative methods is very common. An example of quantitative research in IT could be a study that examines the impact of cybersecurity training on the reduction of security breaches in organizations. In research like this, the researcher might collect data on two groups of organizations: one that implements regular cybersecurity training for its employees and one that does not. The primary data would include numerical measures of security breaches (e.g., the number of attempted cyberattacks, actual breaches, or phishing incidents) over a set period. The researcher would then analyze this data using statistical techniques, such as regression analysis, to determine if there is a significant difference in the number of security breaches between the two groups. This approach could involve secondary data analysis, where the researcher uses existing data from corporate security logs or cybersecurity reports, or primary data collection through surveys or experiments. For instance, the researcher might survey employees to gauge their knowledge before and after a cybersecurity training session and measure how well the training correlates with a reduction in security incidents. By employing quantitative methods like statistical analysis, the researcher can provide objective, measurable outcomes that inform organizations about the effectiveness of cybersecurity training programs and their impact on reducing security threats.

Qualitative Research Method

The second half of this book by Dr. Lingelbach mainly covers qualitative research, a methodology that focuses on exploring deeper insights, behaviors, and perceptions through non-numerical data. It is particularly effective in examining complex social, cultural, or organizational phenomena where numbers alone cannot fully capture the nuances of a situation. Common qualitative methods include interviews, focus groups, and case studies, each offering distinct advantages in gathering rich, detailed perspectives. In interviews, researchers engage one-on-one with participants to explore their personal experiences, beliefs, and attitudes in depth. This method allows researchers to uncover insights that might not emerge in structured surveys. For instance, in the field of IT, an IT researcher might conduct interviews with software developers to understand the challenges they face when adopting new development frameworks or tools. The interview responses could reveal how developers' attitudes toward innovation or their workplace culture influence their technology adoption decisions.

Another key qualitative method is case studies, which involve an in-depth examination of a specific individual, group, organization, or phenomenon within its real-world context. Case studies are especially valuable in IT and computer science research because they allow researchers to investigate complex issues in their natural settings. For example, a case study might focus on how a particular tech company managed a major IT infrastructure overhaul. The researcher could interview employees, review internal documents, and observe the implementation process to understand the organizational challenges, decision-making processes, and outcomes. Such a case study could offer actionable insights for other companies planning similar transformations. By focusing on non-numerical data, qualitative research allows for a deep understanding of the human and social dimensions of technology. Whether through interviews, focus groups, or case studies, it provides rich, contextual insights that are essential for addressing the complex, ever-evolving challenges in the IT and computer science fields. These methods are invaluable for exploring issues such as technology adoption, ethical concerns in AI, user behavior, organizational change, and much more.

Mixed Methods Research combines both quantitative and qualitative techniques to provide a more comprehensive understanding of a research problem. This approach is particularly useful when numerical data alone cannot fully explain a phenomenon, and deeper contextual insights are needed.

Practice Lab 1.1: Map Your Research Journey

Activity

Design a mini research project.

Objective

To guide students through the full research process by having them conceptualize a simple IT or IS research project using the 8-stage framework.

Instructions

1. **Choose a Topic**
   Select a relevant topic in IT or IS (e.g., mobile app usability, cloud adoption in SMEs, AI in cybersecurity).
2. **Define the Research Problem**
   Write a short paragraph (3–5 sentences) describing a real-world problem related to the topic.

3. **Conduct a Mini Literature Review**
   Use Google Scholar or an academic database to find and summarize 2–3 scholarly sources related to the topic.
4. **Formulate a Research Question**
   Develop one clear and focused research question based on the problem and review.
5. **Select a Research Method**
   Choose a method (e.g., survey, experiment, case study) and briefly justify why it's appropriate.
6. **Describe Data Collection Strategy**
   Indicate what kind of data you would collect (quantitative/qualitative), how you would collect it, and from whom.
7. **Outline the Data Analysis Plan**
   Describe how you would analyze the data (e.g., statistical test, coding, visualization).
8. **Synthesize and Plan the Reporting Format**
   Summarize what kinds of insights you expect and how you would report your findings (e.g., paper, dashboard, presentation).

Deliverable

Students submit a 1–2 page mini research plan or present a brief slide deck outlining each stage.

Digital Transformation and Research Methods

DT (Hinterhuber & Nilles, 2021; Vial, 2019) drives significant disruptions across society, industries, and organizations through emerging technologies such as AI, big data and analytics, blockchain, cloud computing, social media, mobile technologies, and the Internet of Things (IoT) (Feroz et al., 2023). As organizations adapt to an increasingly competitive digital landscape, these technologies reshape business operations and value chain processes. Similarly, research tools and methodologies are also evolving due to DT. Advanced analytics, AI-driven insights, and digital data collection methods enhance the research process, enabling more efficient data gathering, real-time analysis, and automated decision-making. As a result, researchers must embrace digital advancements to stay relevant and maximize the impact of their studies. In the age of DT, research has become easier in terms of data collection and analysis. However, the fundamentals of research have not changed.

Research methods have been complemented by the digitalization of research tools. If we look at the DT technologies such as AI, big data analytics, cloud computing, etc., they have accelerated research workflows, enabling faster data collection and processing, deeper insights, and greater collaboration across disciplines and geographical boundaries. Despite all these advances, research is fundamentally about "inquiring." As discussed earlier in the chapter, research is conducted for many different reasons such as innovation, problem solving, and others. In academia, research is primarily focused on knowledge creation and expansion. DT technologies offer new opportunities and better ways of knowledge distribution across academic boundaries.

The Evolving Landscape of Research Methods

In academia, we have all experienced first-hand the impact of information and communication technologies on how research is done, data is accessed, processed, analyzed, and presented (Grosseck & Bran, 2016; Paulus et al., 2017). Because of the newly emerging technologies like AI and big data, we have access to new research methods and tools that were unavailable before. These advancements enable researchers to collect and analyze vast amounts of data with greater speed, accuracy, and efficiency. One example is that of AI-powered tools and machine learning algorithms, and how they can be used to uncover complex patterns, automate data processing, and generate insights that were once labor-intensive and time-consuming. This not only saves time but also increases the quality of the results as human errors are significantly reduced.

Another example is big data analytics, which allows researchers to process and examine massive, unstructured datasets. This capability helps uncover hidden patterns, trends, and correlations across various academic disciplines, from healthcare and social sciences to finance and engineering. For instance, in biomedical research, big data analytics can be used to analyze genetic information and disease patterns, leading to advancements in personalized medicine (Chung Chow, 2015; Dash et al., 2019). Similarly, in business and marketing, companies leverage these tools to study consumer behavior and market trends, enabling data-driven decision-making (Aboelmaged & Mouakket, 2020; Loebbecke & Picot, 2015).

In the fields of IT and computer science, digital analytics provide significant advantages by streamlining data collection, automating processes, and improving analytical accuracy. Researchers in cybersecurity, for example, can utilize digital analytics to detect anomalies in network traffic, helping to identify and mitigate potential security threats. Likewise, AI and machine learning models rely on vast datasets to refine predictive algorithms, improving applications such as speech recognition, image processing, and natural language understanding.

Impact of Digital Technologies on Research Practices

The impact of digital technologies on the research processes in IT and any other scientific field has been very well observed. As alluded earlier, DTs in research practices have streamlined everything from data collection to publication. With increasingly powerful computing information systems and the availability of digital tools, researchers can now simulate scientific phenomena and research scenarios with remarkable precision helping them in studying them. In terms of access, the exponential growth of digital data across interconnected global networks has fundamentally transformed the research landscape, enabling near-instantaneous access to vast repositories of information through the availability of thousands and thousands of research databases and journals. This shift has significantly reduced the reliance on traditional, labor-intensive data collection methods, allowing researchers to allocate more resources to analysis and interpretation. Moreover, advanced computational tools and machine learning algorithms facilitate the seamless integration of heterogeneous datasets from multiple sources in real-time, a capability that was previously unattainable. This enhanced analytical power not only accelerates knowledge discovery but also fosters interdisciplinary research by bridging disparate data domains, ultimately advancing the depth and scope of scholarly inquiry.

For instance, in the field of social sciences, digital survey platforms and web-based analytics tools have dramatically increased the efficiency of data collection and analysis, allowing researchers to gather insights from large populations in a fraction of the time previously required. This contributes to the overall quality of research as more diverse and larger sets of data are gathered. In reference to the field of IT, data scientists can leverage big data analytics and cloud computing to process vast amounts of structured and unstructured data, enabling smart decisions about consumers in industries such as finance and marketing, increasing the ability of businesses to increase their profitability. Predictive analytics models, for example, help businesses forecast customer behavior and optimize operational strategies with unprecedented accuracy.

Furthermore, cloud-based platforms and digital collaboration tools have highly altered the way research is conducted. These technologies enable scholars to collaborate in real time, regardless of geographical location. Platforms such as Google Drive, Microsoft OneDrive, and GitHub facilitate seamless sharing of documents, datasets, and code, making research more efficient and accessible. In addition, online academic communities and virtual research environments allow interdisciplinary teams to work together, accelerating innovation and knowledge dissemination. As DT continues to reshape industries, it also influences research methodologies. Traditional approaches are being enhanced or, in some cases, replaced by data-driven, technology-assisted methods that increase precision and scalability. To remain at the forefront of innovation, researchers must embrace these digital advancements, leveraging them to drive more impactful and insightful discoveries. Additionally, remote access to specialized instruments like telescopes, microscopes, and advanced manufacturing tools has become more accessible through networked connections. Just as significantly, research findings can now be disseminated online much faster than through traditional publishing channels.

Digital Data Collection Methods

So, we saw the incredible impact of DT on the research processes and practices. Now, let's discuss the specifics of how research methods have improved because of digital technologies. In today's highly dynamic and digitalized world, digital data collection methods have become essential for gathering accurate, efficient, and scalable data. These methods leverage technology to collect and analyze information, making research more accessible and adaptable to various fields. Below are some of the most common digital data collection techniques.

Digital Surveys and Questionnaires

Digital survey platforms such as Google Forms, Qualtrics, and SurveyMonkey allow researchers to collect structured responses from a large audience. These tools enable automated data entry, real-time analytics, and easy distribution through email, social media, or websites. I remember a time when traditional paper-based surveys were the norm. Back when I worked for an NGO, I quickly learned just how challenging traditional survey methods could be. As a newly hired research analyst, I was eager to dive into data analysis, but nothing could have prepared me for what happened next. One afternoon, the head of the research department called me into his office. "We've conducted thousands of surveys over the past few years," he said. "I need you to analyze the data." I nodded confidently. "Of course, I'd be happy to." He, then, led me down a hallway, past offices and meeting rooms, until we stopped in front of an old storage room. He unlocked the door, swung it open, and said, "All yours Mr. Feroz!." Inside, stacked from floor to ceiling, were hundreds of boxes filled with paper surveys. My heart sank. I had imagined working with spreadsheets and statistical software, not spending weeks sifting through mountains of paper.

At that moment, I realized just how inefficient traditional survey methods could be. Not only did these paper-based surveys take up an absurd amount of space, but they also made analysis incredibly time-consuming and prone to human error. Fortunately, the organization had a talented software engineer on staff. Recognizing the urgent need for a better system, we teamed up to design a digital data entry system. Slowly but surely, we converted those paper surveys into a structured digital format, making the analysis process infinitely faster and more accurate. What once took weeks of manual work could now be done in a matter of hours. That experience solidified my belief in the power of digital survey methods. They don't just make data collection easier, they completely transform the research process, turning what was once a logistical nightmare into a seamless, efficient system.

Digital survey methods offer significant advantages over traditional survey methods, enhancing efficiency, accuracy, and accessibility. Unlike paper-based surveys, which require extensive time and resources for distribution, collection, and manual data entry, digital surveys can be deployed instantly to a global audience through online platforms and mobile applications. This not only accelerates the data collection process but also reduces human errors associated with manual transcription. Moreover, digital surveys enable real-time data validation and automated analysis, allowing researchers to detect inconsistencies and analyze results instantaneously. Features such as adaptive questioning, where survey logic adjusts based on respondents' answers, improve data quality by ensuring relevant questions are asked. Additionally, digital surveys enhance respondent engagement by offering interactive formats, multimedia integration, and accessibility across various devices. Their ability to reach diverse and geographically dispersed populations further strengthens the generalizability of research findings. Ultimately, digital survey methods streamline the research process, making it more cost-effective, scalable, and analytically robust compared to traditional approaches.

Online Interviews

Rather than relying on traditional in-person interviews, researchers now leverage digital platforms such as Zoom, Microsoft Teams, and Skype to conduct virtual discussions with participants across the globe. This shift not only enhances convenience but also significantly reduces the costs associated with travel, lodging, and logistical coordination. These kinds of expenses can be prohibitive, especially in large-scale or international research projects. Speaking from personal experiences, online interviews were a lifesaver for me during COVID when I was collecting data for my PhD dissertation. It makes it very convenient for you to collect data without any geographical limitations and reduces costs significantly. For example, a study requiring interviews with experts from multiple countries would traditionally involve flying researchers across continents, arranging meeting spaces, and accommodating different time zones. These factors often limit the scope and feasibility of qualitative research. However, with virtual meeting tools, interviews can be conducted seamlessly from anywhere, eliminating geographical barriers and allowing for a more diverse and representative participant pool. Additionally, these digital platforms offer built-in recording and transcription features, streamlining the data analysis process. Researchers can revisit recorded conversations, apply AI-driven transcription services for accurate documentation, and use qualitative analysis software to extract key themes efficiently. This technological advancement has transformed qualitative research, making it more accessible, scalable, and cost-effective than ever before.

Smartphones and Mobile Data Collection

Smartphones and mobile applications have incredibly eased the data collection process by enabling researchers to gather information quickly, efficiently, and in real-time. These technologies support various data collection methods, including GPS tracking, mobile surveys, multimedia uploads, and real-time logging of user activities. This is particularly beneficial in fields like IT, social sciences, public health, and environmental studies, where field data collection is essential. For instance, platforms like SurveyMonkey and Google Forms allow participants to complete surveys anytime and anywhere, even from the comfort of their own beds. Instead of traveling to research centers or filling out lengthy paper forms, respondents can simply tap through a digital questionnaire on their smartphones. This not only improves response rates but also ensures broader and more diverse participation.

Similarly, tools like KoBoToolbox and Open Data Kit (ODK) have become indispensable in field research, especially in remote areas with limited internet connectivity. Public health researchers, for example, can use these platforms to collect real-time data on disease outbreaks, vaccination campaigns, or community health trends. With offline functionality, these tools enable researchers to gather data in rural areas and later sync it to a central database when connectivity is restored. By integrating mobile technologies into the research process, scholars can overcome traditional barriers like geographical limitations, logistical constraints, and participant availability. These tools not only enhance efficiency and accuracy but also expand the scope of research, allowing for richer datasets and deeper insights.

Social Media and Online Forums

Online forums provide researchers with unique data sets that are openly available, and researchers can post surveys for eliciting responses with minimal costs. Social media platforms such as Twitter, Reddit, LinkedIn, and Facebook have become invaluable sources of user-generated content, offering researchers a vast and dynamic dataset for analyzing trends, public opinion, and behavioral patterns. Unlike traditional survey methods, which require time-consuming data collection, social media provides real-time insights into societal sentiments, emerging issues, and shifting public discourse across diverse demographics. For example, Twitter is widely used for sentiment analysis, where researchers apply natural language processing (NLP) techniques to assess public emotions regarding political events, product launches, or social movements. Reddit, with its topic-specific communities, allows researchers to conduct in-depth analyses of niche discussions, making it a valuable resource for understanding consumer preferences, mental health conversations, or technology adoption trends. Similarly, LinkedIn serves as a key platform for studying professional networking patterns, industry trends, and workforce sentiments, while Facebook offers insights into community engagement, brand perception, and social interactions at a large scale.

Social media posts and the huge amount of data generated are goldmines of insights. By leveraging sentiment analysis, researchers can quantify emotional tones in posts, distinguishing between positive, negative, and neutral sentiments to gauge public reactions. Meanwhile, topic modeling techniques, such as Latent Dirichlet Allocation (LDA), help uncover hidden themes within large volumes of text, enabling researchers to identify trending discussions, misinformation patterns, or shifts in consumer interests. With the proliferation of social media data, researchers now have unprecedented access to unfiltered, real-world conversations. This not only enhances traditional qualitative research but also enables predictive analytics, allowing organizations, policymakers, and businesses to make data-driven decisions with greater accuracy and relevance.

Big Data and Cloud-Based Research

DT has made it possible for researchers to rely on cloud-based platforms such as Google Cloud, Amazon Web Services (AWS), and Kaggle to store, access, and analyze vast datasets spanning multiple domains. These platforms provide scalable computing power, robust security, and real-time collaboration tools, making large-scale research more efficient and accessible than ever before. Cloud repositories enable researchers to work with both structured data (such as financial records, customer transactions, or census information) and unstructured data (including social media posts, images, and sensor readings). For example, Google Cloud's BigQuery allows researchers to process terabytes of data using SQL-based queries, making it an essential tool for analyzing large datasets in fields like healthcare, finance, and climate science. Similarly, AWS provides services like S3 (Simple Storage Service) and EC2 (Elastic Compute Cloud), which facilitate massive data storage and high-performance computing for machine learning and AI research.

Kaggle, a cloud-based data science community, offers publicly available datasets on topics ranging from epidemiology to economic trends. Researchers can leverage Kaggle's collaborative environment to build predictive models, perform data visualizations, and apply machine learning techniques without the need for expensive computing infrastructure. For instance, data scientists working on climate change research can access Kaggle's extensive datasets on global temperature shifts and deforestation patterns, enabling large-scale analysis and predictive modeling. By utilizing cloud-based platforms, researchers can bypass the limitations of local storage, streamline data processing, and integrate machine learning algorithms to extract deeper insights. This transformation has made computational research accessible to a wider audience, accelerating innovation across disciplines.

AI and Machine Learning-Based Data Collection

This is a new area and is developing fast. A lot of new AI-based models are emerging that enable researchers to collect, process, and analyze data. AI-driven methods such as NLP, image recognition, and predictive analytics enable researchers to work with vast datasets at an unprecedented scale, uncovering insights that were previously impossible to obtain with traditional methods. For example, NLP allows researchers to analyze massive volumes of text data from news articles, social media, and academic literature, extracting meaningful patterns and sentiments in real time. For instance, NLP algorithms can be used to track public opinion on global issues like climate change by analyzing Twitter discussions, policy documents, and scientific papers. Similarly, image recognition technologies are being applied in fields such as environmental science, where AI can process satellite imagery to detect deforestation patterns, urban expansion, or natural disasters. In healthcare, AI-powered image analysis is accelerating medical diagnostics, helping radiologists identify diseases such as cancer with greater speed and accuracy. Another transformative development is the rise of AI-assisted surveys and chatbots for interactive data gathering. Traditional surveys often suffer from low response rates and engagement issues, but AI-powered chatbots such as those integrated into platforms like Facebook Messenger or WhatsApp, offer a more dynamic, conversational experience for respondents. These AI-driven tools can adapt their questions in real time based on user responses, improving data quality and relevance. For example, a market research firm could deploy an AI-powered chatbot to gather customer feedback on a new product, automatically analyzing sentiment and trends as responses come in. As AI continues to evolve, its role in research will only expand, allowing for more efficient, scalable, and insightful data collection and analysis across a wide range of disciplines.

Practice Lab 1.2: Digital Tools in Modern Research

Objective

Explore how digital tools are changing the way researchers collect and analyze data.

Instructions

1 **Choose ONE digital research tool** from the list below:

- **Google Forms** – Create a short survey (3–5 questions).
- **ChatGPT** – Use it to generate a summary or code for a research task.

- **Kaggle** – Browse a dataset and describe what kind of research it could support.
- **Otter.ai or Zoom** – Record and transcribe a short mock interview (2–3 mins).

2 **Complete a short report (max 250 words)** that includes:

- The tool you used
- What task you completed
- One benefit and one challenge of using this tool
- How this digital method compares to a traditional one

Deliverable

Submit your 250-word report.

Chapter Summary

In this chapter, we examined how research methods had been influenced and reshaped by the ongoing wave of DT. The chapter began by defining the fundamental concept of research, outlining its primary purposes, and describing the structure and function of traditional research methodologies. It emphasized how traditional approaches such as qualitative, quantitative, and mixed methods had long served as the foundation for academic and applied inquiry. We discussed DT, explaining how it had increasingly become a critical force in various fields, including research. DT was described as the integration of digital technologies into traditional processes with the goal of creating new or improved value. Key drivers of DT, such as automation, cloud computing, AI, and the IoT, were highlighted as pivotal in changing how data is collected, analyzed, and interpreted. As research environments evolved in response to these technologies, traditional methodologies were shown to face new challenges. While these methods retained their strengths, they often struggled to address the complexity, speed, and volume of modern data environments. Researchers were required to rethink and adapt their methods to meet the demands of a rapidly changing digital landscape.

The chapter also explored the challenges and opportunities introduced by DT. Among the challenges were the ethical dilemmas associated with big data, concerns around data privacy, and the need for real-time data analysis. On the other hand, DT presented opportunities for richer insights, more efficient research workflows, and broader access to diverse data sources. To respond to these dynamics, the chapter underscored the need for adaptation and innovation in research methodologies. It stressed the importance of flexibility and technological literacy in designing modern research strategies. Finally, the chapter provided an overview of emerging digital data collection methods, such as web scraping, social media analytics, and IoT-based data acquisition. These tools were presented as essential for navigating contemporary research challenges and for unlocking deeper, more actionable insights. Through the integration of these advanced technologies, researchers were positioned to enhance their ability to conduct meaningful investigations and contribute to knowledge creation in a digitally transformed world.

Review Questions

1 What is research? Explain by providing a few examples from your daily life.
2 What are the main research methods?
3 How have digital technologies impacted research processes?
4 What is digital transformation? What is its impact on research?
5 Discuss some digital data collection methods.

References

Aboelmaged, M., & Mouakket, S. (2020). Influencing models and determinants in big data analytics research: A bibliometric analysis. *Information Processing and Management, 57*(4). https://doi.org/10.1016/j.ipm.2020.102234

Aspers, P., & Corte, U. (2019). What is qualitative in qualitative research. *Qualitative Sociology, 42*(2). https://doi.org/10.1007/s11133-019-9413-7

Chung Chow, S. (2015). On big-data analytics in biomedical research. *Journal of Biometrics & Biostatistics, 6*(3). https://doi.org/10.4172/2155-6180.1000236

Dash, S., Shakyawar, S. K., Sharma, M., & Kaushik, S. (2019). Big data in healthcare: Management, analysis and future prospects. *Journal of Big Data, 6*(1). https://doi.org/10.1186/s40537-019-0217-0

Feroz, A. K., Zo, H., Eom, J., & Chiravuri, A. (2023). Identifying organizations' dynamic capabilities for sustainable digital transformation: A mixed methods study. *Technology in Society, 73*(April). https://doi.org/10.1016/j.techsoc.2023.102257

Grosseck, G., & Bran, R. (2016). Script towards research 2.0: The influence of digital and online tools in academic research. *World Journal on Educational Technology: Current Issues, 8*(2). https://doi.org/10.18844/wjet.v8i2.676

Hinterhuber, A., & Nilles, M. (2021). Digital transformation, the Holy Grail and the disruption of business models: An interview with Michael Nilles. *Business Horizons*. https://doi.org/10.1016/j.bushor.2021.02.042

Loebbecke, C., & Picot, A. (2015). Reflections on societal and business model transformation arising from digitization and big data analytics: A research agenda. *Journal of Strategic Information Systems, 24*(3), 149–157. https://doi.org/10.1016/j.jsis.2015.08.002

Otani, T. (2017). What is qualitative research? In *Yakugaku Zasshi* (Vol. 137, Issue 6). https://doi.org/10.1248/yakushi.16-00224-1

Paulus, T. M., Jackson, K., & Davidson, J. (2017). Digital tools for qualitative research: Disruptions and entanglements. *Qualitative Inquiry, 23*(10). https://doi.org/10.1177/1077800417731080

Vial, G. (2019). Understanding digital transformation: A review and a research agenda. *Journal of Strategic Information Systems, 28*(2), 118–144. https://doi.org/10.1016/j.jsis.2019.01.003

2 Understanding Quantitative Research

Chapter Objectives

After reading this chapter, readers should understand:

- Introduction to Quantitative Research in IT
- Characteristics of Quantitative Data
- Information Systems Research Design in Quantitative Studies
- Hypothesis Formulation and Testing
- Variables in Quantitative Research

Introduction to Quantitative Research in IT

Let's talk numbers!

Quantitative research is all about using numerical data to understand things better. It's like when a company wants to know which soda flavor people like the most, so they survey 1000 customers and count how many prefer each flavor. Or when a teacher gives a math test to a class and looks at the average score to see how well students understood the lesson. It's different from just asking opinions because it focuses on facts, measurements, and patterns (things you can count). This kind of research helps businesses, scientists, and even governments make better decisions based on real data instead of just guesses (Rutberg & Bouikidis, 2018; Zyphur & Pierides, 2017).

A quantitative research design focuses on precise measurements to test hypotheses, aiming to create a well-structured study that ensures accurate data collection and statistical analysis. It emphasizes numerical data and larger sample sizes, with most of the planning and structure determined before data collection begins. In contrast, qualitative research delves deeply into a topic, exploring complex details and building an understanding of a problem, often within a broader social or organizational context. It typically involves smaller sample sizes and requires significant analysis after data collection, as the data comes in the form of text, interviews, videos, or observations rather than

DOI: 10.4324/9781003545521-3

numbers. For example, in information technology (IT), a quantitative study might analyze user engagement by collecting data on the number of clicks and time spent on a website, while a qualitative study could involve interviewing users to understand their experiences and challenges with the site. Quantitative research helps in identifying patterns and making predictions, whereas qualitative research provides rich insights into user behavior and decision-making (Järvinen & Karjaluoto, 2015; Saura et al., 2017).

Quantitative Research Designs

Quantitative research can be categorized into several types based on its purpose and methodology (Figure 2.1).

Descriptive Research

Descriptive research plays a crucial role in IT, information systems (IS), and computer science by providing a foundational understanding of trends, patterns, and characteristics within a given domain. This research approach focuses on answering "what is happening?" rather than exploring underlying causes, making it essential for identifying key metrics and informing data-driven decision-making. Common methods include surveys, observations, and analysis of existing datasets to quantify occurrences and behaviors. For instance, in cybersecurity, descriptive research can measure the frequency of cyberattacks on an organization over the past year, helping to assess security risks. Similarly, in software and app development, tracking user engagement metrics such as daily active users provide valuable insights into adoption and usability.

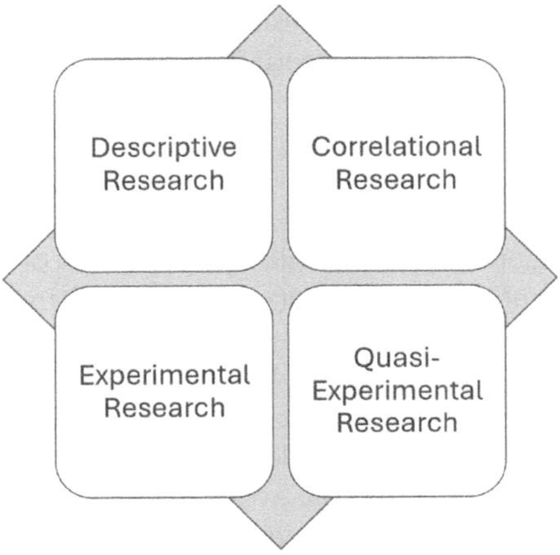

Figure 2.1 Quantitative Research Design Categories

Correlational Research

Correlational research is a valuable approach in IS and IT, as it helps identify relationships between key variables without manipulating them. This method examines whether two or more factors move together (positive correlation) or in opposite directions (negative correlation), providing critical insights without establishing causation. For example, in remote work environments, correlational research can explore the relationship between screen time and productivity, helping organizations understand how digital engagement impacts efficiency. Similarly, in network management, analyzing whether higher bandwidth correlates with faster website loading times can inform IT infrastructure decisions. By uncovering associations between variables, correlational research aids in optimizing technology use, enhancing system performance, and guiding data-driven decision-making in IT and IS.

Experimental Research

This method is highly reliable and delivers the best results. Researchers in advanced stages of their careers often rely on experiments to prove their hypothesis. Novice researchers and emerging academic scholars can use this method to establish a solid foundation for their academic careers. Experimental research is often conducted by researchers in the fields of natural sciences, but it can be a valuable method in IS and IT, as it allows researchers to establish cause-and-effect relationships by systematically manipulating an independent variable and observing its impact on a dependent variable. This approach involves control and experimental groups to ensure valid comparisons, making it a key technique in A/B testing and product evaluations. For example, in user experience (UX) research, an experiment can compare two different UI designs to determine which leads to higher user engagement. Similarly, in system optimization, researchers may measure system performance before and after a software update to assess its effectiveness.

Quasi-experimental Research

Quasi-experimental research is commonly used in IS and IT when full randomization of participants is not feasible due to ethical or practical constraints. While like experimental research, it focuses on studying cause-and-effect relationships without random assignment, making it a valuable tool for real-world scenarios. For instance, in cybersecurity, researchers may compare security awareness levels between employees who received training and those who didn't, but without randomly selecting participants. Similarly, in examining the impact of remote work on IT team performance, quasi-experimental research can assess pre-existing employee groups, providing insights into how different work arrangements affect team dynamics and productivity. This approach is especially useful in IT studies where controlled experiments are difficult to implement but where valuable comparisons and insights are still needed.

The following table highlights how quantitative research methods are used across various fields, emphasizing the versatility and importance of these methods in analyzing numerical data, identifying trends, and making predictions. Each field utilizes specific tools and techniques suited to its unique needs but shares a common goal of generating objective, data-driven insights (Table 2.1).

Table 2.1 The Use of Quantitative Research in Different Fields

Field	*Application*	*Methods Used*	*Common Outcomes*
Information Systems (IS)	Analyzing data, measuring performance, and assessing the impact of technological advancements.	Statistical techniques, data analysis tools, surveys, performance metrics	Identifying trends, evaluating software/hardware efficiency, improving decision-making.
Biology & Chemistry	Analyzing experimental results and validating scientific theories.	Controlled experiments, measurements, statistical analysis	Validating hypotheses, identifying patterns in biological or chemical processes.
Psychology & Sociology	Understanding human behavior through measurable factors.	Surveys, psychological tests, observational studies, statistical methods	Understanding relationships between variables like behavior and demographics, testing behavioral theories.
Economics	Assessing financial trends, consumer behavior, and market dynamics.	Statistical analysis, econometrics, market surveys	Predicting market trends, evaluating financial performance, understanding economic behavior.
Marketing	Evaluating consumer behavior, campaign effectiveness, and business performance.	Surveys, sales data analysis, customer feedback, statistical techniques	Measuring consumer preferences, forecasting demand, analyzing campaign success.
Education	Studying student performance, learning outcomes, and instructional methods.	Standardized tests, longitudinal studies, surveys	Identifying effective teaching methods, measuring student success, predicting educational outcomes.
Healthcare	Evaluating the effectiveness of treatments, patient outcomes, and healthcare practices.	Clinical trials, patient surveys, medical data analysis	Improving healthcare practices, assessing treatment effectiveness, identifying health trends.

Characteristics of Quantitative Research Data

For quantitative research, you are going to need quantitative data which refers to data that can be expressed in numerical terms, allowing for the measurement and analysis of variables in a structured and objective manner. It involves quantities that can be counted, measured, or expressed as numbers, making it ideal for statistical analysis and drawing conclusions based on numerical evidence. This type of data can be used to quantify behaviors, phenomena, or characteristics, and is often collected through tools such as surveys, experiments, sensors, or observation (Hanafi Azman Ong et al., 2017; Schoonenboom, 2023). Quantitative data plays a crucial role in identifying trends, testing hypotheses, and drawing objective conclusions across diverse fields such as IT, social sciences, healthcare, economics, and marketing. It can be categorized into discrete and continuous data. Discrete data consists of distinct, specific values, typically counted in whole numbers, such as the number of users on a website or the number of software bugs reported. In contrast, continuous data can take any value within a given range and is measured rather than counted, including variables like time spent on a website, temperature, or network bandwidth. Understanding these data types is essential for effective data analysis and decision-making.

Numerical Nature

Quantitative data is inherently numerical, meaning it consists of measurable values that can be counted, ranked, or subjected to mathematical operations. This numerical nature allows for precise analysis, statistical modeling, and data-driven decision-making. Because quantitative data can be manipulated mathematically, it enables researchers to calculate averages, identify trends, establish correlations, and make predictions based on patterns. For instance, in IT and digital analytics, website traffic data such as the number of visitors per day, bounce rates, or average session duration provides insights into user behavior and engagement. Similarly, in healthcare, a patient's blood pressure readings or cholesterol levels over time allow for tracking health trends and assessing the effectiveness of treatments. Researchers can leverage the numerical properties of quantitative data across various fields to perform detailed assessments, compare results, and derive meaningful conclusions that drive strategic decisions.

Precision and Objectivity

A major challenge that researchers face when doing their study is objectivity and staying impartial. Quantitative data is objective and precise, as it consists of measurable values that are independent of personal opinions or interpretations. The objectivity ensures that data-driven conclusions are based on factual evidence rather than subjective judgment. Additionally, quantitative data is verifiable and reproducible, meaning that different researchers or analysts measuring the same variables under similar conditions should obtain the same results. For example, in finance, stock prices, interest rates, and exchange rates are recorded as precise numerical values that can be analyzed without bias. Similarly, in engineering, measurements such as the tensile strength of materials or the energy consumption of a system provide exact, repeatable data points that allow for accurate comparisons and performance assessments. Such precision makes quantitative data essential for scientific research, business analytics, and technological advancements.

Collection Methods

Quantitative data is gathered using structured and systematic methods, ensuring consistency, reliability, and comparability across different datasets. These methods include surveys with closed-ended questions, controlled experiments, structured observations, and automated data collection systems, all designed to minimize variability and enhance accuracy. For example, in market research, customer satisfaction surveys often use rating scales (e.g., 1–5) to quantify opinions, allowing businesses to analyze trends and compare results over time. In scientific experiments, researchers collect data using precise instruments, such as measuring the temperature change in a chemical reaction or the response time of a computer system under different loads. Thanks to these structured approaches, quantitative data remains consistent, standardized, and easy to analyze, making it a cornerstone of evidence-based decision-making in fields ranging from economics and healthcare to engineering and IT.

Measurable Variables

Quantitative data consists of measurable variables that can be expressed on a consistent numerical scale, allowing for precise calculations, comparisons, and statistical analysis. These variables can be classified into interval, ratio, ordinal, or nominal data types, depending on their properties and the mathematical operations that can be applied. For instance, in healthcare, a patient's weight, blood pressure, or heart rate are measurable variables that enable doctors to track health progress over time. In sports analytics, variables such as an athlete's sprint time, shooting accuracy, or average heart rate during a game provide valuable performance metrics.

Since these variables are quantifiable, they enable researchers, analysts, and decision-makers to perform statistical analyses, identify patterns, and draw objective conclusions across a wide range of disciplines, from finance and engineering to psychology and social sciences.

Replicability

One of the key strengths of quantitative data is its replicability, meaning that the methods used for data collection are standardized, allowing for studies to be repeated under similar conditions to verify results and ensure reliability. This characteristic is essential in scientific research, business analytics, and technology, where consistency and accuracy are critical for decision-making. For example, in clinical trials, drug effectiveness is tested using controlled experiments with standardized dosages, procedures, and measurement techniques. If another research team follows the same methodology, they should obtain similar results, reinforcing the reliability of the findings. Similarly, in IT performance testing, metrics such as server response time, CPU usage, and network latency are measured using standardized benchmarking tools, ensuring that results can be replicated and compared across different systems. By adhering to structured methodologies and standardized measurement techniques, quantitative data ensures that conclusions are reliable, valid, and universally applicable, making it a foundation for evidence-based research and decision-making.

Large Datasets

Quantitative research often involves analyzing large datasets, enabling researchers to uncover patterns, trends, and relationships across diverse variables. These extensive datasets provide a robust foundation for statistical modeling, machine learning, and predictive analytics, making them essential in fields like finance, healthcare, marketing, and technology. We talked about Kaggle earlier, a well-known platform for data science and machine learning, which hosts massive datasets covering topics such as customer purchasing behavior, financial transactions, and healthcare diagnostics. Data scientists and researchers use these datasets to develop predictive models, optimize algorithms, and gain insights into real-world problems. Similarly, in financial technology (FinTech), companies analyze vast transaction logs to detect fraud patterns, assess credit risk, and optimize investment strategies. In healthcare, organizations leverage extensive patient records to identify disease trends, improve diagnostics, and enhance treatment plans through artificial intelligence (AI)-driven analytics. Large datasets are crucial for conducting longitudinal studies, which track variables over extended periods to analyze changes, trends, and long-term effects. The vast amount of data collected over time ensures that findings are statistically significant, reliable, and applicable to broader populations. For example, in public health research, the Framingham Heart Study has been collecting data on thousands of participants since 1948 to examine risk factors for cardiovascular disease. The large dataset allows researchers to analyze patterns in heart disease prevalence, lifestyle influences, and genetic factors across multiple generations.

Statistical Analysis

Quantitative data is typically analyzed using statistical techniques to summarize, interpret, and draw meaningful conclusions. These methods allow researchers to identify patterns, relationships, and trends within datasets, making data-driven decision-making more precise and reliable. Common statistical techniques include:

- Descriptive statistics, such as mean, median, and standard deviation, summarize key characteristics of a dataset. For example, in finance, the average stock price over a month helps investors assess market stability.
- Inferential statistics, including correlation and regression analysis, which determine relationships between variables. For instance, in marketing analytics, regression models can predict how advertisement spending impacts sales revenue.
- Hypothesis testing, which assesses whether observed effects are statistically significant. In healthcare, clinical trials use hypothesis testing to evaluate whether a new drug is more effective than existing treatments.

Generalizability

One of the key advantages of quantitative data is its generalizability, meaning that findings from a well-designed study can be applied to a larger population. This is particularly true when researchers use random or representative sampling techniques, ensuring that the sample accurately reflects the broader group being studied. For example, in public opinion polling, organizations like Pew Research Center survey a random sample of voters to predict national election outcomes with a high degree of accuracy. Similarly, in healthcare research, clinical trials conducted on a diverse and representative group of patients can provide insights into how a new drug or treatment will work across different demographics. Generalizability is crucial for making data-driven decisions, shaping policies, and developing scalable solutions in fields such as economics, education, and business. When properly designed, quantitative studies allow researchers to draw conclusions that extend beyond the sample group, increasing the real-world applicability of their findings.

Practice Lab 2.1: Exploring Characteristics of Quantitative Data

Objective

To identify and analyze key characteristics of quantitative research data using real-world examples and structured thinking.

Instructions

1. **Choose a Dataset**
   Visit https://www.kaggle.com/datasets and select **any one dataset** that interests you. (You do **not** need to download it – just review its description, columns, and sample values.)
2. **Answer the Following in a Short Report (Max 300 Words):**
   - **Dataset Name** and the **URL**
   - Identify **two types of quantitative data** in the dataset:
     - One **discrete** variable
     - One **continuous** variable
   - Explain how the dataset supports **at least two** of the following characteristics of quantitative data:
     - Numerical Nature
     - Precision & Objectivity
     - Measurable Variables
     - Large Datasets
     - Statistical Analysis
     - Replicability
     - Generalizability
   - Briefly suggest **one type of statistical test or analysis** that could be applied to the data.

Deliverable

Upload your short report (PDF or Word).

Hypothesis Formulation and Testing

In quantitative research, it is essential to clearly define the research questions and hypotheses at the end of the literature review. The purpose of the literature review is to highlight existing gaps in knowledge and establish why the study is necessary. By concluding the review with research questions or hypotheses, researchers effectively bridge the identified gaps with the objectives of their study. A research question is broader and exploratory, seeking to understand a phenomenon without making specific predictions. In contrast, a hypothesis is a testable statement that suggests a potential relationship between variables based on prior research or theory. While quantitative studies can include both research questions and hypotheses, qualitative studies typically focus solely on research questions, as they do not involve statistical hypothesis testing.

Formulating a Hypothesis

For studies that include hypotheses, researchers must clearly define both the null hypothesis (H_0) and the alternative hypothesis (H_1) in a structured format. The null hypothesis suggests no significant relationship or effect, while the alternative hypothesis proposes an expected relationship. The goal of hypothesis testing is to reject the null hypothesis, providing statistical evidence that supports the alternative hypothesis. For example, in IT research, consider a study examining the relationship between cybersecurity training and phishing susceptibility among employees in an organization. The literature review might reveal conflicting findings on the effectiveness of training programs, making it necessary to explore this relationship further. The study could then present the following hypotheses:

- H_1 (Alternative Hypothesis): *Employees who undergo cybersecurity training are less likely to fall victim to phishing attacks compared to those who have not received training.*
- H_0 (Null Hypothesis): *There is no significant difference in phishing susceptibility between employees who receive cybersecurity training and those who do not.*

By testing these hypotheses, researchers can provide data-driven insights that help organizations develop more effective cybersecurity policies. Hypotheses are often based on theoretical frameworks, prior research, or observed patterns. For instance, studies on the Technology Acceptance Model (TAM) might hypothesize that perceived ease of use positively influences technology adoption rates.

Hypothesis Testing Process

Once a hypothesis is formulated, researchers test it using statistical methods to determine whether the observed data supports or contradicts the hypothesis. First, data collection is conducted using structured methods such as surveys, experiments, or database analysis to gather relevant quantitative data. Next, researchers must choose an appropriate statistical test based on the data type and research question. Common tests include T-tests, which compare two groups (e.g., evaluating IT system performance before and after an upgrade), Chi-square tests, which analyze categorical relationships (e.g., device type and security breach frequency), and regression analysis, which examines relationships between variables (e.g., the impact of AI investment on financial performance). Once the statistical test is selected, researchers establish a significance level (α), typically set at 0.05, meaning there is a 5% probability of incorrectly rejecting the null hypothesis. Finally, the results are interpreted based on the p-value. If $p < 0.05$, the null hypothesis is rejected, indicating a statistically significant effect. However, if $p > 0.05$, there is insufficient evidence to reject the null hypothesis, suggesting that the observed effect may have occurred by chance.

Hypothesis testing plays a crucial role in IS research, helping organizations make data-driven decisions. For instance, a company may want to determine whether AI-driven chatbots improve customer satisfaction compared to human representatives. The hypotheses for this study would be:

- H_0 (Null Hypothesis): *There is no difference in customer satisfaction between AI chatbots and human representatives.*
- H_1 (Alternative Hypothesis): *Customers interacting with AI chatbots report higher satisfaction than those assisted by human representatives.*

To test this hypothesis, the company could survey thousands of users and conduct a T-test to compare customer satisfaction scores between the two groups. If the p-value obtained from the analysis is less than 0.05, the company can reject the null hypothesis and conclude that AI chatbots significantly enhance customer satisfaction. Hypothesis testing is a fundamental component of quantitative research that ensures objectivity, reliability, and informed decision-making across various industries. Some of its key benefits include:

- Ensuring Objectivity: By relying on statistical evidence rather than subjective opinions, hypothesis testing eliminates bias and enhances the credibility of research findings.
- Enhancing Predictive Power: It helps organizations forecast trends and make data-driven decisions, such as predicting IT system performance improvements or evaluating the impact of new technologies.
- Supporting Evidence-Based Policies: Hypothesis testing is widely used in business, healthcare, IT, and finance to shape strategic actions. For example, financial institutions use hypothesis testing to analyze the impact of fraud detection algorithms, while healthcare providers assess the effectiveness of telemedicine platforms.

Variables in Quantitative Research

Variables serve as measurable characteristics or properties that can change and impact the outcome of a study. They are crucial for establishing relationships, testing hypotheses, and deriving conclusions. In IT research, understanding variables helps in analyzing trends, system performance, user behavior, and technological effectiveness. Generally, in research, variables are typically classified into independent, dependent, and other supporting categories. Table 2.2 summarizes different types of variables and their roles in IT and IS.

Table 2.2 Types of Variables and Their Roles in Quantitative Research

Type of Variable	*Definition*	*Role in Quantitative Research*	*Example in IT / Information Systems*
Independent Variable	A factor that is manipulated, categorized, or controlled to observe its effect on the dependent variable.	Serves as the cause in a cause-and-effect relationship; the variable being tested.	Type of encryption algorithm (e.g., AES, RSA, Blowfish) in a study measuring system performance.
Dependent Variable	The outcome or response measured to assess the effect of the independent variable.	Represents the effect or result in a study; what is being measured.	Encryption speed (ms) or CPU usage when using different encryption algorithms.
Control Variable	A variable that is held constant to isolate the relationship between the independent and dependent variables.	Prevents confounding results by ensuring consistency in other influencing factors.	Team size and project complexity kept constant in a study comparing Agile vs. Waterfall methodologies.
Moderating Variable	A variable that influences the strength or direction of the relationship between the independent and dependent variables.	Alters how the independent variable affects the dependent variable.	Developer experience level moderates the effect of programming language on development speed.
Mediating Variable	A variable that explains the mechanism through which the independent variable affects the dependent variable.	Acts as a bridge or intermediary step in the causal chain.	User training level explains how cloud computing adoption leads to improved business efficiency.

Independent Variables

Independent variables represent the factors that researchers manipulate, categorize, or control to examine their impact on dependent variables. It serves as the cause in a cause-and-effect relationship, helping researchers determine how changes in one element influence outcomes. In experimental research, independent variables are deliberately manipulated, while in observational studies, they are categorized based on existing characteristics. For instance, let's consider a study evaluating the effectiveness of various encryption algorithms. In this case, the independent variable is the type of encryption algorithm used, such as AES (AES stands for *Advanced Encryption Standard*, which is a symmetric encryption algorithm widely used to secure digital data. It uses the same key for both encryption and decryption, making it fast and efficient for protecting information in storage or during transmission), RSA (RSA refers to *Rivest–Shamir–Adleman*, an asymmetric encryption algorithm that relies on a pair of keys – a public key for encryption and a private key for decryption. It is commonly used in secure data exchange, authentication, and digital signatures.), or Blowfish (VPS stands for *Virtual Private Server*, a type of web hosting service that provides users with a virtualized environment on a physical server. It offers more control, flexibility, and dedicated resources than shared hosting but at a lower cost than a fully dedicated server.). Researchers analyze these different methods to determine their impact on security performance and computational efficiency. Similarly, in a study on website loading speed, the independent variable could be the type of web hosting service, whether shared, VPS, or dedicated hosting. By comparing these categories, researchers can assess their influence on site performance. Another example is an AI-based fraud detection system, where the independent variable is the machine learning model employed, such as a decision tree, neural network, or support vector machine (SVM). The choice of models can significantly affect the accuracy and efficiency of fraud detection.

Dependent Variables

A dependent variable is the outcome or response that researchers measure in a study to determine how it is influenced by changes in the independent variable. It represents the effect in a cause-and-effect relationship, allowing researchers to assess whether variations in the independent variable lead to a measurable impact. By analyzing dependent variables, researchers can gain insights into the effectiveness, efficiency, and performance of different interventions or conditions. For instance, in a study examining encryption techniques, the dependent variables could include encryption speed, measured in milliseconds, and system performance impact, assessed through CPU and memory usage. These factors help determine the efficiency and computational demands of different encryption algorithms. Similarly, in a study on website performance, the dependent variable might be the page load time, measured in seconds. By comparing how different hosting services affect loading speeds, researchers can evaluate their efficiency. In an AI-based fraud detection study, the dependent variable could be the accuracy of fraud detection, expressed as a percentage. The effectiveness of various machine learning models can be assessed based on their ability to correctly identify fraudulent transactions.

Control Variables

Control variables are factors that researchers keep constant to ensure that any changes in the dependent variable are directly attributable to the independent variable. By maintaining these variables at a fixed level, researchers can isolate the true effect of the independent variable and prevent confounding influences. For instance, a study comparing software development methodologies such as Agile versus Waterfall, the project completion time serves as the dependent variable. However, external factors like team size, project complexity, and available resources must be controlled. If these factors vary, they could skew the results, making it difficult to determine whether differences in project completion time are due to the development methodology itself or other influences.

Moderating Variables

Moderating variables, on the other hand, influence the strength or direction of the relationship between the independent and dependent variables. They do not directly cause an outcome but can alter the way an independent variable affects a dependent variable. For instance, in a study on how different programming languages (independent variable) impact software development speed (dependent variable), a key moderating variable is the level of developer experience. Developers with extensive experience may code faster, regardless of the programming language used, while novice developers may take longer regardless of the language. This moderation effect means that the impact of the programming language on development speed may vary significantly depending on the developer's experience level.

Mediating Variables

Mediating variables play a crucial role in explaining the mechanism through which an independent variable influences a dependent variable. Rather than merely modifying the strength of the relationship (like moderating variables), mediating variables provide insight into the process or intermediary steps that connect the cause to the effect. Let's consider a study examining the impact of cloud computing adoption (independent variable) on business efficiency (dependent variable). While cloud computing has the potential to enhance efficiency, its benefits might not be realized unless employees possess the necessary skills to use it effectively. Here, user training level acts as a mediating variable as it explains why or how cloud adoption leads to increased efficiency. Without adequate training, employees may struggle to use cloud-based tools, reducing the expected efficiency gains.

Data Collection Methods

Quantitative data collection involves gathering numerical data that can be measured, analyzed statistically, and used to identify patterns, relationships, or trends. These methods are widely used in research fields such as science, technology, business, and social sciences to test hypotheses and measure variables. Here we discuss a few quantitative data collection methods.

Surveys and Questionnaires

In quantitative research, surveys and questionnaires are widely used data collection tools designed to gather information from a large group of respondents efficiently. These tools typically consist of closed-ended questions, such as multiple-choice questions, rating scales, and Likert-scale items, which allow for quantitative analysis. While open-ended questions may also be included, surveys are primarily structured to facilitate statistical evaluation. These key characteristics make surveys and questionnaires very appealing to researchers.

- They can be administered through online platforms, email (as discussed in Chapter 1), face-to-face interviews, or phone calls.
- Researchers can frequently utilize Likert scales (e.g., 1–5 ratings) to assess attitudes, perceptions, or satisfaction levels.
- They allow for easy data collection, organization, and analysis using statistical tools like SPSS, R, or Python.
- They are suitable for cross-sectional or longitudinal studies, depending on research objectives.

In the IT field, surveys are valuable for assessing UXs, technology adoption, and system effectiveness. For instance, consider a study measuring user satisfaction with cybersecurity awareness training. Researchers might design a survey using a 5-point Likert scale (1 = Very Unsatisfied, 5 = Very Satisfied) to gauge participants' perceptions of the training program's effectiveness. The collected responses can then be analyzed to identify trends, assess overall satisfaction, and determine areas for improvement. Surveys and questionnaires remain a powerful method for obtaining structured data, enabling researchers to derive insights into user behaviors, preferences, and technological adoption trends.

Experimentations

In quantitative studies, experiments and control groups are used to examine cause-and-effect relationships by manipulating one or more independent variables and observing their impact on dependent variables under controlled conditions. These methods are widely used in scientific and technical research, including the field of IT.

- They involve control and experimental groups to compare outcomes effectively.
- They use randomization to minimize bias and ensure objective results.
- They employ statistical tests such as ANOVA (Analysis of Variance), t-tests, and regression analysis to determine the significance of observed differences.
- They ensure replicability, allowing other researchers to verify findings.

A common application of experimental research in IT is evaluating machine learning algorithms for fraud detection. For instance, an experiment could be designed to test the performance of different machine learning models (e.g., Decision Tree, Neural Network, and SVM) in detecting fraudulent transactions. The independent variable would be the type of algorithm used, while the dependent variable would be fraud detection accuracy (measured as a percentage). By comparing the accuracy rates across different models, researchers can determine which algorithm performs best under controlled conditions.

Observations

Observational studies are a type of non-interventional research in which researchers collect quantitative data without manipulating any variables. These studies are designed to observe and record natural occurrences, providing valuable insights when experimental manipulation is not possible or ethical. In this approach, researchers systematically gather data based on predefined criteria without influencing the environment or participants.

- They involve no direct intervention; researchers merely observe and measure existing behaviors or outcomes.
- They are commonly used when experimental manipulation is not feasible due to ethical, logistical, or practical constraints.
- Data collection is often done using checklists, logs, or specialized software tools that automatically track and record information.
- They offer a real-world perspective, providing insights into natural behaviors and phenomena as they occur in everyday settings.

Observational studies allow researchers to collect real-time data in natural settings, making them an essential tool for understanding patterns and trends in user behavior, system performance, and other factors that cannot easily be manipulated in an experimental setting. In the IT and IS field, observational studies are particularly useful for analyzing user behavior and system performance in live environments. For example, researchers might monitor website traffic and user interactions to study the effects of a User Interface (UI) redesign on user engagement. By using Google Analytics, researchers can collect quantitative data such as page views, bounce rates, and session duration. This data provides insights into how users navigate the site before and after the redesign, revealing whether the changes have a positive or negative impact on UX.

Structured Interviews

Structured interviews are a form of data collection in which researchers ask participants a fixed set of standardized questions. This structured format ensures consistency across responses and enables the collection of quantifiable data. While interviews are typically associated with qualitative research, the structured approach is designed specifically for numerical analysis and is commonly used in quantitative research. In the context of the IT field, structured interviews can be used to gather data on technology adoption and usage patterns. For example, researchers might conduct structured interviews with IT managers at various organizations to assess the adoption rate of cloud computing. Each interview could consist of a set of standardized questions, such as: "Has your organization implemented cloud computing?," "What percentage of your infrastructure is cloud-based?," and "What challenges have you faced in adopting cloud computing?" The responses would then be categorized into quantifiable metrics (e.g., percentage of infrastructure adopted, common challenges) that can be analyzed for trends across different companies or industries.

Structured interviews provide a powerful tool for gathering consistent, reliable, and quantifiable data, making them especially valuable for studies that require large-scale data collection or comparisons across multiple respondents. Here are the key characteristics;

- They collected responses that are pre-coded, meaning participants' responses are assigned numerical values for easy statistical analysis.
- In this mode of data collection, all participants are asked the same set of questions in the same order, ensuring that responses are comparable.
- They help reduce interviewer bias by standardizing the interview process; the potential for interviewer influence or variability is minimized.
- They are very efficient in large-scale studies and are often used in large surveys, market research, or when seeking to gather data from a broad sample of respondents.

Secondary Data Analysis

In quantitative research, secondary data analysis is a research method that involves using existing datasets collected by other researchers, organizations, or institutions. Instead of gathering new data through experiments or surveys, researchers analyze previously collected data to answer new research questions or test hypotheses. This approach is highly efficient, as it saves time and resources compared to primary data collection, making it a popular choice in many fields, including IT. This approach saves time and resources, as the data is already available, eliminating the need for new data collection. In this approach, preprocessing may be necessary to ensure the existing data is compatible with the new research question, particularly if the data was originally collected for a different purpose. While it is a little challenging to find data that is exclusively related to your research, there are still a lot of sources for secondary data. Common sources of secondary data include databases like Kaggle, open business data repositories, government open data portals, and industry reports from organizations such as the World Bank or OECD. Secondary data analysis enables researchers to perform large-scale analyses by leveraging extensive datasets that may be difficult or costly to collect firsthand.

In the field of IT and business, secondary data analysis is frequently used for tasks like predictive modeling and data mining. For example, researchers may analyze historical stock market data to develop and test predictive models for algorithmic trading. Using existing datasets, such as those available through financial data providers or open government data portals, researchers can build models that forecast market trends, identify profitable trades, and optimize trading algorithms. Secondary data analysis offers significant advantages, such as access to large datasets and the ability to focus on more complex questions without the logistical challenges of primary data collection. However, researchers must be cautious about ensuring that the data is relevant, accurate, and appropriately processed to address the specific research objectives (Table 2.3).

Table 2.3 Advantages and Disadvantages of Different Quantitative Methods

Method	*Advantages*	*Disadvantages*
Surveys and Questionnaires	• Efficient for collecting data from large groups • Allows statistical analysis using tools like SPSS, R, or Python • Supports both cross-sectional and longitudinal studies • Flexible delivery (online, phone, in-person)	• May suffer from low response rates • Closed-ended questions may limit depth of insight • Risk of respondent bias or misinterpretation of questions
Experimentations	• Establishes cause-and-effect relationships • Uses control and randomization to reduce bias • Highly replicable • Employs powerful statistical tools (e.g., ANOVA, t-tests)	• May be resource-intensive and time-consuming • Requires strict control over variables • May lack real-world applicability due to artificial settings
Observations	• Provides real-world insights without interference • Useful when experiments are not ethical or feasible • Enables automated tracking with software tools	• No control over variables • Risk of observer bias or misinterpretation • May not reveal causal relationships
Structured Interviews	• Ensures consistent data collection across participants • Reduces interviewer bias • Efficient for large samples • Facilitates numerical analysis with pre-coded responses	• Limited flexibility in probing deeper • Time-consuming if conducted face-to-face • May miss context or nuance in participant responses
Secondary Data Analysis	• Saves time and resources • Enables access to large and complex datasets • Useful for longitudinal or big data research • Ideal for predictive modeling and trend analysis	• Data may not perfectly fit new research questions • Quality and relevance of data vary • May require extensive pre-processing and validation

Sampling Techniques

Sampling is a crucial step in quantitative research that determines how well the findings can be generalized to a larger population. The choice of a sampling technique depends on the research objective, population characteristics, and available resources. Sampling techniques in quantitative research are broadly classified into probability sampling and non-probability sampling.

Probability Sampling

1 **Simple random sampling (SRS)** ensures that every individual in a population has an equal probability of selection, reducing bias and enhancing generalizability. For example, in an IT research study on employee productivity in software development firms, a researcher could use a random number generator to select 200 employees from a database of 5000. While this method provides a truly random sample, it may be challenging to implement for large populations due to logistical constraints.
2 **Systematic sampling** involves selecting every nth individual from a population list after determining a random starting point. In a business analytics study evaluating customer satisfaction with an online retail platform, a researcher might survey every 10th customer who made a purchase in the last quarter. This approach simplifies the sampling process but can introduce bias if there is an underlying pattern in the list, such as customers being grouped by demographics.
3 **Stratified sampling** divides the population into subgroups based on a specific characteristic, ensuring representation from each group. In an IS study on cybersecurity awareness among employees, a researcher might first categorize employees based on department – IT, finance, and marketing – then randomly sample proportionally from each group. This guarantees that all departments are represented, but it requires prior knowledge of population characteristics.
4 **Cluster sampling** selects entire groups or clusters instead of individual members, making it cost-effective for large populations. For instance, in a nationwide IT skills assessment, researchers might randomly select 10 major tech companies and survey all employees within those firms. While efficient, this approach risks introducing bias if the chosen clusters are not truly representative of the entire population.
5 **Multi-stage sampling** combines multiple probability sampling techniques to refine the selection process. In a business intelligence study analyzing market trends across different regions, researchers could first randomly select states, then pick cities within those states, and finally choose businesses within the selected cities. While this approach enables large-scale research with improved representation, its complexity requires careful execution to avoid sampling errors.

Non-Probability Sampling Techniques

1 **Convenience sampling** involves selecting participants who are easily accessible, making it a quick and cost-effective approach. For example, in an IT study evaluating UX with a newly developed mobile app, researchers might survey employees within their own department. While this method allows for rapid data collection, it has a high risk of bias since the sample may not accurately represent the broader user base.
2 **Purposive (Judgmental) sampling** focuses on selecting participants based on their expertise or relevance to the study. In a business research project analyzing stock market trends, researchers might specifically interview financial analysts with extensive experience in trading. This approach ensures that insights come from knowledgeable individuals, but the selection process is prone to researcher bias, potentially overlooking diverse perspectives.
3 **Snowball sampling** is useful for reaching hard-to-access populations by relying on existing participants to recruit others. For instance, in an information security study on ethical hacking communities, researchers might start by interviewing a known ethical hacker who then refers others in the field. While effective in locating niche groups, this technique risks sample bias since participants are likely to refer individuals with similar backgrounds or viewpoints.
4 **Quota sampling** involves selecting participants based on predefined quotas to ensure representation of specific characteristics. In a study on digital banking preferences, researchers might aim for a sample consisting of 40% users aged 18–30 and 60% users aged 31–50. While this method guarantees that key demographic groups are included, the lack of randomness increases the likelihood of bias, limiting the study's generalizability.

Practice Lab 2.2: Applying Sampling Techniques in Quantitative Research

Objective

To help students understand and apply different sampling techniques by designing a sampling plan for a hypothetical research study.

Instructions

1 **Choose a Research Scenario** (select one):

- A study on employee satisfaction in tech startups.
- An investigation of user preferences for mobile banking apps.
- A survey on data privacy awareness among university students.

2 **Design a Sampling Plan.** In 300 words or less, respond to the following:
- **State your chosen scenario.**
- **Select one probability** *and* **one non-probability** sampling method that would work well for your study.
- **Explain why** each technique is appropriate, considering your target population, resources, and research goals.
- Identify **one strength** and **one limitation** of each sampling method you chose.

Deliverable

Submit your brief sampling plan as a Word or PDF document.

Chapter Summary

This chapter provided a comprehensive overview of quantitative research and its importance in the field of IT. It introduced the foundations of quantitative research, emphasizing the use of numerical data, statistical analysis, and structured methodologies to explore and solve problems in a data-driven and objective manner. The chapter outlined four primary quantitative research designs: descriptive, correlational, experimental, and quasi-experimental, each serving different investigative purposes in IT contexts. These designs help analyze trends, establish relationships, and test hypotheses in practical, real-world IT scenarios such as user behavior, system performance, and cybersecurity. Key characteristics of quantitative data are explored, including its numerical nature, objectivity, precision, and replicability. The chapter also discusses data collection methods such as surveys, experiments, and secondary data analysis, and stresses the value of large datasets in uncovering patterns and supporting predictive modeling. The importance of statistical analysis is highlighted, with techniques like descriptive and inferential statistics aiding in meaningful interpretation of results. Furthermore, the chapter detailed how variables, whether discrete or continuous, are central to research design, allowing for measurable and repeatable insights across various fields. Lastly, the chapter underscores how sampling and well-designed research frameworks enhance the validity and generalizability of findings in IT studies.

Review Questions

1 What is quantitative research design?
2 Discuss the characteristics of quantitative research data.

3 What are the quantitative data collection methods?
4 Highlight the difference between probability and non-probability sampling techniques.

References

Hanafi Azman Ong, M., Puteh, F., Teknologi Mara, U., & Alam Selangor, S. (2017). Quantitative data analysis: Choosing between SPSS, PLS and AMOS in social science research. *International Interdisciplinary Journal of Scientific Research*, *3*(1).

Järvinen, J., & Karjaluoto, H. (2015). The use of web analytics for digital marketing performance measurement. *Industrial Marketing Management*, *50*. https://doi.org/10.1016/j.indmarman.2015.04.009

Rutberg, S., & Bouikidis, C. D. (2018). Focusing on the fundamentals: A simplistic differentiation between qualitative and quantitative research. *Nephrology Nursing Journal: Journal of the American Nephrology Nurses' Association*, *45*(2), 209–212.

Saura, J. R., Palos-Sánchez, P., & Suárez, L. M. C. (2017). Understanding the digital marketing environment with KPIs and web analytics. *Future Internet*, *9*(4), 1–13. https://doi.org/10.3390/FI9040076

Schoonenboom, J. (2023). The fundamental difference between qualitative and quantitative data in mixed methods research. *Forum Qualitative Sozialforschung*, *24*(1). https://doi.org/10.17169/fqs-24.1.3986

Zyphur, M. J., & Pierides, D. C. (2017). Is quantitative research ethical? Tools for ethically practicing, evaluating, and using quantitative research. *Journal of Business Ethics*, *143*(1). https://doi.org/10.1007/s10551-017-3549-8

3 Survey Research in Information Systems

Chapter Objectives

After reading this chapter, readers should understand:

- Introduction to Survey Research
- Types of Surveys
- The impact of Digital Transformation
- Planning and Designing a Survey
- Best Practices

Introduction to Survey Research

Survey research is widely recognized as a fundamental and well-established methodology within the fields of information technology (IT) and management information systems (MIS). Over the years, it has been extensively utilized by scholars to investigate a broad range of research questions, owing to its structured and systematic approach. The method follows well-defined procedures that, when rigorously adhered to, facilitate the collection of reliable, valid, and easily interpretable data.

The primary objective of survey research is to generate empirical insights that address specific inquiries, resolve identified problems, and provide evidence-based assessments of needs and objectives. Additionally, it serves as a valuable tool for evaluating whether predefined goals have been achieved, establishing benchmarks for longitudinal comparisons, and analyzing patterns and trends over time. Beyond these functions, survey research is instrumental in offering a comprehensive description of existing phenomena, quantifying their prevalence, and situating them within their broader contextual framework. Its applicability across various domains within IT and MIS underscores its significance as a methodological cornerstone for advancing theoretical development and informing practical decision-making.

DOI: 10.4324/9781003545521-4

In survey research, independent and dependent variables serve as fundamental components in defining the scope of the study. However, unlike experimental research, these variables cannot be directly manipulated or controlled by the researcher. Instead, survey research relies on observational and self-reported data to examine relationships between variables as they naturally occur. Prior to administering a survey, the researcher must develop a conceptual or theoretical model that delineates the expected relationships among the variables under investigation. This model provides a structured framework that guides the formulation of hypotheses and research questions. The survey instrument is then meticulously designed to collect data that will empirically test these hypothesized relationships, allowing researchers to assess the extent to which the theoretical assumptions align with real-world observations. Through this process, survey research facilitates a systematic and structured approach to understanding complex phenomena, making it a valuable methodology in MIS and other social science disciplines.

Surveys are widely regarded as one of the most effective and commonly employed research methodologies by researchers in the field of IT and information systems (IS). Their popularity stems from several key advantages as explained below.

Ease of Administration and Data Processing

Surveys are widely valued in IS and IT research due to their ease of administration, making them an efficient and practical choice for data collection. The structured nature of surveys allows researchers to design, distribute, and administer them with relative ease, particularly with advancements in digital survey tools and online platforms such as Qualtrics, Google Forms, and SurveyMonkey. These platforms enable researchers to automate data collection, reducing the time and effort required for manual distribution. Additionally, surveys facilitate efficient data processing, as responses can be automatically recorded and exported in structured formats such as CSV or JSON for further analysis. This automation significantly streamlines scoring and coding, minimizing human error and allowing for rapid data cleaning and transformation. For example, in IT research examining user satisfaction with enterprise resource planning (ERP) systems, surveys can be distributed to employees across various departments, and responses can be instantly aggregated and analyzed to identify system usability issues.

Furthermore, surveys allow for the collection of both quantitative and qualitative data, enhancing their flexibility in research applications. A study investigating cybersecurity awareness in organizations, for instance, can include Likert-scale questions to measure employees' self-reported knowledge while also incorporating open-ended questions to capture nuanced insights into their experiences with security training. The efficiency of surveys extends beyond academic research to industry applications. IT firms frequently conduct user experience (UX) surveys to evaluate software usability, identifying pain points in applications such as mobile banking platforms or AI-driven customer support chatbots. The ability to swiftly process and analyze survey responses helps businesses improve system design and user engagement.

Measurement of Variables and Relationships

Surveys are very effective in systematically measuring key variables and examining the relationships between constructs, enabling researchers to gain empirical insights into complex phenomena in IT and IS. By designing well-structured survey instruments, researchers can quantify abstract concepts such as user satisfaction, technology adoption, cybersecurity awareness, and system usability, allowing for the identification of patterns and causal inferences. For example, in studies on technology acceptance and adoption, surveys are frequently used to measure constructs from established models such as the Technology Acceptance Model (TAM) or the Unified Theory of Acceptance and Use of Technology (UTAUT). Researchers can assess variables such as perceived ease of use, perceived usefulness, and behavioral intention to use a system. By analyzing survey responses, they can determine whether users are likely to adopt a new IT system, such as a cloud-based collaboration tool in an enterprise environment.

Moreover, surveys facilitate the investigation of relationships between multiple variables, allowing researchers to explore correlations, causations, and moderating effects. In cybersecurity research, for instance, surveys can measure the relationship between security awareness training and employees' adherence to security policies. If a positive correlation is found, organizations may be encouraged to invest more in employee training to mitigate risks related to phishing and social engineering attacks. Surveys also help researchers analyze the impact of emerging technologies. For example, in artificial intelligence (AI) and machine learning adoption, survey-based studies can examine the relationship between organizational readiness, perceived trust in AI systems, and actual deployment of AI-driven analytics tools. Such findings provide valuable insights for businesses looking to implement AI-based decision-making solutions. Additionally, surveys allow for longitudinal studies, tracking changes in user behavior or system adoption over time. For instance, a study on remote work technologies could use surveys to analyze how employee productivity and satisfaction with virtual collaboration tools evolve over multiple years, particularly as new features or policies are introduced.

Generalizability, Reusability, and Comparability

A well-designed survey provides researchers with a robust means of collecting data that can be extrapolated to a broader population, thereby strengthening the external validity of a study. By carefully selecting representative samples and employing rigorous statistical techniques, researchers can ensure that findings from survey research reflect trends and patterns applicable to larger or similar populations beyond the initial study sample. This capability is particularly valuable in the field of IT and IS, where technology adoption, user behavior, and system performance need to be assessed across diverse contexts. For instance, in e-commerce research, surveys can measure customer satisfaction with online shopping platforms. If designed properly, findings from a study conducted on a subset of users (e.g., Amazon customers in the U.S.) could be generalized to broader populations (e.g., e-commerce users in other regions) with similar consumer behaviors. This generalizability is crucial for businesses seeking to optimize their platforms for different markets.

Additionally, the reusability of survey instruments across different contexts makes them valuable for longitudinal and cross-sectional studies. Longitudinal surveys allow researchers to track changes in technology adoption, user preferences, and cybersecurity awareness over time. For example, a multi-year study could analyze how organizations adapt to cloud computing over successive phases of implementation, revealing patterns in adoption rates, security concerns, and employee resistance. Cross-sectional surveys, on the other hand, enable researchers to compare different groups at a single point in time. In IT project management research, surveys can assess the effectiveness of agile methodologies across different industries, such as healthcare, finance, and software development. By analyzing responses from professionals in various sectors, researchers can determine whether agile frameworks are universally effective or if industry-specific modifications are required. Surveys also facilitate geographic comparisons, making it possible to examine how technological advancements impact different regions. For example, a survey measuring mobile payment adoption might reveal significant differences between developed and developing countries, providing insights into factors such as infrastructure readiness, regulatory policies, and cultural attitudes toward digital finance.

Predictive Power

Surveys serve as powerful tools for modeling and predicting behaviors based on observed relationships among variables, making them valuable in both theoretical research and practical applications. In the field of IT and IS, predictive survey models are frequently used to anticipate technology adoption trends, cybersecurity risks, and user behavior patterns. For example, in predicting user adoption of new software platforms, surveys can measure variables such as perceived usefulness, ease of use, and trust in the system, applying models like the TAM or UTAUT. The insights derived from these predictive models help organizations forecast adoption rates and design interventions to improve user engagement. Similarly, in cybersecurity research, surveys can assess employees' risk perception and compliance behaviors regarding security policies. Predictive modeling based on survey data can help organizations identify employees at higher risk of engaging in insecure behaviors and implement targeted awareness programs to mitigate cyber threats. In IT project management, surveys that measure past project success factors such as team collaboration, resource allocation, and stakeholder involvement can be used to develop predictive models for assessing the likelihood of success in future projects. These models provide managers with data-driven decision-making tools to optimize project execution strategies.

Empirical Testing of Theoretical Propositions

Surveys play a crucial role in testing and refining theoretical frameworks and hypotheses within IT and IS research. By collecting structured data, researchers can validate or adjust existing models and contribute to the development of new theories that explain digital transformation, system effectiveness, and user interactions with technology. For instance, in the study of AI-driven decision support systems, researchers may hypothesize that trust in AI recommendations is influenced by perceived accuracy, transparency, and UX. A survey-based study can empirically test these relationships, providing evidence for refining AI adoption models. Surveys are also commonly used in agile software development research, where scholars test theoretical models on how agile methodologies impact team performance, software quality, and customer satisfaction. The empirical findings help refine best practices in software development methodologies.

Integration with Qualitative Research

Surveys complement qualitative research methods by confirming, quantifying, and expanding upon insights derived from case studies, interviews, and ethnographic research. This mixed-methods approach strengthens the validity and applicability of research findings. For example, in studies on UX design, qualitative interviews may reveal themes such as frustration with navigation, preference for minimalistic design, or distrust in personalization algorithms. A follow-up survey can quantify the prevalence of these issues across a larger sample, providing statistical evidence that strengthens the qualitative findings. In enterprise digital transformation research, case studies may explore how organizations integrate cloud computing, automation, and AI into their workflows. Surveys can then be deployed across multiple firms to generalize these insights, identifying common challenges and success factors at a broader scale. Surveys also support ethnographic research in cybersecurity by quantifying risk perceptions and security behaviors in different organizational cultures. If interviews suggest that employees in certain industries are more resistant to multi-factor authentication, a survey can measure the extent of this resistance across various sectors.

Technology Acceptance Model (TAM)

The TAM is one of the most widely recognized and influential frameworks for understanding technology adoption. It posits that two key factors, i.e., perceived ease of use and perceived usefulness, shape an individual's intention to embrace new technology. For instance, an older adult who views digital games as overly complex or as an unproductive use of time is unlikely to adopt them. Conversely, if they perceive these games as both easy to learn and beneficial for cognitive stimulation, they may be more inclined to engage with them. Despite criticisms regarding its simplicity and limitations in capturing the full spectrum of technology adoption behaviors, TAM remains a valuable theoretical foundation. It aligns with extensive research exploring the factors that shape technology acceptance among older adults, offering insights into how design and UX can influence their willingness to adopt digital innovations. By understanding these perceptions, developers and policymakers can create more inclusive and accessible technologies tailored to the needs of aging populations (Figure 3.1).

TAM is particularly well-suited for quantitative survey research, as its constructs can be operationalized through structured survey instruments. Researchers frequently use Likert-scale questions to measure these variables, allowing for statistical analysis of relationships between them. TAM's emphasis on measurable constructs aligns well with quantitative methodologies, which seek to identify patterns, test hypotheses, and establish predictive relationships. Studies employing TAM often use techniques such as regression analysis, structural equation modeling (SEM), and factor analysis to assess the model's validity and the strength of associations between its variables.

For example, in the context of older adults and digital game adoption, researchers might design a survey that assesses respondents' perceptions of digital games in terms of ease of learning, perceived benefits (such as cognitive stimulation), and their likelihood of engaging with them. The collected data can then be analyzed to determine whether perceived usefulness and ease of

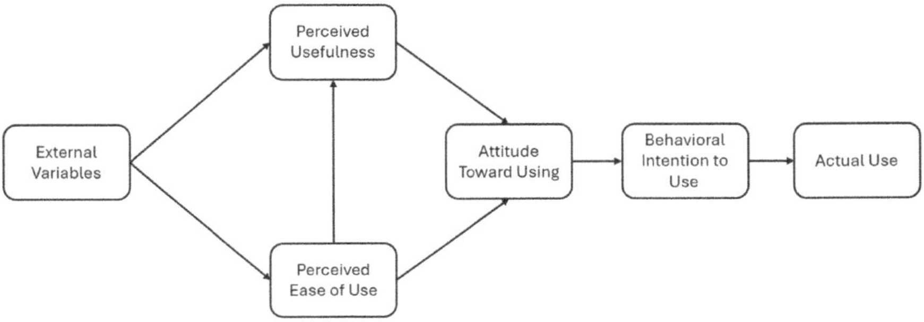

Figure 3.1 Technology Acceptance Model Variables and Factors

use significantly predict adoption intent. By providing a standardized framework for data collection and analysis, TAM enhances the reliability and generalizability of findings in survey-based research. Its structured approach allows for comparative studies across different populations and technologies, making it a powerful tool for understanding and predicting technology adoption trends.

Unified Theory of Acceptance and Use of Technology (UTAUT)

The UTAUT provides a comprehensive framework for understanding technology adoption by positing that an individual's actual use of technology is primarily driven by their behavioral intention. This intention, in turn, is shaped by four key constructs:

- Performance Expectancy: The degree to which an individual believes that using the technology will enhance their performance or provide benefits.
- Effort Expectancy: The perceived ease of use or the level of effort required to learn and operate the technology.
- Social Influence: The extent to which significant others (e.g., peers, family, colleagues) impact an individual's decision to adopt the technology.
- Facilitating Conditions: The presence of organizational or technical support that enables successful technology adoption.

These predictors do not operate in isolation; their effects are moderated by age, gender, experience, and voluntariness of use. For example, older individuals may place greater emphasis on effort expectancy, while younger users might be more influenced by social norms. Likewise, the role of facilitating conditions may be more critical for those with less prior experience using similar technologies. UTAUT is widely applied in quantitative research, particularly through survey-based studies that measure these constructs and analyze their relationships using statistical techniques such as SEM or regression analysis. By integrating multiple determinants of technology adoption and recognizing the role of demographic and situational factors, UTAUT provides a robust, empirically tested model that enhances our understanding of how and why individuals adopt new technologies across different contexts.

Practice Lab 3.1: Designing a Basic Survey

Objective

To help students understand the purpose and structure of survey research by creating a short survey aligned with a specific research question in IT or MIS.

Instructions

1 **Choose a Research Question** (select one or propose your own):
   - How satisfied are employees with the current IT support system in their organization?
   - What factors influence users' adoption of mobile payment applications?
   - How aware are college students of data privacy and cybersecurity practices?

2 **Create a Mini Survey**
   - Design **five structured survey questions** that could be used to collect data related to your chosen research question. Your survey should include:
   - At least **three closed-ended questions** (e.g., Likert scale, multiple choice, yes/no).
   - Up to **two open-ended questions** (optional, for richer insights).
   - Ensure questions are clear, unbiased, and relevant to the research goal.

3 **Brief Justification (150 words max):**
   Explain why survey research is appropriate for your chosen topic. Mention at least **one advantage** of using surveys in IT/IS research (e.g., ease of distribution, ability to quantify results).

Deliverable

Submit your mini survey and justification as a Word or PDF document.

Types of Surveys

There are various types of surveys that researchers can use for different types of studies. Depending on the research objectives, population, and available resources, different types of surveys can be employed. Each type offers unique advantages and limitations, especially when applied in the field of IT.

Cross-sectional Surveys

Cross-sectional surveys are a commonly used research method in both academic and professional settings. They involve collecting data at a single point in time from a sample that is intended to represent a larger population. This approach is particularly effective for evaluating current attitudes, behaviors, or conditions without the need for long-term tracking. In the field of IT, for example, a cross-sectional survey might be conducted to gauge employee satisfaction with a newly implemented customer relationship management (CRM) system across various departments within an organization. This kind of snapshot can provide valuable insights into how the system is being received and whether it meets user expectations. The key advantages of cross-sectional surveys include their speed and cost-effectiveness, making them ideal for projects with limited resources or tight timelines. They are also well-suited for generating descriptive statistics and identifying correlations between variables. However, it's important to recognize their limitations since data is collected at only one point in time, cross-sectional surveys cannot capture trends or changes over time, nor can they be used to establish cause-and-effect relationships.

Longitudinal Surveys

Longitudinal surveys are designed to collect data from the same set of respondents at multiple points over an extended period. This approach enables researchers to observe changes and trends over time and explore potential causal relationships between variables. Longitudinal surveys are particularly useful for studying the evolving impact of technological implementations. For instance, a longitudinal study might monitor employee attitudes toward a new ERP system throughout various phases of its rollout beginning with the pre-implementation stage, continuing through post-training evaluations, and extending to assessments conducted six months after the system has been in use. This method provides valuable insights into how perceptions and behaviors develop in response to the system over time. While longitudinal surveys offer the advantage of tracking dynamic patterns and a better understanding of cause-and-effect linkages, they also come with notable challenges. These studies tend to be time-intensive and more expensive to conduct compared to cross-sectional surveys. Additionally, researchers must address the issue of participant attrition, as individuals may drop out of the study over time, which can affect the reliability and generalizability of the findings.

Descriptive Surveys

Descriptive surveys are used to portray the characteristics of a population, group, or phenomenon at a particular point in time. Rather than delving into the underlying reasons or mechanisms behind certain behaviors or outcomes, these surveys focus on answering the "what" question, like what is happening, what people think, or what practices are in place. In the context of IT and IS, a descriptive survey could be employed to quantify how many organizations within a specific industry sector are currently using cloud-based security solutions. This type of data provides a straightforward, factual snapshot of current practices or trends without attempting to explain why those practices exist or how they developed. One of the main advantages of descriptive surveys is their simplicity since they are relatively easy to design, administer, and analyze, especially when the goal is to summarize information and present it in a clear, digestible format. However, this simplicity also highlights a key limitation: descriptive surveys do not uncover underlying motivations or causal relationships. As such, while they are excellent for providing baseline information or informing future research directions, they should not be relied upon to answer deeper explanatory or predictive questions.

Analytical Surveys

Analytical, or explanatory, surveys are designed to move beyond simply describing a situation. They aim to discover and explain the relationships between variables. These surveys often begin with specific hypotheses and use inferential statistical techniques to test them, making them particularly valuable in research that seeks to identify patterns, correlations, or even potential causal links. For example, an analytical survey might be used to investigate whether there is a significant relationship between the level of IT training employees receive and their compliance with cybersecurity protocols within a large organization. By analyzing data across these variables, researchers can determine whether stronger training programs are associated with better adherence to security standards. The strength of analytical surveys lies in their ability to provide deeper insights that go beyond surface-level observations. However, these benefits come with added complexity. Conducting analytical surveys requires a more rigorous research design and statistical expertise to ensure valid and reliable conclusions. There's also the risk of identifying spurious correlations, relationships that appear statistically significant but are coincidental or influenced by unmeasured factors. Despite these challenges, analytical surveys play a crucial role in evidence-based decision-making and theory development in both academic and applied settings

Planning and Designing a Survey

Planning and designing a survey begins with clearly defined research objectives aligned with broader research questions, followed by identifying the appropriate target population. Researchers must then choose the most suitable survey type and delivery mode (often opting for online), and cross-sectional surveys in IT contexts. Designing the questionnaire involves crafting clear, concise, and relevant questions while avoiding common pitfalls like double-barreled or leading items, and pretesting the instrument ensures clarity and effectiveness. Ethical safeguards, including informed consent and data anonymization, are essential to protect participants. Finally, careful planning of distribution, ongoing response management, and rigorous data quality checks help ensure meaningful and trustworthy results. In Table 3.1, we explain every step and what tools are required to complete the process.

Table 3.1 Steps in Planning and Designing a Survey

No	*Step*	*Explanation*	*Required Tools/Activities*
1	Define Research Objectives	Clearly identify what you aim to learn or test. Align with your research questions or hypotheses. In Chapter 1, we covered this topic in detail.	Research proposal, literature review, conceptual framework tools
2	Identify the Target Population	Decide who will be surveyed (e.g., IT users, professionals, stakeholders). Tailor questions to this group.	Sampling frame, organizational databases, CRM systems
3	Choose the Survey Type and Mode	Select between cross-sectional or longitudinal; online, face-to-face, etc., based on objectives and access.	Survey platform (Qualtrics, SurveyMonkey, Google Forms), email systems
4	Design the Questionnaire	Create questions that are clear, unbiased, and measurable. Use a logical structure.	Survey design software, validated scales, MS Word/Excel
5	Implement Ethical Safeguards	Ensure informed consent, confidentiality, and data protection. Comply with ethical guidelines.	Consent forms, IRB protocols, data anonymization tools
6	Pretest the Survey	Pilot the survey with a small sample to check for clarity, logic, and length.	Survey testing tools, feedback forms, peer reviewers
7	Plan for Distribution and Data Collection	Develop a timeline and strategy to maximize response rates. Send reminders.	Email clients, scheduling tools, response tracking software
8	Ensure Data Quality and Storage	Monitor responses for completeness and consistency. Securely store and clean data.	Data validation scripts, encryption tools, cloud storage, Excel/SPSS/R

Digital Questionnaire Design

Given the impact of digital technologies and the proliferation of digital questionnaires, we will briefly touch on them and the steps involved. Digital questionnaire design refers to the process of creating surveys or data collection instruments using online or electronic platforms such as Google Forms, SurveyMonkey, Qualtrics, or other survey software. This approach leverages technology to efficiently gather responses from participants through computers, tablets, or smartphones. Effective digital questionnaire design requires careful attention to both the content and the UX to maximize response rates and data quality (Table 3.2).

Table 3.2 Steps in Digital Questionnaire Design

Step	*Activity*	*Explanation*	*Required Tools*
Clear and Aligned Questions	Design questions aligned with research objectives	Questions should be clear, concise, and directly related to the research goals. Use mainly closed-ended questions like multiple choice, Likert scales, or dropdowns for easy response and analysis, balanced with open-ended items for richer insights.	Survey platforms (Qualtrics, SurveyMonkey), validated scales
Interactive and Adaptive Design	Use skip logic and branching	Digital surveys can personalize the experience with skip logic, directing respondents to relevant questions based on prior answers. This improves engagement and reduces unnecessary questions, shortening the survey length.	Survey software with branching/skip logic (Qualtrics, SurveyGizmo)
Visual and Mobile Optimization	Create a clean, intuitive layout with mobile responsiveness	Maintain consistent formatting, readable fonts, and include progress bars to motivate respondents and reduce fatigue. Ensure the survey is fully optimized for mobile devices since many participants use smartphones.	Responsive survey platforms, mobile preview tools
Built-in Validation and Pretesting	Implement automatic data validation and conduct pilot tests	Use features like mandatory responses and range limits to improve data accuracy. Pretest the survey with a small sample to identify technical issues, unclear questions, or navigation problems before full launch.	Validation features in survey tools, pilot testing with feedback

Data Cleaning and Preparation

Data cleaning and preparing it for analysis occur in every research form. While there are many ways to clean data depending on the type of software used, here we will provide the general steps involved in it.

Import the Data in Question

The first step in preparing survey data is importing it into a software tool that supports data analysis. Common tools include Excel, SPSS, R, or Python with the Pandas library. Many survey platforms, like Qualtrics or Google Forms, allow direct export in formats compatible with these tools. When importing, it's important to ensure that variable names, question labels, and response codes (e.g., 1 = Yes, 2 = No) are preserved correctly. For example, if you're analyzing user satisfaction with a mobile app in an IT project, incorrect imports might jumble column headers or cause date formats to misalign, which could skew your analysis from the start.

Inspect the Dataset

Once your data is loaded, take time to explore the structure and content. How many responses were collected? Are all expected questions included? What types of data do the variables represent? Are they categorical (like gender), ordinal (like a Likert scale), or continuous (like time spent on an app)? Understanding the types of variables is key because it affects the statistical tests you'll use later. In an IT research context, you might have variables like "frequency of system use" (ordinal) and "response time in milliseconds" (continuous), and these need to be handled differently during analysis.

Remove Incomplete or Irrelevant Responses

Data quality matters. You'll often find that some respondents didn't finish the survey or rushed through it. A good rule of thumb is to remove responses where less than 50% of the questions are answered. Also, look out for duplicates, especially in online surveys where the same person might submit multiple entries. Use metadata like IP addresses or timestamps to identify duplicates. In IT surveys, you may also find "straight liners" who select the same option (like "Strongly Agree") across all questions in a matrix, an indication they didn't engage thoughtfully. Similarly, "speeders" finish the survey much faster than average, raising doubts about response quality.

Handle Missing Data

Missing data is common in surveys and needs careful handling. First, figure out if the missingness is random or if there's a pattern – like younger users skipping income-related questions. Depending on the situation, you can delete those rows or columns (if missingness is extensive), impute the values using averages or predictive techniques (like regression), or leave them as missing if your analysis tool supports that. For example, in an IT usability study, if many users skip the "Would you recommend this software?" question, deleting that variable entirely may lose important insights. In such cases, using mean or mode imputation can help retain valuable information.

Recode and Label Variables

For analysis to work properly, categorical text responses (like "Yes," "No," "Maybe") often need to be converted into numbers. This process is called recoding. You might convert "Yes" to 1, "No" to 0, and "Maybe" to 2. You can also collapse categories like merging "Strongly Agree" and "Agree" into a single category if you have too many low-frequency responses. Additionally, assign clear labels to variables so your output tables make sense later. For instance, in a survey about IT helpdesk performance, rename vague variable names like Q5 to something meaningful like User_Satisfaction.

Detect and Treat Outliers

Outliers are values that are unusually high or low compared to the rest of your data and can distort your results. In IT surveys, suppose you're analyzing time spent on a learning management system, and one user logged 200 hours a week; this might be a system error or an outlier. Use boxplots, z-scores, or the interquartile range (IQR) method to detect such anomalies. Once detected, decide whether to remove, cap, or transform the values based on your research context. Removing them blindly could eliminate useful data; keeping them might skew averages.

Validate and Normalize Data

At this point, you want to make sure all values are within acceptable ranges. For example, if you used a 5-point Likert scale, there shouldn't be any 6s or 0s. Validation also includes checking that numeric data like response times or satisfaction scores make logical sense. If your analysis involves regression or machine learning (common in data-driven IT research), consider normalizing the data, scaling values to a standard range so that one variable doesn't dominate the model simply due to larger values.

Create Derived Variables

Sometimes it's helpful to calculate new variables based on existing ones. For instance, if you asked several questions about user satisfaction, like ease of use, speed, and reliability, you might compute an average satisfaction score from those items. Or if you're preparing data for regression, convert categorical variables (like operating system: Windows, Mac, Linux) into dummy variables (1s and 0s). This step makes your dataset more analysis-friendly and can reveal deeper insights in IT-related survey projects.

Save and Document the Cleaned Dataset

Finally, always save your cleaned data set separately from the raw data. This ensures you have a backup and a traceable audit trail. Just as importantly, document everything: which responses were deleted, how missing values were handled, how variables were recoded, and so on. This documentation supports transparency and reproducibility, key pillars of academic and industry research. In an IT audit or enterprise feedback study, your cleaning log may be just as valuable as your final analysis in supporting decisions or defending results.

Practice Lab 3.2: Cleaning and Preparing Survey Data

Objective

To help students apply basic data cleaning techniques to real-world survey data relevant to IT or IS using Python, Excel, or SPSS.

Instructions

1 **Download a Survey Dataset**
   - Go to Kaggle.com and download a public survey dataset related to IT or tech (e.g., *Kaggle Developer Survey, Tech Salary Survey, Cybersecurity Attitudes Survey*).

2 **Import and Explore the Data**
   - Load the dataset into Excel, Python (Pandas), R, or SPSS.
   - Review the number of responses and variable types (categorical, ordinal, numeric).

3 **Clean the Data**
   - Remove incomplete or irrelevant responses (e.g., <50% complete).
   - Handle missing values (drop, fill with mean/median, or leave as-is).
   - Recode responses where needed (e.g., Yes = 1, No = 0).
   - Detect and treat outliers using visual or statistical methods.

4 **Document and Save**
   - Summarize your cleaning steps in bullet points or short paragraphs.
   - Save the cleaned version of the dataset.

Deliverable

Submit a short report or PowerPoint presentation including:

- The name of the Kaggle dataset used.
- Key cleaning steps taken.
- Before-and-after insights (e.g., % of missing data, outliers removed).
- Reflection on why data cleaning is important in IT research.

Best Practices for Quantitative Survey Research

Effective survey research requires a systematic approach guided by key principles. These include clearly defining the research question, selecting representative samples, balancing costs with errors, designing and pretesting research instruments, implementing quality control measures, ensuring sufficient response rates, applying appropriate statistical methods, upholding ethical standards, and maintaining transparency for evaluation and replication. Together, these principles form a framework for conducting and assessing high-quality survey research. Here we will discuss some of the best practices to follow when it comes to effectively developing and executing surveys.

Best Practice 1: Carefully Craft Your Research Design and Define Research Questions

Remember, your research design will determine the outcome of your research. Also, developing research questions and study objectives requires a thorough understanding of existing literature and available data sources. A well-crafted article should clearly justify the research by contextualizing it with prior work and supporting it with a comprehensive literature review. Researchers often create survey items based on intuition rather than grounding them in a theoretical framework or established model, which can lead to flawed measurement. Additionally, it is essential to consider whether survey research is the most appropriate method or if alternative approaches might yield more reliable or insightful data.

Best Practice 2: Choose Your Research Instrument and Design a Survey

A well-structured survey relies on clear, concise, and unbiased questions with appropriate response options, such as Likert scales or multiple-choice formats. The survey instrument should be fully described, including whether an existing questionnaire was used and, if so, evidence of its reliability and validity from relevant literature. Reliability ensures that the instrument consistently measures the intended variables, while validity confirms that it accurately captures what it is designed to assess. Additionally, the measurement model, including the scale structure and scoring system, should be detailed to facilitate proper interpretation of the results. If open-ended or qualitative questions are included, the methodology for summarizing, coding, analyzing, and reporting text data must be clearly outlined.

For instance, if you are in the IT field and want to develop a survey assessing user satisfaction with cloud computing services, you can go about doing this by including a validated questionnaire. The survey would use Likert-scale questions (e.g., "On a scale of 1 to 5, how satisfied are you with the reliability of your cloud service provider?"). To ensure validity, the questionnaire should be grounded in a theoretical framework like TAM. Additionally, the survey should specify how responses will be analyzed, such as calculating Cronbach's alpha for reliability and conducting factor analysis for scale validation. If open-ended questions are included (e.g., "What challenges have you faced with cloud storage solutions?"), a structured coding approach should be outlined to analyze qualitative data systematically. Below is an example of how the survey would look.

1 **Reliability:** On a scale of 1 to 5, how satisfied are you with the reliability and uptime of your cloud service provider? (1 = Very Dissatisfied, 5 = Very Satisfied)
2 **Performance:** How would you rate the speed and responsiveness of your cloud-based applications? (1 = Very Poor, 5 = Excellent)
3 **Security & Privacy:** To what extent do you feel your data is secure with your cloud service provider? (1 = Not Secure at All, 5 = Very Secure)
4 **Ease of Use:** How easy is it to access, navigate, and manage files or applications on your cloud platform? (1 = Very Difficult, 5 = Very Easy)
5 **Overall Satisfaction:** Would you recommend your current cloud service provider to others? (Yes/No/Not Sure)

Best Practice 3: Do a Pilot Study and Identify Potential Issues

Conducting a pilot study is essential in survey research, allowing researchers to identify ambiguities, biases, and technical issues before full deployment. Pretesting helps refine question wording, improve response options, and enhance overall reliability and validity. By testing with a small focus group or a sample like the target population, researchers can ensure that survey items are interpreted as intended. Additionally, it is increasingly used to explore how participants understand and respond to survey items, ensuring the instrument effectively captures the intended constructs. Let's consider a couple of examples. A company developing an AI-powered customer service chatbot may conduct a pilot study to assess user satisfaction and effectiveness. The survey could include questions about response accuracy, conversational flow, and problem resolution efficiency. During pretesting, participants might report confusion about rating chatbot interactions or difficulty distinguishing between AI and human responses. These insights allow researchers to refine the questionnaire, ensuring that it accurately measures chatbot performance and UX. Similarly, a survey on the adoption of digital analytics tools in marketing decision-making could benefit from a pilot study with marketing professionals. Questions assessing data-driven decision-making, tool usability, and perceived Return on Investment (ROI) might reveal inconsistencies or unclear terminology. Cognitive interviewing could help determine whether respondents understand terms like predictive analytics, attribution modeling, or data visualization. Based on pilot study feedback, the survey can be refined to ensure clarity, improving data accuracy and relevance.

Here is a list of issues that pilot studies can identify and potential mitigation strategies (Table 3.3).

Table 3.3 List of Issues That Pilot Studies Can Identify

Issue	*Description*	*Mitigation Strategy*
Ambiguous questions	Questions that are unclear, vague, or open to multiple interpretations.	Conduct cognitive interviews with participants to clarify wording and ensure questions are understood as intended.
Leading or biased questions	Questions that subtly push respondents toward a particular answer.	Use neutral language and test different phrasings to ensure questions do not influence responses.
Inconsistent response options	Scale points or multiple-choice answers that do not cover all possibilities or create confusion.	Standardize response scales (e.g., Likert scales), ensure response categories are mutually exclusive and exhaustive.
Survey length and fatigue	Excessively long surveys may lead to respondent fatigue, resulting in incomplete or low-quality responses.	Keep the survey concise, prioritize key questions, and pilot test to measure completion time.
Technical issues	Problems with online survey platforms, such as broken links, improper question branching, or formatting issues.	Test the survey on different devices and browsers to ensure functionality before full deployment.
Low response rate in pilot	A low number of responses may indicate lack of participant engagement or survey accessibility issues.	Optimize survey distribution (e.g., personalized invitations, reminders) and check for technical barriers.
Misinterpretation of scale items	Respondents may misunderstand the intent of rating scales or numerical values.	Provide clear instructions and examples, ensuring consistency in scale labeling.
Sampling issues	The pilot study sample may not accurately represent the target population.	Ensure diversity in pilot participants to identify potential biases before full data collection.
Data entry or processing errors	Errors in data recording, missing values, or inconsistencies in responses.	Use automated data validation checks and pretest data analysis procedures.

Best Practice 4: Find Ways to Optimize Response Rates

Achieving a high response rate is essential to reducing nonresponse bias and ensuring the credibility of survey results. Low response rates increase the risk of nonresponse error, where individuals who choose not to participate differ in meaningful ways from those who do, potentially skewing findings. Similarly, response bias occurs when survey respondents are not fully representative of the target population. Below are some ways to ensure a higher response to your surveys (Table 3.4).

Table 3.4 Strategies for Optimizing the Response Rates

Strategy	*Explanation*	*Example*
Personalized Invitations	Personalized emails or messages increase engagement by making participants feel valued. Addressing respondents by name and explaining the survey's relevance can improve response rates.	A university conducting a faculty satisfaction survey sends emails with the recipient's name, a brief purpose statement, and a personalized survey link.
Incentives & Rewards	Offering incentives, such as gift cards, discounts, or entry into a prize draw, motivates participation. Even small incentives can increase response rates.	An IT company surveying customer satisfaction with cloud services offers a $10 gift card for completed responses.
Follow-Ups & Reminders	Sending follow-up emails or messages at strategic intervals helps boost participation, especially from those who may have overlooked the initial invitation.	A healthcare organization conducting a digital health adoption survey sends a reminder one week after the initial request and a final follow-up two weeks later.
Optimized Survey Design	Keeping the survey short, easy to navigate, and mobile-friendly reduces respondent fatigue and dropout rates. Clear instructions and a progress bar help maintain engagement.	A retail company surveying online shopping experiences limits its questionnaire to 10 key questions with an estimated completion time of 5 minutes.
Multi-Channel Distribution	Offering multiple ways to complete the survey – email, SMS, website links, or QR codes – enhances accessibility and response rates.	A financial institution conducting a customer experience survey shares the survey via email, in-app notifications, and printed receipts with QR codes.
Pre-Survey Communication	Informing potential respondents about the survey in advance builds awareness and increases the likelihood of participation.	A software development firm planning a survey on AI adoption in business sends an announcement explaining the purpose and importance of participation.

(Continued)

Table 3.4 (Continued)

Strategy	*Explanation*	*Example*
Survey Timing & Context	Sending surveys at an optimal time when respondents are most likely to engage can improve response rates. Avoiding holidays and busy work periods is crucial.	A cybersecurity company surveying employees on phishing awareness sends the survey mid-week during work hours rather than on weekends.
Anonymity & Confidentiality Assurance	Reassuring participants that their responses will be confidential and used only for research purposes encourages honest and increased participation.	A business school conducting research on corporate ethics assures participants that responses are anonymized and will not be linked to individuals.
Engaging Introduction & Clear Purpose	A compelling introduction that explains the study's significance, expected time commitment, and how results will be used increases motivation to respond.	A tech company surveying software engineers on job satisfaction highlights how the findings will shape workplace policies.
Gamification & Interactive Elements	Making surveys more engaging by incorporating interactive elements, progress tracking, or gamification techniques can enhance participation.	A computer science department conducting a student experience survey includes interactive sliders for rating satisfaction levels and visual elements to make the process enjoyable.

Best Practice 5: Minimize Measurement Error

It is essential to use validated scales, avoid leading or double-barreled questions, and maintain consistency in wording and formatting. Minimizing measurement error is critical in survey design, as it ensures that the data collected truly reflects the respondents' perceptions, attitudes, or behaviors rather than inconsistencies or biases introduced by poorly worded questions. One of the most effective strategies to reduce measurement error is to use validated scales – question sets that have been tested for reliability and validity in prior studies. For example, if you are researching user satisfaction with an ERP system, you might use items from the TAM or Information Systems Success Model instead of writing new questions from scratch. These established instruments help ensure your results are comparable to other studies and grounded in theory.

It's also essential to avoid leading, ambiguous, or double-barreled questions, which can confuse respondents and distort results. A double-barreled question like "How satisfied are you with your organization's IT support and software tools?" combines two distinct concepts, making it unclear what exactly the respondent is evaluating. Instead, break it into two separate questions to isolate the variables. Consistency in wording and formatting further helps reduce cognitive load on respondents. For instance, if you're assessing perceptions of data security protocols, use a uniform Likert scale (e.g., 1 to 5, from "strongly disagree" to "strongly agree") and consistent phrasing to allow for easier interpretation and analysis. Such design discipline ensures higher data quality and more robust statistical insights in IT and IS research.

Best Practice 6: Implement Quality Control Measures

You should always monitor data collection, check for inconsistent responses, and remove duplicate or incomplete entries. Implementing quality control ensures the reliability and integrity of survey data. During and after data collection, researchers should actively monitor responses for patterns that indicate poor data quality. This includes identifying inconsistent answers, such as a respondent claiming to use a system daily but later indicating they are unfamiliar with it. Additionally, attention checks like simple questions embedded within the survey, like "Select 'Agree' for this statement to show you're paying attention," etc., can help detect disengaged or inattentive participants. These measures help filter out responses that could skew the results and compromise the validity of the findings. In IS research, quality control is especially important when surveying users about technical behaviors or attitudes toward technologies like AI tools, data analytics platforms, or cybersecurity policies. For example, if a survey about cloud service adoption receives multiple entries from the same IP address within minutes, this could indicate duplicate submissions, possibly from test runs or fraudulent attempts. Removing such duplicates and incomplete responses not only enhances data quality but also strengthens the credibility of any conclusions drawn from the research.

Best Practice 7: Use Appropriate Statistical Techniques

Using appropriate statistical techniques will help you in extracting meaningful insights from survey data in quantitative research. The choice of statistical methods should align with the research questions, the scale of measurement, and the structure of the data. Descriptive statistics (e.g., means, standard deviations, frequency distributions) are often used to summarize participant responses, while inferential techniques such as t-tests, *Analysis of Variance*, regression analysis, or SEM help test hypotheses and identify relationships between variables. It's also important to check assumptions underlying these techniques (e.g., normality, homogeneity of variance) to avoid drawing invalid conclusions. In IT research, improper statistical treatment can misrepresent the actual UX or system effectiveness. For instance, if you're analyzing how employee training affects information security compliance, a regression analysis can reveal whether training hours predict compliance scores. Additionally, missing data must be handled carefully either through imputation methods or by clearly documenting any deletions to maintain transparency. Ignoring missing responses or using inappropriate techniques can lead to biased results, especially when evaluating technologies like enterprise software adoption, user satisfaction with digital platforms, or AI readiness in organizations. Sound statistical practices ensure the credibility and reproducibility of your findings.

Best Practice 8: Maintain Ethical Standards

Ethical considerations are foundational in any research involving human participants. Researchers must obtain informed consent, which means participants should fully understand the purpose of the study, what their participation involves, and any potential risks or benefits. This is typically achieved through a consent form or an introductory statement at the beginning of the survey. Furthermore, respondent confidentiality must be protected by anonymizing data and ensuring that personal identifiers (such as names, email addresses, or IP addresses) are not linked to survey responses. For IS research students, where questions may probe into system usage, organizational practices, or cybersecurity behaviors, maintaining confidentiality is especially important to prevent potential reputational or security risks for participants or their organizations.

Best Practice 9: Ensure Transparency and Replicability

To strengthen the credibility and usefulness of your study, it is essential to clearly document your survey design, data collection procedures, and analytical methods. This includes providing access to the survey instrument, detailing how variables were measured, and explaining how missing data or outliers were handled. In the field of IT and IS, this transparency allows other researchers to replicate or extend your study, such as validating findings on mobile app usability or examining TAMs across different contexts. Sharing codebooks, analysis scripts, or anonymized datasets, when ethically permissible, fosters a collaborative research culture and enhances the trustworthiness of your work. As noted in the *Journal's* Instructions to Reviewers, there should be a determination of whether the appropriate statistical techniques were used. The article should indicate what statistical package was used and what statistical technique was applied to what variables. Decisions must be made as to how data will be presented, for example, using a pie chart to provide simple summaries of data, but not to present linear or relational data. The authors should provide sufficient detail to allow reviewers to match up hypothesis testing and relevant statistical analyses. In addition, if the questionnaire included qualitative components (e.g., open-ended questions), a thorough description should be provided as to how and by whom the textual responses were coded for analysis.

Best Practice 10: Human Subject Considerations

Although most academic journals now require authors to confirm compliance with Institutional Review Board (IRB) regulations, many survey invitations, especially those conducted via web-based or email methods, still show clear signs of lacking proper IRB review. Indicators of this include invitations that provide insufficient information about the survey, such as unclear estimates of the time required to complete it or inadequate explanations of potential risks and benefits. Some invitations include mandatory questions, which violate participants' rights to skip any item or withdraw entirely. To uphold ethical standards and transparency, authors should clearly state which IRB reviewed and approved their study, the type of approval granted (such as exempt or expedited status), and describe how informed consent was obtained from participants.

Best Practice 11: Transparency

Authors conducting survey research must provide a detailed and transparent description of their methods to allow other researchers to accurately replicate the study. This requirement applies broadly across all aspects of survey research, including instrument development, data collection, and analysis. For instance, simply offering to share the survey instrument upon request does not replace the need to include evidence of the instrument's reliability and validity within the published article itself. Transparency also extends to how the survey was conducted. A review of recent articles in the journal revealed that many studies used mixed methods of survey distribution, such as both internet-based and traditional mail surveys, but failed to specify which data came from each method. In some cases, the description of survey administration was so vague that it only mentioned the survey was "sent" without clarifying the mode of delivery. Such incomplete reporting undermines the study's reproducibility and weakens its scientific rigor.

Additional Considerations Regarding Internet or Web-based Surveys

The use of internet- or email-based surveys has become increasingly popular as a cost-effective and efficient method for conducting survey research. While these digital approaches simplify data collection, it's important to remember that the fundamental principles of survey design and administration remain the same as with traditional mail surveys. Researchers and reviewers should understand that the mode of delivery does not eliminate the careful planning needed before distribution. However, web-based surveys do pose unique challenges, such as the risk of surveys being forwarded to unintended recipients, which can compromise the sample's integrity. Additionally, issues like undeliverable emails, caused by outdated contact lists or incorrect addresses, can affect response rates and make it difficult to determine the correct number of people who actually received the survey invitation. To maintain transparency and credibility, authors should clearly explain how their survey was distributed (for example, via an email containing a link to the questionnaire) and specify which online survey platform was used to collect responses.

Impact of Digital Technologies

In Chapter 1, we talked about the impact of digital transformation on research methods in general. If we look at the landscape of survey research, digital transformation technologies are offering researchers unprecedented ease, reach, and analytical capabilities. Advancements in mobile computing, AI, analytics, and big data have made it easier to design, distribute, and analyze surveys in ways that were unimaginable just a decade ago. Mobile platforms now allow surveys to be completed anytime and anywhere, increasing response rates and reaching diverse populations, including users in remote or international locations. For researchers in the field of IT and IS, this is especially valuable as it enables the collection of real-time user feedback on digital platforms, enterprise systems, or new technologies being piloted across multiple locations. AI has also brought enormous changes in terms of how survey data is prepared and analyzed. AI-powered tools can help clean data, detect patterns, and even generate preliminary insights automatically. For instance, researchers studying user behavior on cybersecurity platforms can now integrate survey responses with behavioral data from user logs, thanks to data analytics and big data platforms. Tools like Qualtrics, Google Forms, and SurveyMonkey now offer built-in analytics dashboards, sentiment analysis, and machine learning-based suggestions to improve question clarity and response quality. This allows IT and IS researchers to quickly identify trends in user satisfaction, adoption barriers, or system performance issues and make data-driven recommendations.

However, these digital advancements also bring challenges. The abundance of digital data can lead to information overload, where researchers may struggle to filter signal from noise without clear hypotheses or frameworks. AI tools may inadvertently introduce biases, especially if trained on non-representative data, leading to skewed insights. Furthermore, the use of tracking tools, cookies, or embedded scripts in online surveys raises ethical concerns about privacy and informed consent. Participants may be unaware that their metadata, like location, device type, or response time, is being collected, complicating efforts to maintain transparency. While digital technologies have greatly expanded the possibilities for survey research, particularly in the agile and fast-paced field of IT, they also require researchers to be more vigilant, ethical, and technically proficient. Leveraging these tools wisely allows for more comprehensive, timely, and impactful research, but it also demands a careful balance between innovation and integrity.

Chapter Summary

Survey research remains a vital methodology in the field of IS, enabling researchers and practitioners to gather structured insights into user behavior, technology adoption, system performance, and emerging digital trends. This chapter introduced the foundational concepts of survey research, including its relevance, historical development, and integration within the IS discipline. We explored various types of surveys, like cross-sectional, longitudinal, and experimental, and discussed how each serves different research purposes. The chapter also examined the profound impact of digital technologies on survey research, highlighting how tools like mobile platforms, AI-driven analytics, and online survey builders have improved efficiency, accuracy, and reach. Planning and designing effective surveys requires aligning questions with research objectives, selecting appropriate sampling methods, and applying principles of clarity, neutrality, and user-centered design. Digital survey tools offer advanced features like skip logic, real-time validation, and mobile optimization, which enhance user engagement and data quality. The chapter concluded with best practices for collecting and cleaning survey data, emphasizing the importance of removing bias, treating missing values, and preparing datasets for robust analysis. By combining traditional research rigor with modern digital tools, survey research in IS continues to evolve, offering powerful means for exploring complex phenomena in today's technology-driven world.

Review Questions

1. What is the primary purpose of survey research in the field of IS?
2. Compare and contrast cross-sectional and longitudinal surveys.
3. How has digital transformation impacted survey research methodologies?
4. You are investigating the effectiveness of a new cybersecurity training program in a company. Which type of survey (cross-sectional, longitudinal, or experimental) would be most appropriate and why?
5. A poorly designed digital questionnaire is receiving very few responses. Based on best practices, what design improvements would you suggest?
6. Explain how skip logic and automatic validation in digital surveys contribute to data quality.
7. Why is it important to detect and remove "speeders" or "straight-liners" in survey data?
8. Describe the steps you would take to clean and prepare a dataset collected from an online survey about UX with a university's learning management system.
9. What role does recoding play in preparing data for analysis in tools like SPSS or Python?
10. Digital technologies like AI and big data analytics are increasingly integrated into survey research. What are the opportunities and potential challenges associated with this trend in IS research?
11. Reflect on the ethical considerations in conducting digital survey research. How would you ensure informed consent, confidentiality, and responsible data handling in a study involving mobile app users?

4 Quantitative Data Analysis in IS

> **Chapter Objectives**
>
> After reading this chapter, readers should understand:
>
> - Nature of Quantitative Analysis
> - Descriptive Statistics and Multivariate Analysis
> - Structural Equation Modeling (SEM)
> - Quantitative Data Visualization

Quantitative Data Analysis

As researchers in information technology (IT) and computer science, we often pause now and then and reflect on the core purpose of research, i.e., uncovering patterns, validating assumptions, and generating insights that drive innovation. At its heart, research in information systems (IS) often begins with something surprisingly basic, that is, quantifying digital interactions. Think of it this way: whether you are analyzing web traffic, user behavior in a mobile app, or server logs, you are fundamentally comparing values like how many users clicked Button A versus Button B, or how long different types of queries take to execute. These comparisons form the basis of deeper insights. They allow us to optimize systems, improve user experience, or detect anomalies in network traffic.

Without a doubt, things grow more complicated as we start layering variables such as time of day, device type, or geographic location. When dealing with massive volumes of data like real-time transaction records from an e-commerce platform or millions of entries in an enterprise resource planning system, visual inspection alone does not cut it. That is where data analysis and statistical methods come into play. Statistical analysis, a vital tool in data science, helps IT professionals make sense of large datasets. It is not just about numbers, but it is also about relationships. For example, an

DOI: 10.4324/9781003545521-5

IS analyst might use correlation techniques to understand the link between system response time and user satisfaction or apply regression models to forecast network demand. Even those without a traditional background in mathematics can contribute meaningfully to this space. With the help of user-friendly tools and programming languages like Python and R, IT specialists can build models that not only explain past behavior but also predict future outcomes such as customer churn in a CRM system or fraud detection in financial transactions. The modern discipline of data science sits at the intersection of computing, statistics, and domain expertise. As we merge these fields, we open doors to predictive analytics, machine learning, and intelligent decision systems capabilities that are increasingly central to modern IS.

The Process of Quantitative Data Analysis

There are several in conducting quantitative data analysis.

Step 1: Define Research Objectives and Hypotheses
Step 2: Prepare and Clean the Data
Step 3: Conduct Descriptive Analysis
Step 4: Perform Inferential Analysis
Step 5: Interpret Results and Derive Insights
Step 6: Communicate and Report Findings

Steps 1 and 2 have been covered extensively in the previous chapters. Quantitative data analysis begins with a clear articulation of the research objectives and, where applicable, the formulation of testable hypotheses. This step is crucial because it guides the entire analytical process, including data collection, selection of variables, and the analytical techniques to be applied. At this stage, activities include identifying independent and dependent variables, determining control variables, and deciding the unit of analysis (individual, group, organization). Once data has been collected, often via digital surveys or system logs, it must be cleaned to ensure quality and accuracy. Raw data is rarely perfect; there may be missing values, inconsistent responses, outliers, or duplicate entries that can distort the analysis. Cleaning is the process of identifying and correcting these errors. Typical activities here include importing data into tools such as Excel, SPSS, R, or Python (Pandas); removing incomplete or irrelevant records; checking for outliers using boxplots or z-scores; recoding variables; and handling missing values through deletion or imputation methods. For example, if survey participants skipped a Likert-scale question on perceived system reliability, imputation using median scores or predictive modeling (KNN, regression) can be applied. Visualization tools like Tableau or Power BI can also be used to inspect the dataset for anomalies visually.

Step 3: Conduct Descriptive Analysis

Descriptive statistics provide a summary of the basic features of the dataset, offering a snapshot of the data's central tendencies, distribution, and variability. In IS research, this might involve calculating the average user satisfaction score for a new mobile banking app, identifying the frequency of system usage across departments, or determining the standard deviation of response times in a network performance evaluation. Activities in this step include generating means, medians, modes, standard deviations, and frequency distributions. Cross-tabulations and pivot tables are also commonly used to explore relationships between categorical variables. Software like SPSS, Excel, R, or Python (with libraries like NumPy and SciPy) can automate these calculations. Visual tools such as histograms, bar charts, and box plots help communicate the findings. For example, using Tableau, an IT researcher might display satisfaction scores segmented by user roles (e.g., admin, analyst, developer) to detect patterns.

Step 4: Perform Inferential Analysis

Inferential statistics allow researchers to make data-driven generalizations about a population based on a sample. This step includes hypothesis testing, confidence intervals, regression analysis, ANOVA, and correlation analysis. In the context of IS, inferential analysis might be used to examine whether there's a statistically significant difference in mobile app adoption rates between two age groups or whether the quality of IT support predicts system usage. Common activities include selecting the appropriate statistical, checking assumptions (normality, independence, homoscedasticity), running the tests using software like SPSS, R, or Stata, and interpreting the results (p-values, effect sizes, confidence intervals). For example, a data analyst might use multiple regression in Python (Statsmodels) to test how perceived ease of use, system reliability, and user training jointly predict satisfaction with a CRM system. Visualization tools like Tableau or R Shiny can present inferential results in dashboards for better stakeholder communication.

Step 5: Interpret Results and Derive Insights

Interpreting results involves translating statistical findings into meaningful insights that align with your research questions and theoretical framework. This is not just a technical exercise; it requires domain knowledge to assess the implications of the findings. In an IT setting, suppose a survey analysis shows that perceived usefulness has the strongest correlation with system usage – this insight can guide future system design and training strategies.

Activities in this step include reviewing statistical outputs, validating whether the hypotheses were supported, and mapping findings back to literature or theoretical models. Tools for this phase include data visualization platforms like Tableau, Power BI, or Excel for creating dashboards, and word processors for crafting narrative interpretations. For advanced analysis, decision trees or feature importance plots from machine learning tools like scikit-learn (Python) can add depth. It's also essential to report limitations, such as sample bias or measurement error, to ensure transparency.

Step 6: Communicate and Report Findings

The final step is to communicate the results clearly and effectively to both technical and non-technical audiences. This includes writing reports, preparing presentations, and creating visual summaries. In the field of Information Systems, stakeholders may include IT managers, software developers, system users, or policymakers, each requiring different levels of technical detail. Activities involve structuring the report (introduction, methods, results, discussion), creating data visualizations, and tailoring messages to your audience. Tools like Tableau, PowerPoint, Canva, and document editors such as Word or LaTeX can assist in this process. For example, presenting survey results on end-user training effectiveness through an interactive dashboard helps IT decision-makers allocate resources or revise strategies quickly. It is also important to include appendices with technical details for reproducibility and maintain ethical standards when presenting data, especially when involving human subjects.

Use Cases of Quantitative Data and Importance

Quantitative analysis involves analyzing numerical data or data that can be converted into numbers without losing its meaning. In IS and IT research, this often includes structured data from databases, surveys, system logs, or user interactions. For example, categorical variables such as programming language preference, software adoption rates, or cybersecurity incident types can be numerically coded like Java as 1, Python as 2, or phishing attacks as 1 and ransomware as 2. Once transformed into numerical form, these data points can be analyzed to identify patterns, trends, and relationships through statistical methods like regression analysis, clustering, and machine learning models. However, while quantitative analysis excels at answering "what" questions such as how many users abandoned their shopping carts, it does not explain "why" they left. To uncover the underlying reasons, qualitative data analysis is needed (discussed later in this book), leveraging methods like open-ended surveys, user interviews, and behavioral observations. Combining both approaches provides a holistic view, empowering businesses and researchers to make data-driven, user-focused decisions (Table 4.1).

Quantitative analysis measures differences between groups, assesses relationships between variables, and tests hypotheses scientifically. In IS and IT research, it helps compare groups by analyzing numerical data, such as evaluating the effectiveness of different cybersecurity training programs by measuring employees' phishing detection rates before and after training.

Table 4.1 Use Cases of Quantitative Data Analysis and Examples

Use Case	*Explanation*	*Example*
System Performance Monitoring	Quantitative analysis helps measure system metrics like response time, uptime, and error rates.	Analyzing server logs to identify peak traffic hours and adjusting load balancing strategies.
User Behavior Analysis	Tracks and quantifies how users interact with software or systems to improve design and functionality.	Measuring click-through rates and session durations on an enterprise web portal.
Fraud Detection	Identifies anomalies in data patterns that may indicate fraudulent activity.	Using statistical models to detect unusual transaction amounts in an e-commerce platform.
Business Intelligence (BI)	Converts raw data into actionable insights for decision-making.	Creating dashboards that show sales trends, customer acquisition rates, and churn rates.
Predictive Analytics	Uses historical data to predict future outcomes and behaviors.	Forecasting inventory needs based on previous purchasing patterns in a supply chain system.

It also identifies relationships between variables, such as the link between server response time and user engagement or the correlation between mobile banking adoption and customer satisfaction in fintech services. Additionally, quantitative analysis is crucial for hypothesis testing, ensuring conclusions backed by solid data rather than based on assumptions. For instance, organizations might test whether AI-driven chatbots improve customer service response times compared to human representatives or evaluate the impact of cloud computing adoption on business efficiency. By leveraging statistical methods, quantitative analysis transforms raw data into meaningful insights, enabling informed decision-making across technology, business, and research domains. Furthermore, quantitative analysis allows researchers and IT professionals to extract actionable insights from data. For instance, an e-commerce platform might use it to determine which user interface changes lead to higher conversions, while a network administrator may analyze system logs to detect anomalies indicative of cyber threats. Data visualization tools such as Power BI, Tableau, or Python's Matplotlib further enhance understanding by presenting complex datasets in intuitive formats.

Descriptive Statistics in Information Systems Research

We live in the age of digital transformation. That means vast amounts of data are generated continuously ranging from web server logs and software usage patterns to e-commerce transactions and database performance indicators. To

Table 4.2 Types of Descriptive Statistics and Examples

Statistic Type	*Purpose*	*Example*
Central Tendency	Identifies the "average" or most common value in a dataset.	Average response time of a customer service chatbot.
Dispersion (Variability)	Measures how spread out the data is around the average.	Standard deviation of page load times across different devices.
Frequency Distribution	Shows how often different values occur.	Number of logins per user role (admin, editor, viewer, guest).
Percentiles & Quartiles	Ranks or categorizes data by position.	Identifying top 10% of users based on transaction volume.

begin extracting meaning from these raw data sources, researchers often rely on descriptive statistics, a foundational toolset that offers concise summaries and visual representations of key data characteristics. For instance, an IT analyst examining system downtime across cloud servers might use measures like mean, median, and standard deviation to quantify average downtime and variability. Similarly, an IS researcher assessing how users interact with a mobile banking app might use frequency distributions and charts to visualize login behavior, peak usage times, or feature adoption rates. Descriptive statistics do not attempt to infer or predict; rather, they focus on what is happening in the dataset. These techniques help uncover basic trends, spot outliers, and provide a clear overview of the data landscape. Whether evaluating support ticket resolution times in an IT service management system or summarizing CPU usage across virtual machines, descriptive statistics offer a crucial starting point, one that prepares the groundwork for more advanced analyses such as hypothesis testing, machine learning, or predictive modeling. Descriptive statistics are typically divided into three main categories: measures of central tendency, measures of dispersion, and frequency distributions. Each serves a unique purpose in summarizing and interpreting data from IS (Table 4.2).

Visualizing Descriptive Statistics

Visualizations transform numerical summaries into interpretable insights. In IS research, common techniques are discussed below. These visualizations are commonly created using tools like Microsoft Excel, Tableau, Power BI, or programming libraries in Python such as matplotlib and seaborn. By turning raw data into intuitive visuals, researchers and IT professionals alike can uncover actionable insights that drive better decision-making and system optimization.

Histograms

Histograms are used for visualizing the distribution of numerical data, making them especially useful in IS research. For instance, a histogram displaying user login times on an enterprise portal can quickly highlight peak access hours and periods of low activity. System administrators might use this insight to optimize resource allocation during high-traffic periods or schedule maintenance during off-peak times. Histograms can also be applied to analyze response times of web services, helping identify patterns in performance that might not be obvious from raw statistics alone.

Boxplots

Boxplots are particularly effective for detecting outliers and understanding variability in datasets. In an IT infrastructure context, a boxplot of system latency across various network zones can reveal regions experiencing significantly higher delays. This visualization can help network engineers pinpoint problematic nodes or connections in a distributed system. In another example, if help desk response times are plotted using boxplots, support managers can quickly identify unusually long resolution times and investigate whether these are due to specific types of tickets or internal workflow inefficiencies.

Bar Charts

Bar charts provide a clear visual comparison between categories and are frequently used in software analytics. For example, a bar chart comparing the number of users accessing different modules in an Enterprise Resource Planning (ERP) system can reveal which features are most or least utilized. This information can guide future development efforts, user training initiatives, or even decisions about deprecating underused components. Similarly, bar charts can be used to visualize incident frequency across departments, helping IT managers allocate resources more effectively.

Heatmaps

Heatmaps are ideal for displaying the intensity of activity over time or space, offering a high-level view of user behavior. In IS research, a heatmap showing hourly user activity on a digital banking platform can help identify engagement trends and unusual usage spikes. For example, a sudden increase in transaction volume during late-night hours might indicate a promotional campaign's success – or raise a red flag for potentially fraudulent activity. Heatmaps are also used in website analytics to show where users click most frequently on a webpage, offering insights into interface design and usability.

Multivariate Analysis Techniques

Due to rapid digital transformation and the expansion of AI, as IS become more complex, so does the data they generate. When you are working with multiple variables at once, like system performance, user behavior, and error

Table 4.3 Common Multivariate Techniques

Technique	*Purpose*	*Example*
Multiple Regression	Predicts a single outcome based on multiple predictors.	Predicting system downtime based on server load, memory usage, and error rate.
Logistic Regression	Predicts a categorical outcome (e.g., success/failure).	Modeling the likelihood of a cybersecurity breach based on multiple risk factors.
Factor Analysis	Identifies underlying variables (factors) that explain data correlations.	Reducing user satisfaction survey items into core dimensions (e.g., usability, reliability).
Cluster Analysis	Group observations based on similarity.	Segmenting users of a cloud platform based on usage behavior.
Principal Component Analysis (PCA)	Reduces dimensionality while retaining variance.	Visualizing high-dimensional network traffic data for anomaly detection.
MANOVA (Multivariate Analysis of Variance)	Examines differences in multiple dependent variables across groups.	Comparing multiple performance metrics across different IT teams.

rates, it is not enough to just look at one or two factors in isolation. That is where multivariate analysis comes in. It helps us explore the relationships between several variables at the same time, uncover patterns we might otherwise miss, and even build models that help us make smarter, data-driven decisions. Unlike univariate or bivariate analysis, which focus on just one or two variables, multivariate techniques acknowledge that real-world data is rarely that simple. Let us say we are trying to understand user satisfaction with a corporate app. It is probably not just about how fast the system responds. We also need to consider how easy the interface is to navigate and how often users encounter errors. Multivariate analysis allows us to study how all these factors interact and impact the overall user experience. When we bring these variables together in one model maybe through a multiple regression or a cluster analysis, we start to see a fuller picture. For example, we might find that users are more forgiving of slow load times if the interface is clean and error-free, or that certain types of users respond differently to specific design changes. These are the kinds of insights that single-variable analysis just cannot provide. So, as you dive into IS research or analytics work, think about the bigger picture (Table 4.3).

Structural Equation Modeling (SEM)

Structural equation modeling (SEM) is a set of statistical techniques used to analyze complex relationships among observed and latent variables (variables that are not directly measured but inferred from other indicators). SEM not only allows researchers to test hypotheses about direct and indirect relationships among variables, but it also accounts for measurement error, making it more robust than traditional regression techniques. In the field of IT, SEM is often used to examine factors influencing user adoption of new technologies. For instance, researchers might model how perceived usefulness and perceived ease of use (latent constructs) affect behavioral intention to use a new software system. This kind of study is often built on the technology acceptance model and is common in IS adoption research. Another example is modeling how security awareness, perceived severity of threats, and organizational support influence employee compliance behavior with cybersecurity policies. Here, SEM can assess both the measurement quality of each construct and the structural paths between them, offering insights into which factors most significantly drive compliance.

Here are some programming languages and software that can be used for SEM.

R

R is a free, open-source programming language widely used in statistical modeling and data analysis. It's especially popular among researchers in social sciences, psychology, and IS for its advanced modeling capabilities. Key R packages for SEM include lavaan (Rosseel, 2012) (user-friendly and powerful for SEM), sem (early SEM package), OpenMx (Merkle & Rosseel, 2018) (ideal for large-scale or advanced SEM), and blavaan (Neale et al., 2016) (Bayesian SEM modeling using lavaan syntax). In IT and IS research, R can be used to test the TAM, where latent variables such as *Perceived Usefulness* (PU) and *Perceived Ease of Use* (PEOU) influence *Behavioral Intention to Use*. The lavaan package lets researchers build these models using simple syntax and provides rich output for path analysis and fit indices. R offers a high level of flexibility, advanced statistical capabilities, rich visualization options, and strong community support. It is particularly valuable for academic and professional researchers who want full control over their analyses.

Python

Python is a general-purpose programming language increasingly used in data science, machine learning, and statistical modeling. Though not originally built for SEM, it now supports SEM through a growing set of libraries. The primary SEM library in Python is semopy (Igolkina & Meshcheryakov, 2020), which allows users to specify SEM models using model description strings. For Bayesian SEM, libraries like PyMC3 or PyMC can be used (Salvatier et al., 2016). While not as mature as R in this domain, Python is gaining ground. Python can be used to model customer satisfaction with IT service platforms. Latent variables like *Service Quality* and *User Support* can be modeled to predict *Overall Satisfaction*, helping IT firms understand key service drivers.

Python integrates seamlessly with data preprocessing, machine learning, and visualization tools (e.g., Pandas, Scikit-learn, Seaborn), making it great for end-to-end data analysis pipelines. It's ideal for data scientists who want to incorporate SEM into broader analytics workflows.

IBM SPSS AMOS

AMOS (Analysis of Moment Structures) is a visual software add-on for IBM SPSS that allows users to draw SEM models graphically rather than coding them. It's especially popular in business, education, and social sciences. AMOS is a standalone software that works with SPSS data files and offers a drag-and-drop interface to build path diagrams, specify relationships, and assess model fit. AMOS is often used to analyze relationships in ERP implementation studies, such as how *IT training quality* and *management support* affect *user satisfaction* and *system usage*. Researchers can visually build and modify models with ease. AMOS is user-friendly, ideal for beginners or those with minimal programming experience. Its visual interface makes it great for teaching SEM concepts and exploring models interactively (Arbuckle, 2017).

Mplus

Mplus is a powerful commercial software package designed for SEM, path analysis, multilevel modeling, and latent class analysis. It operates via syntax-based commands, offering high flexibility and advanced features. Mplus is a standalone program with its own scripting language. It excels in handling complex data structures, missing data, and longitudinal models. Researchers might use Mplus to conduct a multi-group SEM to compare male and female responses to information security policies. It allows testing whether structural relationships differ between groups with precision. Mplus is extremely powerful for handling advanced SEM scenarios, including Bayesian estimation, multilevel modeling, and structural modeling with categorical data. It's a go-to tool for methodologically rigorous research (Muthén & Muthén, 2017).

Stata

Stata is a statistical software package popular in economics, health, and policy research. It includes robust SEM features via the sem and gsem commands, supporting both continuous and categorical latent variables. Stata's SEM features are built into the software itself, with a model builder GUI and syntax-based approach. gsem supports generalized SEM with non-normal outcomes and multilevel models. In public sector IT research, Stata can model how *Transparency, Service Quality*, and *Trust in Government* interact to shape *Citizen Engagement* in e-Government systems. Stata's SEM capabilities are well-integrated with its powerful data management and econometrics features. It's ideal for researchers dealing with survey data, policy modeling, or large datasets.

LISREL

LISREL (Linear Structural Relations) is one of the earliest SEM tools, widely used in early structural modeling research. It uses a matrix-based approach to define and estimate SEM models. LISREL is a standalone program requiring specific syntax. Though it has a steeper learning curve, it remains respected for methodological rigor in SEM. In enterprise systems research, LISREL might be used to assess how factors like *Top Management Support* and *System Quality* affect *IS Success*, measuring direct and indirect effects through multiple latent variables. LISREL is known for its statistical precision and methodological contributions to the field. It's still favored in some academic circles for its formal approach and legacy value.

SmartPLS

SmartPLS is a graphical SEM tool that uses Partial Least Squares (PLS) path modeling, an alternative to covariance-based SEM. It's suited for exploratory models and smaller datasets. SmartPLS is a standalone software with an intuitive drag-and-drop interface. It handles both reflective and formative measurement models and outputs path coefficients, loadings, and model fit statistics. A study on mobile payment adoption can use SmartPLS to model how *Perceived Risk*, *Trust*, and *Ease of Use* affect *Adoption Intentions*, even with small or non-normally distributed samples. SmartPLS is ideal for applied researchers and practitioners. It's user-friendly, handles small samples, and is widely accepted in IS research using PLS-SEM methodology.

JASP

JASP is an open-source GUI-based statistical software built for ease of use. It integrates SEM capabilities through a graphical interface powered by R's lavaan in the backend. While not a package itself, JASP allows users to perform SEM using a point-and-click interface. It automates lavaan code and outputs visualizations and fit indices. In introductory IS courses, JASP can be used to model student satisfaction in e-learning platforms by exploring relationships between engagement, perceived learning, and satisfaction. JASP is beginner-friendly and great for educational use. It provides clean visuals, real-time updates to output, and supports reproducible research without requiring coding expertise.

Data Visualization in Information Systems Research

In IT and IS research, data visualization serves as a cornerstone functioning as both an analytical tool and a communication medium. As organizations increasingly depend on digital infrastructures that produce massive volumes of data, the ability to transform raw data into comprehensible and actionable insights becomes essential. Visualization tools ranging from dashboards in decision support systems to real-time analytics in enterprise applications play a pivotal role in guiding strategic decisions. These tools bridge the gap between data complexity and managerial intuition, allowing researchers and practitioners alike to identify patterns, detect anomalies, and validate hypotheses with greater clarity and precision. The following tools in Table 4.4 collectively provide IS and IT researchers with a diverse suite of visualization capabilities that support both qualitative and quantitative analyses. From the technical rigor of Python and R to the accessibility of Tableau and Power BI, and the specialized capabilities of Gephi, Cytoscape, and NVivo, these platforms enhance both the analytical depth and communicative clarity of research findings.

Table 4.4 Tools for Visualization in IT Research

Tool / Language	*Key Features*	*Typical Use Cases in IS/IT*	*Example Applications*
R (ggplot2, plotly, shiny)	Offers robust statistical graphics; supports interactive web-based visualizations via Shiny	Exploratory Data Analysis (EDA), statistical modeling, user behavior analytics	Visualizing user interactions within ERP systems; dynamic dashboards for academic research (Healy, 2018; Wickham, 2016)
Python (matplotlib, seaborn, altair, plotly)	Widely adopted in data science; supports static and interactive graphics	Visualizing machine learning results, simulations, and time-series data	Plotting fintech data to analyze stock performance, fraud detection, and portfolio risk analysis
Tableau	Drag-and-drop interface; strong support for real-time data connections	Business Intelligence (BI), executive dashboards, KPI monitoring	Used in IT project management dashboards and operational reporting in CRM systems
Power BI	Integration with Microsoft ecosystem; customizable DAX expressions	Strategic planning, financial reporting, user adoption metrics	Visualizing IT budget allocations and ROI on information systems investments
Gephi	Open-source software for network analysis and graph visualization	Analysis of network structures, cybersecurity threats, IT infrastructure dependencies	Mapping social network relationships in collaborative platforms; visualizing server interconnectivity in enterprise networks
Cytoscape	Specialized for biological and complex networks; extensible through plugins	IT governance, network vulnerability visualization	Illustrating dependencies in enterprise architectures or communication networks
NVivo	Qualitative analysis software with rich visualization tools	Thematic coding, discourse analysis, qualitative case study research	Word frequency plots from interview transcripts; cluster maps of emergent themes in IT adoption studies

Graphical Representation of Data in Information Systems Studies

Lab Practice 4.1: Quantitative Data Analysis with Tableau

Objective

To equip students with practical skills in visualizing and interpreting quantitative survey data using Tableau. Students will learn how to explore data distributions, identify trends, and generate insights relevant to IS or IT-related research.

Instructions

1 **Download Sample Dataset:**
- Visit Kaggle.com and download a relevant cleaned survey dataset. Suggested keywords:
  - *"Technology Adoption Survey"*
  - *"Cybersecurity Awareness Survey"*
  - *"Remote Work IT Survey"*
- Alternatively, you can use a dataset provided by your instructor.

2 **Import Data into Tableau:**
- Open Tableau Desktop or Tableau Public.
- Load your CSV or Excel survey data file.
- Familiarize yourself with the dataset: Identify key variables, such as demographic data (e.g., age, role), Likert scale responses, usage frequency, or satisfaction scores.

3 **Create Basic Visualizations:**
Create the following charts using appropriate fields:
- **Bar Chart**: Show the distribution of responses for a Likert-scale question (e.g., satisfaction with IT support).
- **Pie or Donut Chart**: Show proportions of categorical data (e.g., preferred mobile payment platforms).
- **Histogram**: Display distribution of numerical responses (e.g., hours spent using a system).
- **Cross-tab or Heat Map**: Compare satisfaction levels across different user groups (e.g., students vs. staff).
- **Line or Area Chart** *(if time-based data is available)*: Visualize trends over time (e.g., weekly system usage).

4 **Generate Insights and Takeaways:**
- Identify two to three key patterns or trends in the data.
- Suggest what these trends might imply for IT decision-makers or system developers.

Deliverables

- A Tableau Dashboard with at least **three different visualizations** and **interactive filters**
- A short **summary report (200–300 words)** explaining:
    - What the data shows
    - How it relates to your research question or IS/IT topic
    - Recommendations or interpretations

Chapter Summary

This chapter introduced core concepts and techniques used to analyze numerical data in IS contexts. It began by emphasizing the role of descriptive statistics in summarizing data patterns and variability, and then explored inferential techniques like regression, correlation, and hypothesis testing for uncovering relationships and making generalizations. We also discussed SEM, a method for testing theoretical models and relationships among latent variables. The chapter also highlighted the value of data visualization tools (e.g., Tableau, SPSS, R) for communicating insights clearly and effectively. Throughout, the importance of aligning analysis with research objectives was emphasized, starting from cleaning data to reporting results ethically and understandably. Real-world IS applications like fraud detection, system performance monitoring, and user behavior analysis were discussed to illustrate how quantitative methods support data-driven decisions. This chapter equips IS researchers with foundational knowledge and modern tools to conduct rigorous quantitative analysis and contribute meaningfully to both academic and professional practice.

Review Questions

1 What is the main purpose of quantitative data analysis in IS research?
2 How do descriptive statistics differ from inferential statistics in analyzing IS data?
3 Give two examples of how quantitative data can be used in system performance monitoring.
4 What are the key steps involved in the quantitative data analysis process?
5 Explain the role of SEM in IS research.
6 Why is data cleaning important before conducting any statistical analysis? Provide two common data cleaning techniques.
7 What is the significance of data visualization in reporting quantitative findings? Name two tools used for this purpose.
8 How can regression analysis help in understanding relationships within IS datasets?
9 Describe one real-world use case of predictive analytics in Information Systems.

References

Arbuckle, J. L. (2017). IBM® SPSS® AmosTM 25 User´s Guide. In *IBM SPSS Amos 25 User's Guide*.

Healy, K. (2018). *Data visualization: A practical introduction*. Princeton University Press.

Igolkina, A. A., & Meshcheryakov, G. (2020). semopy: A Python package for structural equation modeling. *Structural Equation Modeling, 27*(6). https://doi.org/10.1080/10705511.2019.1704289

Merkle, E. C., & Rosseel, Y. (2018). Blavaan: Bayesian structural equation models via parameter expansion. *Journal of Statistical Software, 85*. https://doi.org/10.18637/jss.v085.i04

Muthén, L. K., & Muthén, B. O. (2017). *Mplus user's guide* (8th ed). Los Angeles, CA: Muthén & Muthén.

Neale, M. C., Hunter, M. D., Pritikin, J. N., Zahery, M., Brick, T. R., Kirkpatrick, R. M., Estabrook, R., Bates, T. C., Maes, H. H., & Boker, S. M. (2016). OpenMx 2.0: Extended structural equation and statistical modeling. *Psychometrika, 81*(2). https://doi.org/10.1007/s11336-014-9435-8

Rosseel, Y. (2012). Lavaan: An R package for structural equation modeling. *Journal of Statistical Software, 48*. https://doi.org/10.18637/jss.v048.i02

Salvatier, J., Wiecki, T. V., & Fonnesbeck, C. (2016). Probabilistic programming in Python using PyMC3. *PeerJ Computer Science, 2016*(4). https://doi.org/10.7717/peerj-cs.55

Wickham, H. (2016). *ggplot2: Elegant graphics for data analysis* (2nd ed.). Springer.

5 Longitudinal Studies in Information Systems and IT

> **Chapter Objectives**
>
> After reading this chapter, readers should understand:
>
> - Types of Longitudinal Studies
> - Designing a Longitudinal Study
> - Applications of Longitudinal Studies
> - Data Management and Analysis
> - Techniques

Longitudinal Studies

Longitudinal study is a research approach that involves collecting data from the same subjects or entities repeatedly over a period of time. The key feature of this method is its ability to track changes, trends, and cause-and-effect relationships as they unfold, offering insights that a one-time snapshot (cross-sectional study) simply can't provide. Longitudinal studies can span days, months, or even decades, depending on the research goals. In everyday life, we encounter longitudinal studies in areas like public health, education, and social sciences. For instance, medical researchers might follow a group of individuals over 20 years to observe how their lifestyle choices such as diet, exercise, or smoking impact the development of chronic diseases. Similarly, educational researchers may track students from kindergarten through high school to understand how early childhood education affects long-term academic achievement and social development. These studies help establish patterns and detect causal relationships that emerge only over time. In Table 5.1, we provide a few examples of longitudinal studies that are currently ongoing.

In the field of information systems (IS), one example of a longitudinal study might involve tracking user adoption of a new enterprise resource planning (ERP) system over a 12-month period. Researchers or information technology (IT) managers could observe how employees interact with the system during

DOI: 10.4324/9781003545521-6

Table 5.1 Examples of Prominent Longitudinal Studies

Study Name	*Purpose*	*Conducting Institution*	*Initiation Date*	*Current Status*	*Website*
Framingham Heart Study	To identify common factors contributing to cardiovascular disease by following participants over time.	National Heart, Lung, and Blood Institute (NHLBI) in collaboration with Boston University	1948	Ongoing	Framingham Heart Study
1970 British Cohort Study	To study the social, educational, and health development of individuals born in a single week in 1970 in the UK.	Centre for Longitudinal Studies, UCL Social Research Institute	1970	Ongoing	1970 British Cohort Study
Dunedin Multidisciplinary Health and Development Study	To investigate the health and development of a cohort born in Dunedin, New Zealand, in 1972-1973.	University of Otago, New Zealand	1972	Ongoing	Dunedin Study
Nurses' Health Study	To explore risk factors for chronic diseases in women, particularly among nurses.	Harvard T.H. Chan School of Public Health	1976	Ongoing	Nurses' Health Study
Korea Nurses' Health Study (KNHS)	To assess health status, lifestyle, occupational environment, and disease-related characteristics among Korean female nurses.	Korea Disease Control and Prevention Agency (KDCA) and Ewha Womans University	2013	Ongoing	KNHS

different stages like initial rollout, training, adaptation, and eventual integration into daily workflows. By collecting usage data, support requests, and user satisfaction surveys at multiple time points, they can determine whether specific interventions (like additional training or interface updates) improve user adoption and performance. Another compelling example comes from data science in IT, where longitudinal studies can be used to track changes in model performance over time. For instance, a retail company using a predictive model to forecast sales might monitor that model's accuracy and precision over several quarters. As new products, customer behaviors, and market conditions evolve, the model's effectiveness may degrade, a phenomenon known as model drift. By conducting a longitudinal analysis, data scientists can detect when and why the model's predictions start to diverge from actual outcomes, prompting retraining or refinement. This long-term monitoring ensures that data-driven decisions remain accurate and aligned with current realities. Longitudinal studies in IS and IT allow researchers and professionals to observe complex, dynamic systems over time, identify patterns, test hypotheses, and make data-driven decisions that align with long-term goals (Table 5.2).

Table 5.2 Applications of Longitudinal Studies in IT and IS

Application Area	*Example*	*Explanation*
Technology Adoption and Diffusion	Tracking adoption of cloud computing among SMEs over a 5-year period	Measures how awareness, perceived benefits, and actual use of cloud services spread over time, identifying adoption patterns and barriers.
User Behavior Over Time	Studying employees' use of a new ERP system at 1-month, 3-month, and 12-month intervals	Helps reveal learning curves, usage consistency, or resistance to change as users become more familiar or dissatisfied with the system.
IT Project Implementation and Effects	Monitoring system usage and performance outcomes following the rollout of a CRM system	Captures both short- and long-term effects of system implementation, including issues during transition and sustained value post-adoption.
Organizational Change andDigital Transformation	Examining how business processes and employee roles shift over time during digital transformation	Tracks the evolving impact of digital tools on workflow, decision-making, and organizational culture through different transformation phases.
Security and Compliance Evolution	Evaluating compliance with cybersecurity policies across departments over several audit cycles	Assesses whether training, policy changes, or incidents affect long-term compliance and security behaviors.
Long-term Impact on Performance or Strategy	Studying how the use of business intelligence tools affects strategic decision-making over 3 years	Determines whether IT investments lead to measurable improvements in decision quality, agility, or competitive advantage over the long term.

Practice Lab 5.1: Discovering and Analyzing a Longitudinal Study in IT

Title

Finding and Analyzing a Real-World Longitudinal Study in Information Systems or IT

Objective

Students will locate a current or recent longitudinal study in the IT/IS domain, analyze its methodology, and write a short report summarizing their findings.

Learning Outcomes

By completing this lab, students will:

- Identify and interpret the design and scope of a longitudinal study.
- Evaluate the methodology used in a real-world IS context.
- Reflect on the challenges and benefits of longitudinal research.

Instructions

Step 1: Locate a Longitudinal Study

Search for a **peer-reviewed article**, **working paper**, or **research project** that clearly uses longitudinal methods in the field of **Information Systems**, **Information Technology**, or **related areas.**

Step 2: Read and Analyze the Study

Focus on the following key elements in your analysis:

- **Research Question(s):** What is the study trying to find out?
- **Timeframe:** Over how many periods/years was the data collected?
- **Sample and Method:** Who or what is being studied? How was the data collected?
- **Key Variables:** What are the independent and dependent variables?
- **Findings/Trends:** What patterns or trends did the study reveal over time?
- **Implications:** What is the significance of the findings for IT/IS professionals?

Step 3: Write a Short Report (500–700 words)

Deliverable

A 500–700 word report (PDF or DOCX).

Instructor Tips

- Encourage students to pick diverse domains (e.g., artificial intelligence adoption, cybersecurity behavior, IT usage in education).
- Offer 2–3 example papers to get them started.
- You can allow collaboration in pairs for deeper discussion.

Types of Longitudinal Studies

There are various longitudinal study types that offer distinct advantages depending on the research question and data availability. By applying these methods to IT and IS, researchers and practitioners can move beyond static analyses and gain dynamic, actionable insights that evolve with the technologies and environments they aim to understand.

Panel Studies

Panel studies involve collecting data from the same individuals, systems, or entities at multiple time points. This type of study provides deep insights into how variables change within the same units over time, making it ideal for exploring cause-and-effect relationships. The ability to control for individual-level differences enhances the validity of observed trends and patterns. Consider a university tracking a panel of students across eight semesters to study how their interaction with a cloud-based learning management system (LMS) evolves. Researchers might measure login frequency, use of different LMS tools (forums, quizzes, gradebook), and academic outcomes over time. This helps assess whether increased LMS use improves academic performance or how system interface changes affect user behavior. Similarly, an organization might conduct a panel study of system administrators' performance before and after the deployment of a new monitoring tool, allowing them to evaluate the tool's effectiveness in real-world use.

Cohort Studies

Cohort studies follow a group of people (or systems) who share a defining characteristic or experience within a specific time period. Unlike panel studies, cohort participants do not necessarily need to be assessed at the same intervals or be the exact same individuals throughout the study. The key feature is the shared starting point, which allows comparisons across time within the same contextual framework. For example, a software company could initiate a cohort study of users who signed up for its new productivity app during the first quarter of a year. This group might be tracked over several months to assess patterns in feature adoption, retention rates, and support needs. Insights can then be compared with later cohorts introduced to updated versions of the app, helping developers understand the long-term impact of onboarding strategies or interface changes. In higher education, a cohort study might follow a specific class of computer science majors to evaluate how early exposure to data analytics tools affects their career paths and technical competencies.

Trend (Repeated Cross-Sectional) Studies

Trend studies examine changes in the same population over time, but with different samples at each time point. This design is particularly useful when studying large populations where following the same individuals is impractical or unnecessary. Trend studies are excellent for capturing macro-level shifts, such as changes in attitudes, policies, or technologies. To illustrate an example from the IT field, a consulting firm may conduct annual surveys of IT professionals working in healthcare to monitor changes in their attitudes toward cybersecurity protocols. Even though different individuals may respond each year, the surveys consistently target the same population group. This allows researchers to track trends such as increased adoption of multifactor authentication, rising concerns about data privacy, or shifting budget allocations toward cloud security. Similarly, a university IT department could analyze semester-by-semester survey data on student satisfaction with campus Wi-Fi, identifying service improvements or recurring issues over time.

Retrospective Longitudinal Studies

Retrospective studies look backward in time using existing historical data to identify trends and relationships. These studies are particularly valuable when immediate real-time data collection is not possible or when researchers aim to understand the long-term outcomes of past events or policies. An analytics team in a data-driven organization might examine five years of archived server logs and user data to analyze how system load has changed in response to new product releases or infrastructure changes. For instance, they might discover that a cloud migration in year three significantly reduced downtime and latency. Likewise, a retrospective study might evaluate historical bug reports, system updates, and user complaints to assess how the introduction of a new software development lifecycle (e.g., Agile vs. Waterfall) impacted product quality and delivery time (Table 5.3).

Table 5.3 Advantages and Disadvantages of Each Type

Type of Study	*Advantages*	*Disadvantages*
Panel Study	• Tracks the same subjects over time, enabling rich, individual-level insights. • Controls for individual variability. • Useful for causal inference.	• Participants may drop out over time. • Maintaining consistent data collection can be costly and time-consuming. • Panel fatigue may reduce data quality.
Cohort Study	• Focuses on groups with s hared characteristics, making it ideal for studying policy or system implementation impact. • Allows comparisons across cohorts.	• Cannot always track the same individuals, reducing the ability to analyze individual change. • May face confounding variables if not carefully designed.
Trend Study	• Efficient and less resource-intensive than panel studies. • Ideal for observing macro-level changes in IT/IS populations. • No attrition bias.	• Different samples each time means you can't track individual changes. • Changes in sampling or measurement over time may compromise comparability.
Retrospective Study	• Makes use of existing historical data, saving time and resources. • Can quickly assess long-term effects of IT interventions.	• Limited by data availability and quality. • Potential for recall or recording bias. • May lack control over data collection methods used in the past.

Analytical Techniques for Longitudinal Studies

Analyzing longitudinal data requires specialized analytical techniques due to issues like correlation within subjects, missing data, and time-dependent changes. Here are common analytical techniques for longitudinal studies.

Descriptive and Inferential Statistics

Descriptive statistics summarize data across different time points using measures such as means, standard deviations, and graphical representations like line graphs to visualize trends. Inferential statistics, in contrast, help test hypotheses about changes over time, associations between variables, or differences between groups. For longitudinal data, special care must be taken to account for the repeated-measures nature of the data. For example, in a study examining employee satisfaction with a newly deployed help desk system over 12 months, descriptive statistics can reveal mean satisfaction scores at quarterly intervals, while inferential tests like paired t-tests or linear regression with time as a predictor can assess whether satisfaction significantly increases or decreases over time. However, since longitudinal data violates the assumption of independence between observations, traditional statistical methods must be adapted or replaced with more sophisticated models, which will be discussed in the sections below.

Repeated Measures ANOVA

Repeated measures analysis of variance (ANOVA) is a widely used technique for comparing means across multiple time points within the same subjects. This method accounts for the correlation between repeated observations and provides insight into whether changes over time are statistically significant. In the IT/IS domain, suppose a researcher wants to evaluate how user proficiency with a new project management software evolves over a 6-month training program. By measuring usability ratings at baseline, 3 months, and 6 months, repeated measures ANOVA can test whether there is a significant improvement in perceived usability. This technique assumes sphericity (equal variances of the differences between all combinations of related groups), and violations of this assumption require corrections such as the Greenhouse-Geisser adjustment. One limitation is that it becomes less practical with more complex time structures or when there are missing data points. Nonetheless, it is a robust tool for straightforward within-subject comparisons over a few time intervals.

Growth Curve Modeling/Latent Growth Modeling

Growth curve modeling (GCM), including its more flexible variant latent growth modeling (LGM) within the structural equation modeling (SEM) framework, is designed to examine individual trajectories over time. These techniques model both the average growth trend and individual variations in growth patterns. In the context of IT/IS, consider a study analyzing the development of digital literacy among employees following the introduction of a company-wide digital transformation initiative. GCM can be used to model the increase in digital literacy scores over time, capturing both the overall trend and differences among departments or demographic groups. LGM is particularly powerful because it can incorporate latent variables and measurement errors, and allow for predictors of growth parameters (e.g., initial literacy level predicting rate of improvement). These models are ideal when the research interest lies not only in whether change occurs but also in understanding the shape of that change (linear, quadratic, etc.) and the factors influencing it.

Fixed and Random Effects Models

Fixed and random effects models, commonly used in panel data analysis, address longitudinal data by modeling both time-invariant and time-varying components. A fixed effects model controls for all unobserved, time-invariant differences between individuals, thus isolating the impact of time-varying predictors. Conversely, random effects models assume that individual-specific effects are uncorrelated with the predictors and include them as random variables, allowing for estimation of both within- and between-subject variation. In an IS study investigating the impact of teleworking frequency on IT productivity over two years, a fixed effects model could be used to control individual characteristics such as age, role, or education, focusing on the effect of changes in teleworking behavior over time. Alternatively, a random effects model could be used if those individual-specific factors are assumed to be randomly distributed and uncorrelated with teleworking. The choice between fixed and random effects models typically depends on the assumptions about the correlation between the individual effects and predictors, often tested using the Hausman test.

Time-Series Analysis

Time-series analysis is particularly suited for examining data collected at regular intervals over time, focusing on identifying trends, seasonal patterns, and potential autocorrelation in the data. It is widely used when there is interest in forecasting or understanding temporal dynamics. In IT and IS, time-series techniques can be applied to monitor network traffic or server load over time to predict future usage spikes or detect anomalies. For instance, an IT operations manager might use autoregressive integrated moving average (ARIMA) models to analyze daily login attempts to a corporate system, identifying recurring patterns that signal increased activity during specific times of the year. Time-series analysis is also useful in evaluating the effects of interventions, such as a software update or security patch, by comparing performance indicators before and after the change. These methods require stationarity in the data, or adjustments through differencing or detrending, to ensure valid inferences.

Survival Analysis/Event History Models

Survival analysis, also known as event history modeling, is a technique used to analyze the timing of events and the probability that a certain event occurs over time. Unlike other longitudinal techniques, survival analysis deals specifically with time-to-event data and can handle censored data (i.e., when the event has not occurred for some subjects by the end of the study). In IT/IS research, survival analysis might be used to model the time until a user abandons a new enterprise application, or how long a server runs before experiencing a critical failure. For example, in a study evaluating the adoption of a cybersecurity awareness platform, researchers might use a Cox proportional hazards model to estimate the time it takes for employees to complete a mandatory training module, accounting for factors such as department, age, and prior security incidents. This approach provides valuable insights into not just whether an event occurs, but when it is likely to happen, which is critical for planning interventions or system upgrades.

Designing a Longitudinal Study

Designing a longitudinal study involves careful planning to ensure that data collected over time effectively addresses the research objectives. Unlike cross-sectional studies, longitudinal research tracks the same subjects across multiple time points, allowing researchers to observe changes, identify patterns, and make stronger inferences about causality and temporal dynamics. This approach is particularly valuable for studying development, behavior, or system evolution over time, whether in health, education, or technology fields. A well-designed longitudinal study requires thoughtful decisions about the study population, frequency of data collection, measurement tools, and analytical strategies, as well as proactive planning to handle challenges such as participant attrition, missing data, and maintaining consistency across measurement waves (Table 5.4).

Table 5.4 Longitudinal Study Design Framework

Step	*Explanation*	*Tools / Resources*
1 Define Research Objectives	Clarify what you're studying over time. For example, in IT, you might examine how developers' productivity changes after adopting a new software development methodology (e.g., Agile vs. Waterfall) over 12 months.	Research frameworks, logic models, literature reviews
2 Choose Study Design Type	Decide on the study format: • *Prospective*: You follow a team of software engineers starting from the rollout of a new version control system. • *Retrospective*: You analyze archived bug reports and commit logs over the past 3 years to track software reliability. • *Panel*: You follow the same group of IT professionals over time. • *Cohort*: You track different cohorts based on when they adopted a specific tool (e.g., GitHub).	Epidemiological design guides, software engineering case studies
3 Sampling Strategy	Select the participants and determine sample size. For an IT study, this might include selecting developers from various organizations using different DevOps pipelines. Consider attrition if developers change jobs or projects during the study.	G*Power (power analysis), Qualtrics, REDCap
4 Timing & Frequency of Data Collection	Define how often data will be collected. For example, measure system performance and user satisfaction monthly after a cybersecurity upgrade, or collect developer survey responses quarterly to assess burnout or satisfaction.	Study timeline planners, Gantt charts

(Continued)

Table 5.4 (Continued)

Step	*Explanation*	*Tools / Resources*
5 Select Measures & Instruments	Choose reliable tools to measure outcomes. In IT, this could include: • Performance metrics (e.g., code churn, pull request time) • System logs (uptime, latency) • Developer self-reports (e.g., DASS-21 for stress, job satisfaction scales) • Ensure tools are valid across time and context.	PROMIS tools, developer productivity surveys, psychometric databases
6 Data Collection Methods	Decide on data sources and modes. IT studies may involve: • Automated collection of software metrics via APIs • Online surveys of user experience • Interviews with IT staff after major software updates	GitHub/GitLab APIs, REDCap, SurveyMonkey, Trello/JIRA logs
7 Ethical Considerations	Address consent, privacy, and data protection, especially with workplace monitoring or system logs. Example: If you're tracking employee system usage, ensure anonymization and organizational approval.	IRBs, data use agreements, consent forms
8 Data Management Plan	Organize data securely and consistently. Use long format for repeated measures (e.g., each row is a developer at a specific time). Track code versions and survey timestamps. Plan how to handle missing data due to system outages or nonresponse.	SPSS, R, Python (pandas), NVivo (for qualitative log data)
9 Analysis Strategy	Use statistical models suited for repeated measures: • Linear Mixed Models to track changes in team velocity • Generalized Estimating Equations for binary outcomes (e.g., defect/no defect) • Latent Growth Modeling for cognitive load over multiple software release cycles	R (lme4, nlme, lavaan), Stata (xtmixed), Mplus
10 Anticipate and Mitigate Challenges	Plan for issues like: • Developer turnover (attrition) • Inconsistent data logging across projects • Tool migration (e.g., switching from JIRA to Azure DevOps). Mitigation may involve periodic reminders and data normalization protocols.	Reminder systems, cloud-based tracking dashboards, retention strategies
11 Pilot Testing	Run a small test to catch issues with survey design, software instrumentation, or scheduling. Example: Test your code logging setup on a small development team to ensure accurate data collection before scaling.	Usability checklists, pilot participant feedback forms

Data Management and Quality Control

Effective data management and quality control are essential components of longitudinal studies, given the complexity and volume of data collected over extended periods. These processes ensure the integrity, consistency, and reliability of the data, which directly affect the validity of the study's conclusions. Data management in longitudinal research involves creating a structured plan for organizing, storing, and accessing data across multiple time points. This includes assigning unique identifiers to each participant, maintaining consistent data formats (typically in long format, where each row represents one time point per participant), and establishing secure storage protocols to protect sensitive information. For example, in an IT-related longitudinal study tracking software developer productivity, timestamped logs, survey responses, and system usage data must be integrated and linked accurately across repeated measurements.

Quality control focuses on ensuring the accuracy and completeness of data. This starts with standardized data collection procedures, such as training staff or automating data capture tools (e.g., APIs, monitoring software) to reduce variability. Regular audits, validation checks, and monitoring for anomalies (such as impossible values or duplicate entries) are essential. In IT contexts, ensuring consistent logging formats across different software tools (e.g., GitHub vs. JIRA) helps maintain data quality over time. Moreover, handling missing data is a critical part of longitudinal data quality. Dropouts, skipped questions, or system failures can lead to incomplete datasets. Techniques such as multiple imputations, full-information maximum likelihood (FIML), or model-based approaches like mixed models help address this issue without introducing significant bias (Table 5.5).

Table 5.5 Potential Issues with Longitudinal Studies and Mitigation Strategies

Issue	*Impact*	*Mitigation Strategies*
Participant Attrition	Loss of participants over time reduces sample size, threatens validity, and may introduce bias if dropout is non-random.	• Offer incentives and maintain engagement • Collect contact updates regularly • Use retention strategies like newsletters and reminders • Apply statistical methods to handle missing data (e.g., multiple imputation, FIML)
Missing Data	Leads to biased estimates, reduced statistical power, and incomplete trend analysis.	• Design user-friendly data collection tools • Monitor data quality in real-time • Use advanced modeling techniques (e.g., mixed models, GEE) that handle missingness • Perform sensitivity analyses

(Continued)

Table 5.5 (Continued)

Issue	*Impact*	*Mitigation Strategies*
Measurement Inconsistency	Changes in measurement tools or methods over time can threaten reliability and validity.	• Use validated, stable instruments • Train data collectors consistently • Test for measurement invariance • Document all changes to tools and protocols
Practice Effects or Reactivity	Participants may change behavior due to repeated exposure to the same tests or awareness of being studied.	• Rotate or vary question formats • Space data collection intervals appropriately • Include control groups if possible
Time and Cost Constraints	Long durations and repeated measures increase financial and logistical demands.	• Seek phased funding • Use digital tools for remote data collection • Optimize study design (e.g., accelerated longitudinal design)
Technological Changes	Software, platforms, or devices used in the study may become obsolete or evolve.	• Use adaptable, open-source tools • Plan for technology updates • Ensure backward compatibility of data formats
Staff Turnover	Loss of trained personnel may disrupt data collection and quality assurance.	• Document protocols thoroughly • Crosstrain team members • Maintain a knowledge base or operations manual
Data Security and Privacy Risks	Long-term storage of personal data increases exposure to breaches or non-compliance with regulations.	• Encrypt and securely store data • Use access controls and audit trails • Update consent forms and comply with data protection laws (e.g., GDPR)
Temporal Confounding Variables	External events (e.g., policy changes, pandemics) may influence outcomes across time.	• Record contextual variables • Include time as a covariate in models • Use interrupted time series or segmented analysis if needed

Chapter Summary

Longitudinal studies are a critical research strategy for examining how information systems and technologies evolve over time. This chapter introduced the core types of longitudinal studies like panel, cohort, and trend, and their relevance to various research goals in IT. Key design considerations were discussed, including defining research questions, maintaining consistent measurements, and selecting appropriate time intervals. The chapter outlined effective data collection methods such as repeated surveys, system usage logs, and transactional records, while stressing the importance of data reliability and quality across time points. Analytical techniques like repeated measures ANOVA, mixed-effects models, and time-series analysis were introduced, with real-world applications in areas like digital transformation, cybersecurity monitoring, and user satisfaction trends. While longitudinal designs offer unique advantages such as trend detection and stronger causal inference, they also pose challenges, including participant attrition, long durations, and complex data handling. Overall, the chapter provided practical guidance for planning, executing, and analyzing longitudinal research in IS, empowering researchers to generate impactful, time-sensitive insights.

Review Questions

1. What are the three primary types of longitudinal studies, and how do they differ?
2. Why are longitudinal studies particularly valuable in IS/IT research?
3. What are some common research questions that are best suited for longitudinal designs?
4. Describe key steps in designing a longitudinal study.
5. What are some advantages and limitations of using system logs or transactional data in longitudinal studies?
6. How does consistent measurement over time contribute to the reliability of a longitudinal study?
7. What are the major statistical techniques used to analyze longitudinal data in IS/IT research?
8. Give an example of how a longitudinal study might be applied to track user behavior over time.
9. What challenges might researchers face in maintaining participant engagement in a longitudinal study?
10. How can longitudinal studies help identify causal relationships in IT adoption or digital transformation research?

6 Publication Process, Tools, and Strategies for Quantitative Research

Chapter Objectives

After reading this chapter, readers should understand:

- Selecting a Suitable Journal for Quantitative Research
- Manuscript Preparation and Submission
- Formatting Guidelines for Journal Submission
- Writing the Manuscript: Structure and Content
- Preparing Figures, Tables, and References
- Submission Process and Online Submission Systems
- Peer Review Process
- Overview of the Peer Review Process
- Roles of Reviewers, Editors, and Authors
- Responding to Reviewer Comments
- Tools and Software for Quantitative Research

Introduction

The landscape of academic publishing has evolved significantly in recent decades, particularly within the field of information systems (IS) and information technology (IT), where the convergence of technology, business, and society presents a unique set of challenges and opportunities for researchers. Quantitative research, which emphasizes empirical investigation through statistical, computational, and mathematical techniques, plays a foundational role in generating evidence-based insights in IS. Yet, navigating the path from research ideas to publication remains a complex endeavor, especially for early-career scholars and practitioners transitioning into academia. In the context of IS, researchers often grapple with the dual demands of methodological rigor and practical relevance. For instance, a study employing structural equation modeling (SEM) to examine the adoption of mobile payment systems must not only demonstrate statistical validity but also

DOI: 10.4324/9781003545521-7

address pressing questions of usability, security, and socio-technical acceptance. Similarly, a researcher exploring data breach impacts using panel data analysis must contend with the need for high-quality secondary data and a theoretical framework that aligns with both IS and managerial domains. The challenge lies in presenting such work in a manner that meets the expectations of academic journals, which vary widely in their focus, audience, and review criteria.

In academic programs like Master's and Doctor of Science in IT, the student population reflects a rich mix of traditional and non-traditional learners, and faculty engagement in applied, practice-oriented research is both encouraged and necessary. This emphasis on bridging theory with practice mirrors a broader trend in IS research, where scholars are increasingly called upon to demonstrate the real-world utility of their work. However, transforming rigorous research into publishable manuscripts that resonate with top-tier journals requires more than technical proficiency. It demands a strategic understanding of the publication process, familiarity with tools that streamline research workflows, and a nuanced approach to academic writing.

The motivation for this chapter stems from my years of mentoring students, collaborating on multidisciplinary projects, and reviewing manuscripts across IS, management, and computing journals. One recurring theme is the uncertainty many researchers face when preparing to publish: Where should I submit this manuscript? How do I meet the journal's formatting expectations? What should I expect during the peer review process? How do I respond to contradictory reviewer feedback? These questions are not merely procedurally reflect the underlying anxiety that comes with subjecting one's work to public and professional scrutiny.

In quantitative IS research, the complexity of data collection and analysis further amplifies these concerns. Consider a study investigating the effect of algorithmic decision-making on consumer trust in e-commerce. Beyond the technical tasks of operationalizing constructs and validating models using software such as SPSS, R, or SmartPLS, the researcher must also craft a narrative that effectively communicates findings to a diverse readership. This includes journal editors, who are often looking for theoretical contributions; peer reviewers, who are concerned with methodological integrity; and practitioners, who seek practical implications.

This chapter seeks to uncover the publication journey for quantitative IS researchers by offering a structured overview of the key steps involved, i.e., from journal selection and manuscript preparation to submission, review, and post-review revision. It also introduces essential tools and strategies for enhancing research quality and visibility. Practical insights, drawn from real-world academic experiences, are interwoven throughout to ground the discussion in the realities of publishing in the IS discipline. Ultimately, the aim is not merely to help researchers get published, but to empower them to contribute meaningfully to scholarly discourse in IS. By embracing both the science and the craft of publishing, scholars can more effectively engage with the broader academic community, influence policy and practice, and shape the evolution of the discipline.

Selecting a Suitable Journal for Quantitative Research

First thing is first. Ask yourself, where do you want to publish your paper? Selecting the right journal is an important decision in the publication process. It influences not only the potential visibility and impact of a study but also determines the level of scrutiny the work will undergo, the expectations for theoretical contribution, and the standards of methodological rigor. For scholars in IS, journal selection is especially nuanced due to the interdisciplinary nature of the field. Researchers must often balance outlets that emphasize technical innovation, managerial relevance, and theoretical advancement. In quantitative research, where the study design is grounded in statistical analysis and empirical data, alignment with a journal's methodological orientation and audience expectations is essential. For example, a researcher employing a logistic regression model to examine cybersecurity awareness among employees in small businesses may find a better fit in *Information & Management* or *Journal of Organizational and End User Computing* than in *MIS Quarterly*, which typically favors studies with strong theoretical grounding and sophisticated modeling techniques (Table 6.1).

A common mistake early-career scholars make is to pursue high-impact factor journals without fully considering the thematic and methodological fit. While publishing in a journal like *Journal of the Association for Information Systems (JAIS)* may be desirable, doing so without understanding its editorial expectations – such as contribution to IS theory, multi-method rigor, and relevance to current discourse – can result in desk rejection. Conversely, practice-oriented journals like *Journal of Information Technology Teaching Cases* may offer a more suitable outlet for studies with an applied focus, particularly those conducted in educational technology, learning analytics, or IT service management settings.

For example, consider a quantitative study examining the adoption of blockchain-based supply chain platforms among logistics firms in the southeastern United States. If the research uses survey data and SEM to test hypotheses derived from the Technology-Organization-Environment (TOE) framework, suitable journals might include Electronic Markets, Technological Forecasting and Social Change, or Journal of Enterprise Information Management. Each of these journals explicitly encourages empirical work that blends theory and application in emerging digital contexts.

Alternatively, for a predictive analytics project using machine learning techniques (e.g., decision trees, random forests) to classify IT project risks,

Table 6.1 List of Top 10 IS Journals by Impact Scores

Rank	*Journal Name*	*Publisher*	*Impact Factor*	*Website*
1	Journal of Strategic Information Systems (JSIS)	Elsevier	8.7	https://www.journals.elsevier.com/the-journal-of-strategic-information-systems
2	Information & Management	Elsevier	8.6	https://www.journals.elsevier.com/information-and-management
3	Journal of Management Information Systems (JMIS)	Taylor & Francis	7.7	https://www.jmis-web.org/ranking
4	European Journal of Information Systems (EJIS)	Taylor & Francis	7.3	https://www.tandfonline.com/journals/tjis20
5	MIS Quarterly (MISQ)	MIS Research Center (U. of MN)	7.0	https://misq.umn.edu/about/
6	Decision Support Systems (DSS)	Elsevier	6.7	https://www.journals.elsevier.com/decision-support-systems
7	Information Systems Research (ISR)	INFORMS	6.45	https://pubsonline.informs.org/journal/isre
8	Information Systems Journal (ISJ)	Wiley	6.4	https://onlinelibrary.wiley.com/journal/13652575
9	Journal of Information Technology (JIT)	SAGE Publications	5.8	https://journals.sagepub.com/home/jin
10	Journal of the Association for Information Systems (JAIS)	Association for Information Systems	5.8	https://aisel.aisnet.org/jais/

the researcher may look toward journals such as *Decision Support Systems* or *Information Systems Frontiers*, which are more receptive to computational modeling and predictive analytics. Ultimately, the goal is not merely to get published but to ensure that the research contributes to an ongoing academic conversation, reaches the appropriate audience, and has the potential to influence practice or policy. By carefully evaluating journal characteristics and aligning them with the purpose and nature of their study, IS researchers can greatly enhance their chances of a successful and impactful publication.

To aid researchers in this decision-making process, the following table outlines a checklist of criteria to consider when evaluating journals for submission (Table 6.2):

Table 6.2 Journal Selection Checklist for Quantitative IS Research

Criteria	*Description*	*Questions to Ask*
Scope and Aims	Focus areas of the journal: technical, managerial, educational, theoretical, etc.	Does my study align with the journal's themes?
Methodological Fit	Acceptable research designs and analysis techniques.	Does the journal publish quantitative studies like mine (e.g., SEM, regression)?
Target Audience	Academic, professional, or hybrid readership.	Who reads this journal? Will my findings be relevant to them?
Impact Factor and Indexing	Citation metrics and visibility in databases such as Scopus, Web of Science, or ABDC.	How visible is the journal in my field? Is it indexed in major databases?
Acceptance Rate and Review Time	Probability and timeline of publication.	What is the average time from submission to first decision?
Open Access or Subscription	Accessibility and cost implications.	Will readers be able to access my work easily?
Past Articles	Review of recently published papers for style, structure, and topics.	Do the recent publications resemble the approach or subject of my paper?
Editorial Board and Reviewer Profile	Expertise and academic standing of editors and reviewers.	Do the editors have experience in my methodological or topical area?
Reputation in the Field	Perception by peers, ranking by professional bodies (e.g., AIS, ABDC).	How is this journal perceived within the IS/IT research community?

Manuscript Preparation and Submission

Once a suitable journal has been selected, the next critical phase in the publication process is the preparation and submission of the manuscript. This stage is where the clarity of the research design, the precision of the analysis, and the coherence of the writing converge to shape the first impression of the work. In quantitative IS research, where methodological rigor is scrutinized closely, effective manuscript preparation requires meticulous attention to both content and presentation.

A well-prepared manuscript does more than report findings; it demonstrates a logical progression from theoretical framing to hypothesis development, data analysis, and interpretation. For instance, a study exploring user resistance to enterprise system upgrades might begin by establishing a theoretical foundation (e.g., status quo bias or protection motivation theory), followed by hypothesis construction and survey instrument development. The manuscript must then present the sampling approach, the statistical methods used (e.g., confirmatory factor analysis, regression analysis), and the results in a manner that is transparent, reproducible, and accessible to readers with varying statistical expertise.

A common pitfall among IS scholars, particularly those transitioning from practice or applied fields, is to focus disproportionately on the results, while offering minimal attention to theory and method. Top journals require a balanced manuscript that speaks to the "why," "how," and "so what" of the study. In practice, this means devoting sufficient space to the literature review and research design, while ensuring that the discussion section interprets results through the lens of prior research and future implications. In the IT domain, studies involving advanced analytical tools, such as neural networks, clustering algorithms, or ensemble models, must also justify their choice of methodology. For example, when using supervised learning to predict IT service desk ticket resolution times, the author should not only report predictive accuracy metrics (e.g., RMSE, R^2) but also explain the interpretability of the model and its practical significance in IT operations management. Before submission, authors should carefully review the journal's author guidelines, which typically outline expectations for manuscript structure, formatting style, citation method (e.g., APA, Chicago, Harvard), and length. Many journals also provide templates or sample papers to guide authors. Failing to adhere to these guidelines can result in immediate desk rejection, even for methodologically sound studies.

Table 6.3 shows a practical list of best practices to guide manuscript preparation in quantitative IS research.

Table 6.3 Checklist: Manuscript Preparation for Quantitative IS Research

Step	*Recommendations*
Follow the Journal's Author Guidelines	Use the exact formatting, structure, and citation style specified by the journal.
Use Standardized Section Headings	Common sections include; Introduction, Literature Review, Research Methodology, Results, Discussion, and Conclusion.
Ensure Theoretical Alignment	Frame the research questions and hypotheses within an established IS theory or conceptual model.
Detail the Research Methodology	Include sampling approach, instrument development, validity checks, and statistical tests used.
Present Results Clearly	Use tables, charts, and standardized reporting (e.g., significance levels, confidence intervals).
Interpret, Not Just Report	Discuss what the findings mean, how they relate to existing literature, and implications for IS/IT practice.
Check for Coherence and Flow	Ensure transitions between sections are smooth and the argument is logically constructed.
Proofread and Peer-Review	Have colleagues or co-authors review the draft before submission to catch overlooked errors.
Use Plagiarism Checkers and Grammar Tools	Tools like Turnitin, Grammarly, or MS Word Editor can help polish the manuscript.
Prepare for Multiple Formats	Be ready to submit PDF and Word versions; some systems also request metadata and author bios.

Most journals today use web-based submission systems such as ScholarOne, Editorial Manager, or Elsevier's EVISE. These platforms typically require authors to register, upload their manuscript and supplementary files, and complete a metadata form detailing the article's title, abstract, keywords, and suggested reviewers. While the submission interface may vary by publisher, the underlying expectations remain consistent: authors must ensure completeness, professionalism, and compliance. A final but often overlooked aspect is the cover letter. This short document should concisely explain the significance of the work, its fit with the journal, and affirm that the manuscript is not under consideration elsewhere. While brief, the cover letter is a key communication channel with the editorial team and should be crafted with care. By investing the necessary time and attention in manuscript preparation and understanding the submission protocol of the chosen journal, researchers position their work for serious consideration. In quantitative IS research, where detail, transparency, and methodological soundness are paramount, this phase is not just procedural but foundational to publication success.

Formatting Guidelines for Journal Submission

Formatting may appear to be a purely mechanical aspect of academic publishing, yet it plays a surprisingly influential role in shaping a manuscript's initial reception. A well-formatted manuscript signals professionalism, attention to detail, and respect for the editorial process. Conversely, poor formatting, even when the content is of high quality, can detract from the paper's credibility and lead to delays or even desk rejection. Each journal has its own detailed submission guidelines that often include specific instructions for margins, font styles, line spacing, section headings, citation formats, and figure/table placement. In IS and IT journals, formatting expectations can vary significantly depending on the journal's publishing house (e.g., Elsevier, Springer, Taylor & Francis, IEEE) and disciplinary orientation. As an example, a submission to *Journal of Strategic Information Systems* (published by Elsevier) must adhere to APA 7th edition citation style and include a structured abstract with clear headings such as "Purpose," "Design/methodology/approach," and "Findings." In contrast, IEEE-affiliated journals such as *IEEE Transactions on Engineering Management* require the use of IEEE style referencing, where citations are numbered in brackets and listed in the order of appearance.

Moreover, many journals have moved toward the use of manuscript templates. Authors submitting to *MIS Quarterly* are encouraged to use the official template provided on the journal's website, which includes formatting for major headings, subheadings, and tables. Failing to use the prescribed format is often grounds for immediate return without review. The checklist in Table 6.4 summarizes common requirements across journals and provides reminders that are often overlooked.

Table 6.4 Checklist: Common Formatting Requirements for IS Journal Submissions

Formatting Element	*Guidelines*	*Common Issues to Avoid*
Title Page	Include title, authors' names, affiliations, and contact details (unless an anonymous submission is required).	Including author info when double-blind is required.
Abstract	150–250 words; structured or unstructured depending on the journal.	Too vague or jargon-heavy abstracts.
Keywords	4–6 keywords that reflect the core concepts of the paper.	Using overly general terms (e.g., "technology," "business").
Main Text Formatting	Typically 12 pt. Times New Roman, double-spaced, justified alignment.	Inconsistent fonts, spacing, or indentation.
Headings and Subheadings	Use numbered or hierarchical headings as required (e.g., 1.0, 1.1).	Mixing styles (e.g., bold + underline) or skipping levels.
Figures and Tables	Label and number sequentially (e.g., Table A and Figure B; provide titles and source notes.	Omitting units, unclear labels, or inaccessible formats (e.g., images instead of editable tables).
In-text Citations	Match the journal's citation style (APA, IEEE, Chicago, etc.).	Incorrect citation formats, missing references in the list.
Reference List	Alphabetically ordered or numerically listed per journal guidelines.	Incomplete or improperly formatted entries.
Appendices (if used)	Include supplementary data, surveys, or derivations as appendices with appropriate labels.	Failing to reference appendices in the main text.
File Format and Naming	Most systems require Microsoft Word (.doc/.docx) or LaTeX files.	Uploading PDFs only or using non-descriptive filenames.

In IT and IS quantitative research, special care should also be taken with tables and figures that present statistical results. For example, when reporting regression models or PLS-SEM output, authors should follow standards for precision (e.g., reporting coefficients to two or three decimal places), significance levels (e.g., $p < 0.05$), and model fit indices. Tables should be self-contained, allowing readers to interpret results without referring back to the text. Consider a study investigating the impact of AI chatbots on service satisfaction in higher education IT helpdesks. If the author reports an ANOVA table comparing student satisfaction scores across chatbot, email, and phone support channels, the table should clearly indicate sample size, degrees of freedom, F-values, and effect sizes. Equally important, the caption should describe what the table shows and what test was used. Finally, journals increasingly request or require *data availability statements, conflict of interest declarations*, and *author contributions* using the CRediT taxonomy (e.g., "Conceptualization," "Data curation," "Formal analysis"). These components, though administrative in nature, are integral to the formatting and ethics of submission. By ensuring adherence to formatting guidelines, authors not only demonstrate professionalism but also reduce the editorial burden and improve the odds of favorable reviewer engagement. In the highly competitive environment of IS publishing, these details can make the difference between an immediate rejection and a paper that proceeds to peer review.

Writing the Manuscript: Structure and Content

Writing a manuscript for publication in IS journals is not simply a matter of describing what was done. Rather, it is a disciplined exercise in argumentation, clarity, and scholarly engagement. The manuscript should tell a compelling research story, anchored in theory, guided by rigorous methodology, and delivered with precision, while making an original contribution to the literature. Successful IS and IT manuscripts typically follow a well-defined structure: Introduction, Literature Review, Research Methodology, Results, Discussion, and Conclusion. Some journals may merge or re-label these sections, but the underlying logic remains constant.

Introduction

The introduction should immediately establish the significance of the research problem. A common and effective strategy is to begin with a real-world phenomenon that exemplifies the research issue. For example, an IS researcher may highlight the rising failure rate of digital transformation initiatives in mid-sized enterprises despite high IT spending. This sets the stage for discussing gaps in understanding and leads into the research questions or hypotheses.

Example:

"Despite a 23% annual increase in digital investment among U.S. healthcare providers, recent studies report stagnant user adoption of new health information systems. This study examines how perceived information transparency influences adoption behavior in electronic health record (EHR) systems using a quantitative survey approach."

This opening quickly outlines the context, the problem, and hints at the methodology – an approach favored by journals like *Information & Management* or *Journal of Information Technology*.

Literature Review and Theoretical Framing

The literature review should not be an exhaustive catalog of prior work. Instead, it must be a focused synthesis that identifies gaps or contradictions in the literature, justifies the theoretical framework, and leads logically to the hypotheses or research questions. For quantitative IS research, integrating an established theory such as the Technology Acceptance Model (TAM), Unified Theory of Acceptance and Use of Technology (UTAUT), or Protection Motivation Theory (PMT) is essential. The review should also clearly identify the constructs, explain their relationships, and provide citations from peer-reviewed sources.

Tip: Avoid overly descriptive reviews. Instead, engage critically with the literature. For instance, if existing studies find inconsistent results regarding the role of trust in mobile payment adoption, use this inconsistency to justify your study.

Research Methodology

This section must be detailed enough for replication. Authors should specify the research design (e.g., cross-sectional survey, experimental study), population, sampling method, instrument development, and data collection procedure. The statistical techniques used (e.g., regression, SEM, machine learning classifiers) should be justified and clearly explained. For IT-based studies, especially those involving system logs or transactional data, include information about data cleaning, variable construction, and platform architecture if relevant. For instance, in a study predicting IT support ticket resolution time using supervised learning, authors should describe data preprocessing (e.g., removing duplicates, handling outliers), feature engineering (e.g., time-to-close, number of reassignments), and model validation techniques.

Note: Include ethical considerations and institutional review board (IRB) approval if the study involved human subjects.

Results

Present the findings clearly and concisely using tables and figures where appropriate. For survey-based studies, include descriptive statistics, reliability tests (e.g., Cronbach's alpha), validity checks (e.g., AVE, CR), and model fit indices. Use consistent notation and explain all symbols and abbreviations.

Example:

In a regression table examining predictors of cybersecurity compliance behavior among employees, authors should report standardized coefficients, *p*-values, and R^2 values. A brief interpretation of each result in plain language should follow the table.

Discussion

This section interprets the results, links them back to the research questions and theoretical framework, and explains their implications. Avoid restating results; instead, emphasize their meaning. Discuss whether the findings support or contradict previous studies and why.

Example:

"The finding that organizational commitment had no significant effect on compliance intention diverges from previous studies (e.g., Posey et al., 2015). One possible explanation is that in high-turnover industries such as retail, commitment is short-term and does not translate into secure behavior."

This type of insight shows scholarly maturity and strengthens the contribution.

Conclusion and Implications

Conclude with a summary of key findings, limitations, theoretical contributions, practical implications, and future research directions. Be specific rather than generic.

Practical Implication Example:

"For IT managers deploying chatbots in university help desks, the study suggests that perceived usefulness alone is insufficient; incorporating training to increase self-efficacy may improve acceptance among less tech-savvy users."

Theoretical Contribution Example:

"This study extends the UTAUT2 framework by integrating cognitive load as a moderating factor, providing a more nuanced understanding of mobile learning system adoption."

Writing a strong manuscript requires attention to both macro-structure (overall flow) and micro-structure (clarity of sentences, transitions, and argument logic). While each section has its function, coherence across sections is equally critical. The hypotheses proposed in the literature review must match those tested in the results; the variables discussed in theory must align with those measured in the methodology. Ultimately, a successful IS manuscript tells a clear, evidence-based story that contributes something new to both theory and practice. It demonstrates analytical rigor while remaining readable to a broader scholarly audience – an equilibrium that experienced authors work hard to master.

Practice Lab 6.1: Finding the Right Journal for Your Research

Learning Goals

- Identify a suitable journal for your research.
- Understand journal expectations (scope, format, style).
- Write a journal-aligned abstract.

Step 1: Pick a Topic (10 mins)
Choose one research idea (your own or one of these):

- Blockchain in healthcare
- Chatbots in education
- IT project failure prediction

Step 2: Find Two Journals (15 mins)
Search online or use examples provided. Use Table 6.2 to compare:

- Scope fit
- Methodology accepted
- Audience
- Submission format

Mark your preferred journal.

Step 3: Review Author Guidelines (15 mins)
Go to the journal website. Note:

- Abstract style
- Manuscript structure
- Formatting/citation style
- Any "must-follow" rules

Step 4: Write a Mini-Abstract (15–20 mins)
Write a **150–200 word abstract** based on your topic, tailored to the selected journal.

Step 5: Present & Get Feedback (10–20 mins)
Share:

- Chosen journal
- Abstract
- One thing you learned about submitting to that journal

Classmates give feedback on journal fit and abstract clarity.

Preparing Figures, Tables, and References

Well-designed figures, tables, and references are clear indications of a strong quantitative manuscript. They not only convey findings efficiently but also reflect the professionalism and rigor of the research. In IS research, where statistical outputs, model diagrams, and dataset summaries are commonplace, these components must be thoughtfully constructed and consistently formatted.

Figures

Figures in IS manuscripts often include conceptual frameworks, model diagrams (e.g., SEM models), and data visualizations such as histograms, scree plots, or ROC curves. When designing figures, clarity and precision should guide the process. Visuals should support, not replace, the narrative in the text. For instance, in a study applying PLS-SEM to explore factors influencing mobile banking adoption, a model diagram like Figure A would typically show latent variables (e.g., perceived ease of use, trust, perceived risk), paths with β-values and significance levels, and R^2 values for endogenous constructs. Such figures should use consistent shapes and labels, and ideally be created using software such as SmartPLS, AMOS, or R's semPlot package.

Tips

- Ensure all axes, legends, and units are labeled.
- Use grayscale or color-blind–friendly palettes if publishing in color.
- Avoid overly complex or decorative designs.

Tables

Tables are vital for reporting descriptive statistics, reliability and validity measures, correlation matrices, and regression or SEM results. They should be self-explanatory, and readers should understand a table's contents without referring to the main text. For example, a table reporting factor loadings and AVE for constructs in a TAM-based study should be structured as follows:

Table A Convergent Validity and Reliability of Constructs

Construct	*Items*	*Factor Loadings*	*AVE*	*CR*	*Cronbach's α*
Perceived Usefulness	PU1–PU4	0.78–0.91	0.72	0.89	0.85
Trust	TR1–TR3	0.81–0.87	0.68	0.86	0.80
Behavioral Intention	BI1–BI3	0.84–0.90	0.75	0.91	0.88

Note: All factor loadings are significant at $p < .001$.

Tables should be sequentially numbered and cited in the text (e.g., "As shown in Table 6.2…"). Avoid splitting tables across pages or embedding them as images, which reduces readability and indexability.

References

Accurate and complete referencing is both an ethical and scholarly obligation. Each journal specifies a preferred citation style, commonly APA (like the one used in this book), IEEE, or Chicago, and the manuscript must conform to it consistently. Many high-ranking IS journals (e.g., *Information Systems*

Research, *MIS Quarterly*) follow APA, while engineering-leaning journals (e.g., *IEEE Transactions*) use IEEE style. When done correctly, figures, tables, and references enhance the manuscript's clarity, reinforce the integrity of the research, and ease the workload of reviewers. They are not supplementary; they are essential elements of scholarly communication. As such, authors should dedicate as much care to preparing them as they do to writing the core text.

Key Points:

- Every citation in the text must appear in the reference list and vice versa.
- Use reference management tools like EndNote, Mendeley, or Zotero to maintain consistency and reduce errors.
- Double-check DOI numbers, publication years, and author names.

Common Pitfalls to Avoid:

- Citing outdated sources as foundational (e.g., using a 2002 source as a sole reference for current cybersecurity trends).
- Inconsistent formatting across entries (e.g., switching between title case and sentence case).
- Overreliance on non-peer-reviewed sources (e.g., whitepapers or blog posts) unless explicitly justified.

Example of APA Reference

Venkatesh, V., Thong, J. Y. L., & Xu, X. (2012). Consumer acceptance and use of information technology: Extending the unified theory of acceptance and use of technology. *MIS Quarterly*, 36(1), 157–178. https://doi.org/10.2307/41410412

Example of IEEE Reference

[1] V. Venkatesh, J. Y. L. Thong, and X. Xu, "Consumer acceptance and use of information technology: Extending the unified theory of acceptance and use of technology," *MIS Q.*, vol. 36, no. 1, pp. 157–178, Mar. 2012.

Submission Process and Online Submission Systems

The submission phase is where months, sometimes years, of research and writing culminate in a formal request for consideration by a scholarly journal. In the field of IT, this process typically unfolds through highly structured online platforms, which manage submission, peer review, and editorial decision workflows. Navigating these systems effectively requires a careful combination of preparation, attention to detail, and strategic thinking.

Table 6.5 Checklist: Final Submission Checklist for IS Journals

Item	*Description*
✓ Manuscript File	Clean version (no author-identifying info), usually in Word or LaTeX
✓ Title Page	Separate file with full title, author names, affiliations, ORCID iDs, and acknowledgments
✓ Abstract and Keywords	Typically 150–250 words and 4–6 keywords
✓ Figures and Tables	Uploaded as separate high-resolution files or embedded (depending on journal)
✓ References	Fully formatted according to journal's style guide
✓ Cover Letter	Brief letter summarizing the manuscript's contribution and fit for the journal
✓ Conflict of Interest and Funding Disclosures	Required by most reputable journals

Preparing for Submission: Final Checks

Before logging into any submission system, authors must ensure their manuscript package is complete and conforms precisely to the journal's formatting and structural guidelines. The final checklist, as shown in Table 6.5, typically includes:

Failure to comply with even minor formatting instructions (e.g., exceeding page limits, incorrect reference style, or submitting an anonymized manuscript without removing metadata) may result in an automatic desk rejection.

Common Submission Platforms

Most IS journals use one of several established online submission systems:

- **Editorial Manager**: Used by *Information & Management, Decision Support Systems*, and many Elsevier journals.
- **ScholarOne Manuscripts**: Popular with journals from Springer, Taylor & Francis, and the Association for Information Systems (AIS) family (e.g., *JAIS, CAIS*).
- **Manuscript Central**: A variant of ScholarOne; used by *MIS Quarterly* and *Journal of MIS*.

Each system requires users to register an account, input manuscript metadata (title, abstract, author details, keywords), and upload required files in the specified formats. Authors are often prompted to select subject classifications and recommend reviewers.

Example:

When submitting to *Decision Support Systems* via Editorial Manager, authors must:

- Choose appropriate article type (e.g., "Research Article"),
- Indicate whether the paper is part of a special issue (if applicable),

- Provide a short highlight of the contribution (max 85 characters), and
- Confirm that ethical requirements (e.g., IRB approval) have been met.

The Role of the Cover Letter

While optional in some systems, the cover letter is often the first document the editor reads. It should be concise – ideally no longer than one page – and include the following elements:

- Title of the manuscript
- Statement of originality and significance
- Explanation of why the paper fits the journal's scope
- Assurance that the work is not under review elsewhere

> **Example Excerpt:**
>
> "This manuscript titled *'Digital Nudging in E-Commerce: A Quantitative Study of Interface Design and Purchase Behavior'* investigates how interface-level cues influence conversion rates across two e-commerce platforms using a field experiment with 1,248 users. The study extends the literature on digital nudging by incorporating real-time user data and contributes to both theory and practice in IS. We believe it aligns well with the aims of *Information Systems Journal*, particularly its emphasis on user behavior and system design."

Author Declarations and Metadata

Most journals now require authors to declare:

- Ethical approval and informed consent
- Data availability (including links to repositories, if applicable)
- Conflicts of interest
- Author contributions (using CRediT taxonomy, in many cases)

Authors should also ensure all co-author names, affiliations, and email addresses are entered correctly. Errors here can delay the review process or create confusion with indexing services post-publication.

What Happens After Submission?

Once submitted, the manuscript enters a multistage editorial workflow:

1. **Initial Editorial Check**: Desk evaluation for scope, formatting, and fit. Many papers are rejected here.
2. **Assignment to an Associate Editor (AE)**: If the editor-in-chief deems the paper worthy of review, it is assigned to an AE.

3 **Reviewer Selection and Invitation**: AEs select and invite 2–3 reviewers based on subject expertise.
4 **Review Process Begins**: This typically takes 6–12 weeks, though timelines vary.

Throughout this period, authors can monitor the manuscript's status via the submission portal. It is acceptable to send a polite inquiry if there is no update after three months. Mastering the submission process requires more than just uploading files, but it demands strategic attention to detail, a professional tone, and an understanding of the editorial environment. A smooth, well-organized submission not only increases the likelihood of passing the initial screening but also sets a positive tone for the entire peer review journey.

Peer Review Process

The peer review process is the backbone of academic publishing, serving as a critical mechanism to ensure the rigor, validity, and originality of research. In IS, the peer review process is typically double-blind or single-blind, with the former being more common in high-impact journals. Understanding how this process works and how to engage with it effectively is crucial for successful publication.

Overview of the Peer Review Process

The peer review process generally follows these steps:

1 **Submission**: The author submits the manuscript, and it undergoes an initial editorial screening by the journal's editorial team.
2 **Reviewer Assignment**: If the manuscript passes the initial check, the editor assigns it to 2–3 reviewers who are experts in the field. These reviewers are selected based on their expertise and their ability to provide an objective, constructive evaluation.
3 **Review and Feedback**: Reviewers evaluate the manuscript on various dimensions, such as the originality of the research, methodological rigor, relevance to the journal's scope, clarity of writing, and the validity of results. They may suggest revisions or reject the manuscript if it fails to meet standards.
4 **Editorial Decision**: Based on the reviewers' comments, the editor makes a decision. The manuscript may be accepted, revised (major or minor), or rejected. In cases of major revisions, the editor may ask for a resubmission after the authors address reviewer comments.
5 **Revisions and Resubmission**: The authors revise the manuscript in line with the reviewers' feedback and resubmit it. If the reviewers accept the changes, the manuscript moves to the final stages.
6 **Final Decision**: Once the revisions are accepted, the manuscript proceeds to publication.

Roles of Reviewers, Editors, and Authors

The success of a manuscript depends on the constructive collaboration between authors, reviewers, and editors. Each has a critical role in the process.

The Role of Reviewers

Reviewers are experts in the field who assess the manuscript's validity, methodology, and contribution to the literature. They are tasked with:

- **Assessing the quality of the research**: Reviewers examine whether the research question is clear, the methodology is appropriate, and the results are robust.
- **Providing constructive feedback**: Reviewers suggest improvements in the analysis, structure, or writing style, helping authors refine their manuscript.
- **Ensuring ethical standards**: Reviewers flag potential ethical issues, such as plagiarism or issues with data integrity.

While reviewers are experts, they are not infallible. They may overlook minor errors or make subjective recommendations based on their personal biases. For this reason, responding to reviewer comments is a delicate task that requires professionalism and objectivity.

The Role of Editors

The editor is responsible for managing the peer review process and making the final editorial decision. They:

- **Ensure fair and transparent reviews**: Editors act as gatekeepers, ensuring that the process is fair, unbiased, and transparent. They resolve disagreements between reviewers or between reviewers and authors.
- **Make editorial decisions**: Editors make the final decision on the manuscript based on the reviewers' feedback, taking into account the manuscript's quality, relevance to the journal, and potential impact.

For example, in journals like *MIS Quarterly* or *Journal of Information Technology*, the editor might consult with an Associate Editor (AE) who specializes in the manuscript's specific subfield, such as e-commerce or information security, to make a more informed decision.

The Role of Authors

As the authors, it is your responsibility to:

- **Prepare a high-quality manuscript**: Submitting a polished manuscript that adheres to journal guidelines will make the review process smoother.

- **Engage with the review comments constructively**: Responding to reviewer feedback is a key part of the process. Authors must carefully address each comment, providing clear explanations for any changes made or justifying why certain suggestions may not have been incorporated.
- **Revise and resubmit promptly**: If the editor requests revisions, it is important to act quickly and thoroughly. Delaying resubmission can harm the chances of acceptance.

Responding to Reviewer Comments

Once the manuscript is reviewed, authors will receive feedback in the form of reviewer comments. These comments can be broadly classified as **minor revisions**, **major revisions**, or **rejection**. Each type of feedback requires a different response strategy.

Minor Revisions:

- Acknowledge the reviewers' feedback and make the necessary changes. Often, reviewers may simply request small adjustments, such as clarifying points, fixing typos, or adding missing citations.
- Respond politely and professionally. For example:

  "Thank you for your insightful suggestion to clarify the definition of 'digital transformation' in the context of small enterprises. We have revised Section 3.1 *to include a more precise definition and additional citations."*

Major Revisions:

- For more substantial revisions (e.g., revising methodology, adding additional analyses), authors must demonstrate that they have thoroughly considered the feedback. This is where detailed responses are required.
- Provide a detailed point-by-point response to the reviewer's comments. It is important to not only justify the changes made but also to explain why certain suggestions may not have been incorporated if they were not feasible or aligned with the study's scope.
- **Example Response**:
  "Reviewer 1 suggested expanding the discussion of the theoretical framework. We have added an entire section in the Discussion chapter (Section 5) to explicitly tie our findings back to the Resource-Based View (RBV) and its implications for IS implementation in emerging markets."

  "Reviewer 2 raised concerns about the statistical analysis. We have conducted additional robustness checks using multigroup analysis, and the results are now presented in Table 6.4. *The changes are reflected in the revised manuscript."*

Rejection:

- While rejections are part of the academic publishing process, they can be disheartening. It is important to maintain professionalism in response.
- If the rejection is based on the manuscript's fit with the journal's scope, consider submitting the paper to a more suitable journal. If the rejection is due to quality concerns, carefully revise the paper and consider resubmission either to the same journal (after revisions) or a different one.
- **Example Response**:

  "We appreciate the reviewers' thoughtful feedback, which helped us identify key weaknesses in our original manuscript. We have thoroughly revised the paper and believe that the changes address the concerns raised. As suggested, we are now submitting the revised version to another journal better aligned with the scope of our research."

Final Submission and Acceptance

Once revisions are made and accepted, the manuscript will undergo a final round of editorial checks. If the manuscript passes, the editor will send an acceptance letter, and the paper will be scheduled for publication. Authors are typically given a chance to review the proofs before the final publication. The peer review process is an essential part of academic publishing that requires not just high-quality research but also an ability to engage in constructive dialogue with reviewers and editors. Understanding the roles of each participant and responding to feedback in a professional and thoughtful manner will greatly enhance the chances of successful publication.

Tools and Software for Quantitative Research

In quantitative research, particularly in IS and IT, data analysis is a central activity that requires specialized software tools for collecting, analyzing, and presenting data. These tools provide researchers with the ability to manage large datasets, perform complex statistical analyses, and ensure the validity and reliability of results. Selecting the right software is crucial to the success of a study, as it can significantly impact both the quality of the analysis and the efficiency of the research process.

Statistical Analysis Software

The backbone of quantitative research in IS/IT often involves statistical analysis, and several software packages are widely used in the field for this purpose. These tools allow researchers to perform tasks such as regression analysis, hypothesis testing, SEM, and more.

- **SPSS (Statistical Package for the Social Sciences):**

  SPSS is one of the most widely used tools for quantitative research in social sciences, including IS. It provides a user-friendly interface for performing a wide range of statistical tests, including t-tests, ANOVA, regression analysis, and factor analysis. Researchers in IT fields often use SPSS to analyze survey data or performance metrics from experiments.

  Example:

  An IS researcher studying the impact of user interface design on e-commerce website usability may use SPSS to analyze survey responses regarding user satisfaction, performing a regression analysis to identify significant predictors of usability scores.

- **R:**

  R is a free, open-source software environment used for statistical computing and graphics. It is particularly popular in fields that require complex data analysis and visualization, such as machine learning, time-series analysis, and big data analytics. R's flexibility, coupled with its extensive libraries (e.g., ggplot2 for visualization, dplyr for data manipulation), makes it ideal for researchers dealing with large datasets or advanced methodologies.

  Example:

  In IT research, R can be used to conduct sentiment analysis on large datasets of user reviews of software products, allowing researchers to uncover patterns in user experiences and perceptions.

- **Stata**:

  Stata is another powerful statistical software that is particularly effective for econometrics and statistical modeling. It is highly favored in quantitative IS research for analyzing data from large-scale surveys and experiments, and it offers robust support for panel data analysis, instrumental variable regression, and survival analysis.

  Example:

  An IS study analyzing factors that affect the adoption of cloud computing might use Stata to analyze longitudinal survey data from multiple organizations to identify significant variables influencing adoption rates.

- **MATLAB**:

  MATLAB is often used in IT research for more specialized tasks like algorithm development, numerical simulations, and modeling. Its ability to handle complex mathematical and statistical problems makes it a go-to tool for researchers studying system dynamics, network behavior, or data-driven algorithms.

Example:

Researchers studying network security might use MATLAB to simulate the behavior of intrusion detection systems under varying network conditions, employing statistical methods to evaluate system performance.

Structural Equation Modeling Tools

For IS researchers, particularly those conducting research on technology adoption models (e.g., UTAUT, TAM), SEM is a critical technique for assessing the relationships between observed and latent variables. Several software tools are tailored for SEM analysis:

- **Amos:**

  Amos, part of the IBM SPSS family, is an intuitive tool for SEM. It allows researchers to develop path models and assess the fit of their models through various indices such as RMSEA, CFI, and TLI. Amos is particularly popular for its ease of use and graphical interface, making it accessible to researchers new to SEM.

  Example:

  A study exploring how perceived ease of use and trust impact customer satisfaction with a mobile banking application might use Amos to test a model where these variables influence customer loyalty.

- **SmartPLS:**

  SmartPLS is a popular tool for partial least squares structural equation modeling (PLS-SEM). It is particularly useful for exploratory research or when data violates normality assumptions. SmartPLS is widely used in IS research for analyzing complex models with many constructs, and it is an excellent tool for researchers studying user behavior or organizational IT adoption.

  Example:

  An IS researcher investigating the factors influencing the adoption of enterprise resource planning (ERP) systems could use SmartPLS to build and test a model with multiple constructs such as perceived usefulness, ease of use, organizational support, and system quality.

Data Management and Visualization Tools

In addition to statistical analysis software, effective data management and visualization are key elements of quantitative research. Researchers in IS and IT fields need tools to clean, organize, and visualize their data, particularly when dealing with large datasets or big data applications.

- **Excel:**

  Microsoft Excel remains one of the most popular tools for data analysis, especially for simpler tasks like basic descriptive statistics, correlation analysis, or creating charts. While it may not be suitable for more complex analyses, Excel is incredibly efficient for small-to-medium-sized datasets and is a go-to tool for initial exploratory analysis.

  Example:

  Researchers studying the performance of IT systems might use Excel to summarize and visualize operational data, such as response times or system uptime, through basic charts or pivot tables.

- **Tableau:**

  Tableau is a leading data visualization tool that allows users to create interactive dashboards and reports. It is particularly useful for exploring large datasets and identifying patterns through dynamic visualizations. In IT research, Tableau can be employed to visualize complex data from system logs, user interactions, or experimental outcomes.

  Example:

  An IS researcher analyzing the effectiveness of different software interfaces might use Tableau to create an interactive dashboard that shows how various design elements influence task completion times across different user demographics.

- **Power BI:**

  Microsoft Power BI is another powerful tool for business intelligence and data visualization. It is particularly useful for researchers who need to integrate data from multiple sources and perform more advanced analysis through customizable visualizations. Power BI can connect directly to databases, spreadsheets, and cloud-based services.

  Example:

  Researchers in cloud computing might use Power BI to visualize and analyze performance metrics from various cloud service providers, comparing cost, uptime, and service reliability across platforms.

Qualitative Analysis Software

Though primarily focused on quantitative analysis, IS researchers may also collect qualitative data through interviews or open-ended survey responses. In such cases, software designed for qualitative data analysis can be invaluable.

- **NVivo:**

  NVivo is widely used for qualitative research, helping researchers code, analyze, and visualize qualitative data. In IT studies, NVivo can be used to analyze interview transcripts or open-ended survey responses, identifying themes related to technology adoption, system satisfaction, or organizational change.

  Example:

  A study on the implementation of a new enterprise system in an organization might use NVivo to analyze employee feedback gathered through interviews, identifying key factors influencing system acceptance.

Strategies for Enhancing the Quality of Quantitative Research

The quality of quantitative research in IS and IT is determined not only by the validity and reliability of the results but also by the robustness of the research design, methodology, and the clarity of communication. High-quality research can lead to more credible findings, greater visibility in the academic community, and a higher likelihood of acceptance in prestigious journals. The following strategies focus on refining the overall quality of research from design through publication.

Strengthening Research Design and Methodology

The foundation of high-quality quantitative research lies in a sound research design and methodology. A robust design ensures that the research questions are answered comprehensively and that the results are valid and reliable.

- **Clear Research Questions:**

  A well-defined research question is the starting point for any study. In IT and IS research, this could involve exploring factors such as user behavior, technology adoption, or system performance. It is critical to clearly articulate the hypothesis or research problem at the outset, ensuring it is both feasible and researchable.

  Example:

  A study examining the factors influencing the adoption of mobile banking might have a research question like, *"What are the key factors that determine the adoption of mobile banking in rural areas?"*

- **Use of Control Variables:**
  When designing experiments or surveys, ensure that control variables are considered to isolate the impact of the independent variables on the dependent

variables. For example, in a study on the effectiveness of cloud-based solutions, it may be important to control for factors such as company size, industry, and previous technological investments to ensure that the results are not biased.

- **Appropriate Sampling Techniques:**

  The reliability of research findings depends on the sampling technique used. For large-scale surveys or experiments, ensure that the sample size is statistically adequate to allow for generalization of findings. Consider techniques such as random sampling or stratified sampling to ensure a representative sample.

  Example:

  A study on system usability across different user demographics should ensure that the sample includes users from various age groups, skill levels, and technological backgrounds to avoid biased results.

Ensuring Validity and Reliability

In quantitative research, validity and reliability are two essential measures of research quality. Validity refers to the accuracy of the measurements and whether the study is actually measuring what it intends to measure. Reliability refers to the consistency of the measurements.

- **Internal Validity:**

  This refers to the extent to which the results of the study can be attributed to the variables being studied and not to other confounding factors. To ensure internal validity, researchers should use controlled environments, clearly defined variables, and standardized procedures.

  Example:

  When conducting usability testing of a new software tool, researchers must ensure that participants have similar levels of prior experience with similar tools to prevent user experience differences from skewing the results.

- **External Validity:**

  This concerns the extent to which the results of the study can be generalized to real-world settings. Ensuring external validity may involve using larger or more diverse sample sizes and replicating the study across different contexts or environments.

  Example:

  In a study on the impact of artificial intelligence in predictive analytics, researchers should aim to conduct the study across multiple industries to ensure the findings apply broadly, not just within one sector.

- **Reliability Testing:**

  Researchers must ensure that their instruments (e.g., surveys, tests) consistently measure the intended variables across time and subjects. Techniques like test-retest reliability, inter-rater reliability, or split-half reliability can help assess and improve consistency.

  Example:

  For a survey measuring employee satisfaction with a new IT system, researchers should test the survey on a small group first to ensure the questions are clear and that results are consistent over multiple administrations.

Advanced Analytical Techniques

The application of advanced statistical techniques can further enhance the quality of quantitative research. As data becomes more complex, researchers need to move beyond basic statistical analyses to employ techniques that better address the nuances of the data.

- **Multivariate Analysis:**

  Using techniques like multiple regression, factor analysis, or cluster analysis can help analyze the relationships between several variables simultaneously. In IS research, multivariate techniques are useful when studying complex phenomena such as organizational IT adoption, user satisfaction, or the relationship between different IT capabilities.

  Example:

  A study exploring factors affecting the success of an enterprise resource planning (ERP) implementation may use multiple regression analysis to identify how variables like training, system customization, and user support influence overall success.

- **Structural Equation Modeling:**

  SEM is increasingly used in IS research to explore complex relationships between variables, including both direct and indirect effects. SEM allows researchers to test theoretical models and assess the goodness of fit, which is critical when evaluating models like TAM or UTAUT.

  Example:

  In a study on the factors influencing e-commerce adoption, SEM could be used to test a model where perceived ease of use, trust, and perceived usefulness impact consumers' intention to purchase online.

- **Machine Learning and AI:**

  Researchers can employ machine learning techniques to analyze large datasets, identify patterns, and predict outcomes. In IT research, machine learning is especially useful when working with big data, system performance metrics, or real-time analytics. Tools such as Python's scikit-learn or R's caret package can aid in these efforts.

  Example:

  A study examining the effectiveness of recommendation algorithms on e-commerce platforms might apply machine learning to analyze clickstream data and predict which factors most strongly correlate with purchase behavior.

Improving Data Presentation and Communication

The clarity with which research findings are presented can significantly affect their impact and acceptance. Researchers must ensure that their data is presented in a way that is easy to understand, visually appealing, and directly tied to the research questions.

- **Effective Use of Tables and Figures:**

  Tables and figures are key tools for presenting complex data in a digestible format. Researchers should strive for clarity and simplicity in presenting their data, avoiding excessive complexity or redundant information. Using appropriate scales, labels, and legends ensures that readers can easily interpret the results.

  Example:

  A study on cloud computing adoption might use bar graphs to compare adoption rates across different regions or industries, ensuring that axes are labeled and legends are clear.

- **Data Visualization Software:**

  Tools like Tableau, Power BI, or even R and Python libraries (ggplot2, matplotlib) can help create compelling visualizations that allow readers to quickly grasp trends, patterns, and anomalies in the data.

  Example:

  Researchers in network security may use visualizations to display the frequency of cyberattacks over time, or to show the effectiveness of various intrusion detection systems, making their findings more accessible.

Ethical Considerations and Transparency

Ensuring ethical integrity in quantitative research is critical for maintaining credibility and contributing to the scientific community. Transparency about data collection methods, analysis techniques, and results enhances the research's trustworthiness and reproducibility.

- **Ethical Data Collection**:

  Researchers should obtain informed consent from participants, ensure data privacy, and avoid bias in survey instruments. For example, when conducting studies involving user behavior, researchers must be clear about the purpose of the study and ensure that participants' data is anonymized.

- **Data Transparency and Reproducibility**:

  Journals are increasingly requiring authors to provide open access to datasets and analysis scripts. This promotes reproducibility and transparency in research, allowing others to verify the findings and build upon them. Providing well-documented code and clear explanations of data preprocessing and analysis methods enhances the overall credibility of the study.

Chapter Summary

This chapter provided a practical roadmap for publishing quantitative research in the IS and IT fields. It began by helping researchers identify suitable journals that match their methodological and topical focus. Readers learn how to prepare and structure a manuscript, including how to properly format text, figures, tables, and references according to journal guidelines. The chapter outlines the entire submission process, emphasizing the use of online systems and the steps involved from submission to decision. A key focus is on the peer review process, explaining the responsibilities of authors, editors, and reviewers, and offering effective strategies for responding to reviewer feedback. Additionally, the chapter introduces essential tools and software that support various stages of quantitative research, from data analysis to citation management. Finally, the chapter presents strategies for increasing the visibility and impact of published work, making it a valuable resource for scholars aiming to publish high-quality, influential research in IS.

Review Questions

1 What are three key factors to consider when selecting a journal for your quantitative research?
2 How does aligning your manuscript with a journal's scope improve your chances of acceptance?
3 Name three structural components typically required in a quantitative research manuscript.
4 What are the common formatting guidelines researchers must follow when submitting to IS journals?

5 What is the role of tables and figures in enhancing the clarity of quantitative research?
6 Describe the main stages of the online submission process for an academic journal.
7 What are the roles of the editor and reviewers in the peer review process?
8 How should an author respond to critical or conflicting reviewer feedback?
9 List two software tools that support quantitative data analysis and two for reference management.
10 What are two strategies researchers can use to increase the visibility and impact of their published work?

Section II

Qualitative Research in Information Technology and IS

7 Qualitative Research in Information Systems

Chapter Objectives

After reading this chapter, readers should understand:

- Definition and Use of Qualitative Research
- The Different Types of Qualitative Research
- The Process of Qualitative Research, Data Collection & Analysis Approaches
- Mixed Methods Approaches & Future Trends and Advancements in Qualitative Research

Introduction and History of Qualitative Research

Qualitative research is a methodological approach that seeks to understand the human experiences, behaviors, and social phenomena from the perspectives of those involved. Unlike quantitative research, which focuses only on numerical data and statistical analysis, qualitative research emphasizes the depth and richness of data, exploring the meanings, interpretations, and complexities of human life. Qualitative research focuses on life experiences; they are more about the "why" and "how" rather than the "how many" or "how often." This approach is rooted in the naturalistic paradigm, aiming to capture the subjective reality of the participants through methods such as interviews, focus groups, observations, and content analysis.

History

Qualitative research has roots in anthropology and sociology fields; however, the modern form of Qualitative research began to emerge at the beginning of the 20th century with the influence of psychoanalysis. By 1945, the recognized father of qualitative research, Paul Lazerfield had shown how the field of psychology could provide a framework to explain and interpret human behavior.

DOI: 10.4324/9781003545521-9

He introduced the world to unstructured interviews and group discussions, and then stressed the importance of asking the question, why? With key developments such as grounded theory, qualitative research solidifies its position in research, making it a rather recent field compared to other research approaches.

Key Points in the Historical Timeline of Qualitative Research

Qualitative research has an evolving history shaped by shifts in social science inquiry, philosophical thought, and methodological innovation. Its roots can be traced back to early anthropological studies that emphasized observation and description of human cultures. Over time, qualitative research developed into a formalized approach, particularly through the contributions of sociologists and theorists who emphasized lived experiences, narrative, and meaning-making. This timeline outlines the key milestones in the evolution of qualitative research, from its emergence in the 19th century to its expansion in the digital age, highlighting foundational methods, major theoretical developments, and the growing recognition of diverse perspectives and ethical practices in the field.

Early 19th Century

- Qualitative research practices are seen in early anthropological fields with observations and descriptions of cultures laying the foundation for qualitative methods.

Early 20th Century

- Robert Park and Ernest Burgess, Chicago School of Sociology, began to use qualitative techniques to study urban communities, contributing to the development of participant observation as a method.
- Early forms of life story interviews emerge, focusing on individual narratives and experiences.

Mid-20th Century (1920s–1940s)

- The concept of qualitative research is formalized, explicitly defined, and recognized as a distinct form of research.
- Grounded Theory is introduced by Barney Glaser and Anselm Strauss. Grounded theory approach emphasizes the iterative process of data collection and analysis to develop a unique theory from the data itself. So, the theory is grounded in the data.

Post-World War II

- Qualitative Research gains acceptance and application in various disciplines like psychology, education, and health sciences.

- With wider application, ethical consideration in qualitative research, such as informed consent and participant privacy becomes a major focus.

Late 20th Century to Present

- Computer software tools for qualitative analysis, called QDAS (Qualitative Data Analysis Systems), emerge facilitating large-scale data management and analysis. Popular QDAS tools include: NVivo, ATLAS.ti, MAXQDA, Dedoose, and Quirkos.
- Approaches like feminist and postcolonial qualitative research emerge, focusing on social inequalities and power dynamics.

Qualitative Research in Information Systems Field

Information systems (IS) research is a relatively recent interdisciplinary field, however, it gained significant traction in the latter half of the 20th century. IS Research borrows heavily from methodologies rooted in social sciences, anthropology, and sociology. Methods normally used are case studies, interviews, and participant observation to understand the social and contextual aspects of technology implementation and use within organizations. Case study and grounded theory remain the prominent qualitative approaches in IS research. The case study method allows for deep exploration of specific organizations or situations, providing contextual details about technology use and impact. Whereas grounded theory is a method for developing theory inductively from the data that enables researchers to uncover emerging themes and patterns from the data, it is most useful for understanding organizational processes related to technology.

Orlikowski & Markus contributed as pioneers in applying qualitative methods to IS research in social constructions of technology and organizational practices, and the use of qualitative methods to study technology implementation and user resistance. Critical issues and debates have centered around rigor and reliability. However, there have been some concerns regarding the subjective nature of qualitative data and its potential lack of generalizability have been raised early on. A growing trend is to combine qualitative and quantitative research approaches to gain a richer and more in-depth understanding of the phenomena in IS research to overcome these issues. Overall, qualitative research has become an essential tool in IS research, allowing for the nuanced exploration of human-computer interaction, organizational dynamics, and social implications of technology, providing valuable insights beyond the use of numbers and statistical testing of quantitative methods alone.

Seminal Qualitative Researchers

Understanding the foundations of qualitative research requires familiarity with the pioneers who shaped its development. The researchers featured in this table have made seminal contributions to qualitative methodology, influencing how studies are designed, data are collected and analyzed, and theories are developed. Their works – often cited and widely used in academic training – established key approaches such as grounded theory, narrative inquiry, and systematic qualitative analysis. Whether through methodological innovation, conceptual clarity, or practical guidance, these scholars have profoundly impacted the evolution of qualitative research across disciplines such as sociology, education, health sciences, and communication. Table 7.1 highlights

Table 7.1 Seminal Qualitative Researchers and Their Contributions

Researcher	*Seminal Work*	*Summary of Contribution*
Barney Glaser	Glaser & Strauss (1967). *The Discovery of Grounded Theory*. Aldine Publishing	Co-founder of grounded theory. Emphasized generating theory from data through iterative coding and analysis. Revolutionized qualitative research with a rigorous, data-driven approach.
Anselm Strauss	Glaser & Strauss (1967). *The Discovery of Grounded Theory*. Aldine Publishing	Co-developed grounded theory. Advocated for constant comparative analysis. Later refined the method in *Qualitative Analysis for Social Scientists* (1987), emphasizing its use in health and organizational studies.
Juliet Corbin	Strauss & Corbin (1990). *Basics of Qualitative R esearch*. Sage Publications	Expanded grounded theory with practical guidelines for coding and theoretical sampling. Made grounded theory more accessible to researchers in nursing, education, and sociology.
Kathy Charmaz	Charmaz (2006). *Constructing Grounded Theory*. Sage Publications	Introduced constructivist grounded theory. Emphasized the researcher's interpretive role and made grounded theory more flexible and widely used in social and health sciences.
John W. Creswell	Creswell (2013). *Qualitative Inquiry and Research Design* (3rd ed.). Sage Publications	Provided a structured overview of five qualitative approaches. Widely used textbook for designing qualitative research, especially in education, health, and social science.
Michael Huberman	Miles & Huberman (1994). *Qualitative Data Analysis* (2nd ed.). Sage Publications	Developed systematic tools for data analysis, including coding strategies and visual data displays. Promoted rigor in qualitative analysis.
Matthew B. Miles	Miles & Huberman (1994). *Qualitative Data Analysis* (2nd ed.). Sage Publications	Co-developed visual and iterative methods for qualitative analysis. His work helped structure and standardize qualitative data interpretation.
Paul F. Lazarsfeld	Lazarsfeld et al. (1944). *The People's Choice*. Duell, Sloan and Pearce	Early pioneer in using qualitative interviews in voter behavior research. Known for the two-step flow model of communication. Influenced both qualitative and mixed-methods research.

their most influential works and summarizes their lasting contributions to the field. The seminal works of the following qualitative pioneers were selected based on their influence in qualitative research, as evidenced by high citation counts and frequent references in methodological literature.

The seminal works were selected based on their foundational impact in qualitative research, as evidenced by high citation counts (Google Scholar trends), frequent references in methodological texts (e.g.,), and their role in shaping qualitative paradigms. There are some overlaps in qualitative work with Glaser and Strauss, who share the same seminal work as do Miles and Huberman due to their collaborative contributions. Lazarsfeld is primarily known for qualitative methods but has significant qualitative components. Strauss & Corbin are recognized for work on grounded theory, where Creswell is a prominent researcher in mixed methods, and Lazarsfeld is considered to be the "father of qualitative research."

Key Contributors to Qualitative Research Methodology

The development and refinement of qualitative research have been significantly influenced by several key scholars. Their contributions span foundational methodologies, practical data analysis techniques, and the integration of qualitative and mixed methods approaches. Below are brief profiles of some of the most influential figures in the field.

Anselm Strauss & Juliet Corbin

- Key Contribution: *Grounded Theory Methodology*
- Impact: Together, Strauss and Corbin advanced the grounded theory approach, which emphasizes developing theory directly from data through systematic procedures. Their co-authored book *Basics of Qualitative Research* (1990) is a cornerstone text in qualitative methodology, widely used in health, education, and organizational research.
- Legacy: They formalized key processes like coding, memo-writing, and theoretical sampling, making grounded theory more accessible and structured.

Kathy Charmaz

- Key Contribution: *Constructivist Grounded Theory*
- Impact: Charmaz introduced a constructivist approach to grounded theory, highlighting the interpretive role of the researcher and the co-construction of meaning in qualitative data. Her work offered a more flexible and reflective alternative to the original grounded theory models.
- Legacy: Her book *Constructing Grounded Theory* (2006) is especially influential in health and social science disciplines for its practical and philosophical insights.

John W. Creswell

- Key Contribution: *Qualitative and Mixed Methods Design*
- Impact: Creswell has written extensively on qualitative research design, often bridging it with mixed methods. His widely used book *Qualitative Inquiry and Research Design: Choosing Among Five Approaches* outlines narrative, phenomenology, grounded theory, ethnography, and case study.
- Legacy: His work provides clarity, structure, and guidance for researchers across disciplines, making it a staple in academic curricula.

Michael Huberman & Matthew B. Miles

- Key Contribution: *Qualitative Data Analysis Techniques*
- Impact: This duo co-authored *Qualitative Data Analysis: An Expanded Sourcebook*, which introduced visual tools such as matrices and flow charts to help analyze complex qualitative data systematically.
- Legacy: Their work brought rigor and transparency to qualitative analysis, and remains a foundational reference for researchers in education, program evaluation, and applied social sciences.

Paul Felix Lazarsfeld

- Key Contribution: *Pioneering Empirical Qualitative and Communication Research*
- Impact: Known for blending qualitative interviews with early survey methods, Lazarsfeld's work, especially *The People's Choice* (1944), laid the foundation for communication and media studies. He also developed the two-step flow model of communication.
- Legacy: Though often associated with quantitative methods, his early integration of qualitative interviews helped shape the trajectory of mixed-methods research. He is often referred to as one of the "fathers" of modern qualitative research.

Table 7.2 indicates some of the top seminal authors in various qualitative research methodologies.

Table 7.2 Top Seminal Qualitative Methods Contributors

Qualitative Methodology	*Author or Researcher*
Mixed Methods	Creswell, Lazarsfeld
Action Research	Kurt Lewin
Case Study	Yin or Stake
Grounded Theory	Charmaz, Glaser, and Strauss, or Cobin and Strauss
Narrative	Connelly and Clandinin
Phenomenology	Van Manen or Moustakas
Qualitative Data Analysis	Huberman, Miles
Ethnography	Geertz, Mead
Critical Qualitative Inquiry	Denzin, Lincoln

Philosophical Underpinnings of Qualitative Research

Below is an integrated overview of key philosophical foundations and assumptions underlying qualitative research, including distinctions between epistemological and ontological stances and the paradigms of interpretivism, positivism, constructivism, and social constructivism.

Philosophical Foundations

Philosophical foundations in research involve considering fundamental questions about the nature of reality (ontology), how we come to know that reality (epistemology), and the values and purposes guiding the inquiry (axiology). These foundations influence the choice of methodology, methods, and interpretations in both qualitative and quantitative research traditions.

Ontological Assumptions

Ontology refers to beliefs about the nature of reality. Ontological assumptions concern whether reality is viewed as a stable, external entity waiting to be discovered, or as multiple, context-dependent realities constructed by individuals and groups.

- Realism (Associated with Positivism): Realists hold that a single, objective reality exists independent of human perception. This stance underpins positivist research, which seeks to uncover universal laws and patterns. Researchers assume phenomena have an existence external to the human mind (Guba & Lincoln, 1994).
- Relativism (Associated with Interpretivism and Constructivism): Relativists believe that realities are multiple, constructed, and context-bound. Reality is interpreted differently by individuals who bring their own experiences, cultures, and histories to understanding phenomena (Denzin & Lincoln, 2011).

Epistemological Assumptions

Epistemology concerns the nature and the scope of knowledge – what it means to know something and how knowledge can be acquired, validated, and communicated.

- **Objectivism (Associated with Positivism)**: Objectivist epistemology posits that knowledge exists independently of the knower and can be discovered through the careful application of the scientific method. Researchers strive for neutrality and aim to reduce subjectivity, assuming that bias-free inquiry is both desirable and achievable (Crotty, 1998).

- **Subjectivism (Associated with Interpretivism, Constructivism, and Social Constructivism)**: Subjectivist epistemology holds that knowledge is shaped by the knower's perspectives, contexts, and interactions. It rejects the notion of an objective reality entirely separate from human consciousness, emphasizing understanding meaning through engagement with participants' lived experiences (Lincoln & Guba, 1985).

Interpretivism vs. Positivism

Positivism emerged from the natural sciences and is grounded in the idea that the world operates according to universal laws discernible through objective observation and measurement. Positivist researchers strive for value-free inquiry, controlled experimentation, quantification, and hypothesis testing (Bryman, 2016). In this tradition, the researcher is viewed as an external observer, studying phenomena without influencing them.

Interpretivism, on the other hand, developed as a critique of positivism's applicability to the social world. Interpretivists argue that the social realm cannot be understood using the same methods as the natural sciences because human actions are infused with meaning, intentions, and interpretations. Through qualitative methods such as interviews, observations, and textual analysis, interpretivist researchers seek to understand how individuals interpret their experiences and construct their social realities (Schwartz-Shea & Yanow, 2012). The researcher is seen as a co-constructor of meaning, engaged deeply with the participants and their contexts.

Key Differences:

- **Ontology**: Positivism assumes a single objective reality; interpretivism acknowledges multiple, socially constructed realities.
- **Epistemology**: Positivism aims for objective, replicable knowledge; interpretivism seeks understanding and interpretation of contextual meanings.
- **Methods**: Positivism relies on measurement, experiments, and surveys; interpretivism employs interviews, participant observations, and narrative analysis.

Constructivism and Social Constructivism

Constructivism holds that individuals construct their own understanding of the world through experiencing things and reflecting on those experiences. Each person's reality is shaped by their unique perspectives, cultural contexts, and historical backgrounds (Crotty, 1998). Constructivists focus on how individuals generate meanings and knowledge through interaction with their environment. The emphasis is on understanding how personal experiences and cognitive processes lead to one's constructed reality.

Social Constructivism, closely related to constructivism, extends the idea of reality construction to the social sphere. Knowledge and reality are not just individually constructed but are co-constructed through social interactions, language, and cultural norms (Berger & Luckmann, 1966). Social constructivists study how collective sense-making processes, discourse, and institutional structures shape what is considered "true" or "real" in a given community. This perspective recognizes that power relations, ideologies, and historical conditions influence how groups co-create shared understandings.

Key Aspects of Constructivism and Social Constructivism:

- **Ontology**: Multiple constructed realities, influenced by personal experiences and social interactions.
- **Epistemology**: Knowledge is created collaboratively between individuals or within communities, rather than discovered.
- **Methods**: Qualitative and interpretive approaches that delve into meaning-making processes, cultural narratives, and social interactions.

These philosophical foundations guide the research design, methods, and interpretations in the social and information sciences. Positivism's claim to objectivity and predictive power contrasts with interpretivism's recognition of subjectivity and contextual understanding. Constructivism and social constructivism further highlight that knowledge and reality are not fixed entities but are constructed individually or collectively. Each perspective – whether positivist, interpretivist, constructivist, or social constructivist – offers valuable insights, and the choice often depends on the research questions, aims, and contexts under investigation.

Key Characteristics of Qualitative Research

Exploratory in Nature

Qualitative research is particularly useful when investigating new or poorly understood phenomena. It does not begin with a hypothesis to test but instead allows themes and insights to emerge from the data. This makes it especially valuable in the early stages of research or in areas lacking prior study. For example, in IS, researchers might explore how information technology (IT) professionals adapt to agile methodologies in software development. Through interviews and focus groups, qualitative studies can uncover team dynamics, role changes, and communication challenges that structured surveys might overlook.

Holistic Perspective

This approach aims to understand phenomena within their full context, taking into account the interrelationships among social, cultural, organizational, and technological elements. For instance, when studying the implementation of an enterprise resource planning (ERP) system in a multinational company, a qualitative study might examine not just the technical process but also user resistance, organizational culture, leadership support, and cross-cultural communication. This broad perspective can reveal why similar systems succeed in one environment but fail in another.

Participant-Centered

Qualitative research values the lived experiences and perspectives of participants. It emphasizes giving voice to those being studied by closely engaging with them through methods like in-depth interviews, focus groups, and observations. In IT and IS, for example, researchers studying cybersecurity awareness might interview employees across departments to understand their real-world experiences, perceptions of digital risk, and the effectiveness of training programs. These insights can inform the design of more relevant and user-friendly security protocols.

Flexible and Adaptive

One of the strengths of qualitative research is its ability to evolve during the study. As new insights emerge, researchers can adapt their questions and focus areas to explore unexpected findings. In an IT context, a researcher studying virtual collaboration might start with an interest in how teams use tools like Slack or Microsoft Teams but shift to explore how trust and team cohesion develop remotely, based on insights that emerge during early interviews.

Descriptive and Interpretive

Rather than merely cataloging behaviors or events, qualitative research provides detailed, nuanced descriptions and seeks to interpret underlying meanings and patterns. For instance, in a case study of a failed digital transformation project in a government agency, a researcher might not only describe the sequence of technical rollouts and management decisions but also interpret the deeper causes such as cultural resistance, lack of stakeholder alignment, or fear of job displacement. These interpretive insights are crucial for understanding the complexity of IT implementations in real-world contexts.

Common Methods of Data Collection

Qualitative research relies on diverse methods of data collection to capture rich, detailed insights into human experiences, behaviors, and social contexts. Each method offers unique advantages depending on the research questions and context. In the fields of IT and IS, these methods help researchers explore how individuals and groups interact with technologies, interpret digital

Table 7.3 Common Methods in Qualitative Research

Method	*Description*	*Example in IT/IS*
Interviews	One-on-one conversations to deeply explore participants' thoughts, feelings, and experiences. Can be structured, semi-structured, or unstructured.	Interviewing IT staff about their experiences transitioning to cloud infrastructure to uncover challenges and attitudes.
Focus Groups	Group discussions that reveal collective views and group dynamics. Useful for exploring shared experiences and social norms.	Conducting a focus group with app users to discuss usability and gather feedback on a new mobile interface.
Observations	Watching participants in their natural settings to understand behaviors and interactions in real-time.	Observing help desk staff during peak hours to identify workflow inefficiencies and informal problem-solving strategies.
Content Analysis	Systematic examination of texts, media, or digital artifacts to identify themes and patterns.	Analyzing user feedback from an open-source platform to uncover common issues and feature requests.

environments, and make decisions. Table 7.3 outlines some of the most commonly used qualitative data collection methods, along with their descriptions and examples relevant to IT and IS research.

Applications and Implications

Qualitative research is widely used in fields such as sociology, anthropology, psychology, education, health sciences, and marketing. It is particularly valuable for understanding complex social issues, developing theories, and informing policy and practice. By providing rich, contextualized insights, qualitative research helps to capture the diversity of human experiences and contributes to a more comprehensive understanding of social reality. In summary, qualitative research offers a powerful toolkit for exploring and understanding the intricacies of human life. Its emphasis on depth, context, and participant perspectives makes it an essential approach in the social sciences and beyond, fostering a deeper appreciation of the complexities that quantitative methods may overlook.

When to Use Qualitative Design for Research

Qualitative research designs are particularly effective in situations where a nuanced understanding of human behavior, contextual dynamics, or emerging phenomena is needed. Qualitative research is particularly well-suited for exploring new, complex, or under-examined phenomena, especially in the early stages of investigation. It enables researchers to generate initial insights and hypotheses that may later be tested quantitatively. Additionally, qualitative methods are valuable for understanding the context and processes behind behaviors and outcomes, allowing researchers to delve into the "how" and "why" rather than just the "what." This approach is especially effective for examining personal experiences, emotions, beliefs, and social interactions, offering a participant-centered view that captures the nuances of lived realities. Beyond individual experiences, qualitative research is instrumental in uncovering social and cultural norms, revealing how individuals interpret and navigate their social worlds. Its strength lies in producing rich, detailed data that highlights complexity and depth – crucial for developing theories or models, such as through grounded theory approaches. It also plays a critical role in evaluating programs and interventions by illuminating the factors influencing their success or failure. Finally, qualitative methods can complement quantitative research by providing contextual understanding and explaining the underlying mechanisms behind numerical trends, resulting in a more holistic and robust analysis.

Below are key scenarios where qualitative research is the most suitable approach, especially within the domains of IT and IS.

1. ***Exploring New or Complex Phenomena***
   Qualitative research is ideal for studying emerging technologies, such as artificial intelligence (AI) or blockchain, where little prior research exists. It enables researchers to explore user adoption patterns, ethical concerns, and real-world challenges without relying on predefined hypotheses.
2. ***Understanding Context and Process***
   In IT and IS, context matters. For example, when examining how an organization transitions to a new enterprise system, qualitative research helps capture the organizational culture, workflow changes, and resistance to change, factors that quantitative methods might overlook.
3. ***Studying Human Experiences and Perspectives***
   When exploring user satisfaction with remote work platforms or the emotional impact of cybersecurity breaches, qualitative methods like interviews and narrative analysis allow researchers to delve into personal experiences, emotions, and attitudes.
4. ***Investigating Social and Cultural Norms***
   Cultural and social factors often influence how technologies are adopted. For example, in cross-national IS studies, qualitative research can uncover cultural differences in privacy expectations, communication styles, or technology acceptance.
5. ***Generating Rich, Detailed Data***
   For topics like digital transformation or IT governance, researchers often need rich descriptions of decision-making processes and stakeholder dynamics. Qualitative methods provide the depth needed to capture these complex and layered realities.

6 ***Developing Theories***
Grounded theory is frequently used in IS research to develop theories around topics like user behavior, system adoption, or IT leadership. Rather than starting with a hypothesis, researchers build theories based on insights emerging directly from the data.

7 ***Evaluating Programs and Interventions***
Qualitative research helps evaluate IT training programs, user experience improvements, or software implementation projects. It reveals how interventions are perceived, what challenges users face, and which aspects lead to successful outcomes.

8 ***Complementing Quantitative Research***
In mixed-methods studies, qualitative data can contextualize and explain findings from surveys or experiments. For example, if a quantitative survey shows low engagement with an e-learning platform, follow-up interviews can uncover usability issues or motivational barriers.

Here's Table 7.4, which highlights different scenarios when to use qualitative methods, with relevant examples from the field of IT and IS, along with the most appropriate qualitative methods for each scenario.

Table 7.4 Recommended Qualitative Methods for Different Scenarios

Scenario	*Example from IT and IS*	*Recommended Qualitative Method*
Exploring New or Complex Phenomena	Investigating user perceptions of emerging technologies like blockchain or generative AI	Exploratory Interviews, Open-Ended Surveys
Understanding Context and Process	Studying how an organization implements a new enterprise system and adapts internal workflows	Case Study, Ethnographic Observation
Studying Human Experiences and Perspectives	Understanding users' emotional responses to cybersecurity threats or remote work fatigue	In-depth Interviews, Narrative Analysis
Investigating Social and Cultural Norms	Exploring digital privacy expectations in different cultural settings	Focus Groups, Thematic Analysis
Generating Rich, Detailed Data	Examining stakeholder dynamics during a digital transformation project	Case Study, Participant Observation
Developing Theories	Building a theory of user resistance to change in IT system rollouts	Grounded Theory, Constant Comparative Method
Evaluating Programs and Interventions	Evaluating the effectiveness of an IT training program for non-technical staff	Semi-Structured Interviews, Focus Groups
Complementing Quantitative Research	Explaining low survey scores in user satisfaction with a new CRM platform	Follow-up Interviews, Document Analysis

Practice Lab 7.1: "Pick Your Question, Match Your Method!"

Objective

To help you understand how to match qualitative research methods with real-world research scenarios in IT and IS.

Instructions

1. **Pick a Theme**
   Choose one of the broad research areas from the list below or create your own:
   - Digital transformation
   - AI in workplaces
   - Cybersecurity behavior
   - Remote work and burnout
   - Tech adoption in education
   - Privacy in social media
   - IT training and learning platforms
2. **Create a Research Question**
   Think about what you're curious about in your chosen theme. Try to write one open-ended research question.
   Tip: Start your question with "How," "What," or "Why."
3. **Match Your Scenario**
   Read through the scenarios in Table 7.4 and identify which one best matches your question.
4. **Choose the Method**
   Based on the matching scenario, select **one or two qualitative methods** you would use to answer your research question. Briefly explain **why** you chose it.

Submission

Turn in a short paragraph with the following:

- Your chosen theme
- Your research question
- The scenario you matched it to
- The method(s) you chose and why

Specific Scenarios for Using Qualitative Design

Qualitative design is employed when the research objectives involve understanding deeper meanings, capturing the richness of human experience, and exploring phenomena in context. It is particularly valuable in fields where the complexity of human behavior and social interactions demands a flexible, adaptive, and detailed approach to data collection and analysis. By choosing qualitative methods, researchers can achieve a comprehensive and nuanced understanding of their subjects, providing a foundation for meaningful and impactful conclusions. Qualitative research design is especially valuable across a wide range of disciplines where understanding human experiences, perceptions, and social contexts is critical. In health research, qualitative methods are used to explore patient experiences, adherence to treatment regimens, and the personal impact of illness on everyday life. These insights are often gathered through in-depth interviews or focus groups, helping to inform patient-centered care. In education, qualitative approaches allow researchers to examine teaching methods, student engagement, and learning outcomes from the perspectives of both students and educators. Observations and case studies are common here, providing a deeper understanding of classroom dynamics and instructional effectiveness.

In business and marketing, qualitative research is employed to investigate consumer behavior, brand perception, and organizational culture. Focus groups and content analysis help businesses understand market sentiments and employee experiences. In social work, researchers use qualitative methods to understand the lived experiences of vulnerable populations and to assess the effectiveness and cultural relevance of social interventions. In psychology, qualitative studies delve into mental health challenges, therapeutic relationships, and subjective emotional experiences, often through narrative interviews and thematic analysis. Finally, in IS, qualitative research is essential for studying the human and organizational factors that influence the adoption, use, and impact of IS technologies. Methods like ethnography and case studies help uncover how systems are integrated into real-world environments, capturing user experiences and contextual challenges that quantitative approaches may overlook (Table 7.5).

Information Systems and Qualitative Research

In the field of IS research, qualitative research can be particularly valuable in several scenarios. These scenarios often involve exploring the human, organizational, and contextual aspects of IS that are not easily captured through quantitative methods. Here are some specific scenarios where qualitative research is appropriate in IS research:

Table 7.5 Qualitative Design Across Different Disciplines

Field	*Purpose of Qualitative Research*	*Common Methods Used*
Health Research	Understand patient experiences, treatment adherence, and impact of illness on daily life	In-depth interviews, focus groups
Education	Explore teaching methods, student engagement, and learning outcomes from participant perspectives	Observations, case studies, semi-structured interviews
Business & Marketing	Investigate consumer behavior, brand perception, and organizational culture	Focus groups, content analysis, ethnography
Social Work	Understand lived experiences of vulnerable populations and effectiveness of social programs	Narrative interviews, participant observation
Psychology	Explore mental health issues, therapeutic processes, and subjective experiences	Thematic analysis, in-depth interviews

Understanding User Experiences and Behaviors

When the goal is to gain a deep understanding of how users interact with IS, qualitative methods such as interviews, focus groups, and ethnographic studies can provide rich insights into user experiences, challenges, and behaviors.

Exploring Implementation and Adoption Processes

Qualitative research is useful for studying the processes involved in the implementation and adoption of IS within organizations. It can uncover the factors that facilitate or hinder successful implementation, the strategies used by stakeholders, and the contextual influences on these processes.

Investigating Organizational Impact

To understand how IS impact organizational processes, culture, and performance, qualitative methods can provide detailed accounts of the changes brought about by IS, the responses of different stakeholders, and the long-term effects on organizational dynamics.

Developing and Refining Theories

Qualitative research is valuable for developing new theories or refining existing ones related to IS. Grounded theory, for example, can be used to generate theories based on data collected from participants, leading to a deeper understanding of phenomena like user acceptance, technology diffusion, and system usage.

Examining Technological Innovations

When studying new or emerging technologies, qualitative research can help explore how these innovations are perceived, adopted, and integrated into existing systems and practices. This approach can reveal insights into the social and technical challenges associated with technological change.

Evaluating Information Systems

Qualitative methods can be used to evaluate the effectiveness, usability, and impact of IS. This includes gathering detailed feedback from users and stakeholders about their experiences, satisfaction, and the benefits and drawbacks of the systems in use.

Investigating Ethical, Legal, and Social Issues

Qualitative research can explore the ethical, legal, and social implications of IS, such as privacy concerns, data security, and the digital divide. It can provide a nuanced understanding of how these issues affect different groups and inform policy and practice.

Understanding Cultural and Contextual Differences

IS are often used in diverse cultural and organizational contexts. Qualitative research can uncover how cultural differences influence the design, implementation, and use of IS, providing insights that can lead to more culturally sensitive and context-appropriate solutions.

Examples of Qualitative Research in IS

- **User Experience Research**: Conducting interviews and usability studies to understand how users interact with a new software application, identifying pain points and areas for improvement.
- **Case Studies of System Implementation**: Using case studies to explore the process of implementing a new ERP system in a multinational corporation, focusing on the challenges faced and strategies used to overcome them.
- **Ethnographic Studies**: Performing ethnographic research in an organization to observe how employees use a particular information system in their daily work and how it affects their productivity and collaboration.

- **Focus Groups on Technology Adoption**: Organizing focus groups with different stakeholders to gather perspectives on the adoption of a new technology, such as a mobile health application, and understanding the barriers to its widespread use.
- **Content Analysis of Online Communities**: Analyzing discussions in online forums or social media to understand user sentiments and experiences related to a specific information system or technology.

Qualitative research in IS is essential for exploring the complex, contextual, and human aspects of technology use and implementation. It provides a rich, detailed understanding of how IS are perceived, adopted, and utilized within different contexts, helping researchers and practitioners design more effective, user-friendly, and context-appropriate systems.

Research Design in Qualitative Studies

According to research guidance published by SAGE journals, the research design in qualitative studies is generally characterized by flexibility, context-sensitivity, and an iterative, emergent process rather than a rigid, predetermined blueprint. SAGE resources emphasize that qualitative research design evolves from the interplay between the researcher's initial inquiry and the unfolding data collection and analysis. It is guided by the nature of the research question, the context of the study, and the theoretical framework informing the inquiry. Key features highlighted by SAGE include:

- ***Emergent Structure:***
  Unlike quantitative designs, which often follow a fixed sequence of steps, qualitative research designs develop and refine their approach as the study progresses. Initial research plans might outline broad methods and objectives, but the specifics – such as which participants to include, how to probe deeper into certain themes, or which analytical strategies to apply – may shift over time.
- ***Contextual Orientation:***
  Qualitative designs pay close attention to the context in which phenomena occur. SAGE emphasizes that understanding experiences, behaviors, and social processes requires situating them within their natural contexts. This involves considering cultural, social, organizational, and historical factors that shape the meanings participants assign to events or issues.
- ***Reflexivity and Researcher Involvement:***
  SAGE guidance underscores the importance of reflexivity in qualitative research design. Researchers acknowledge their own positionality, biases, and assumptions, continuously reflecting on how these factors influence the research process and interpretation of findings. This reflexive stance is integral to maintaining ethical awareness and methodological rigor.

- ***Iterative Data Collection and Analysis:***
  Qualitative research designs typically integrate data collection and analysis in an ongoing, cyclical manner. Early analysis may guide the selection of new participants, the refinement of interview questions, or the pursuit of additional data sources. This iterative approach helps the researcher deepen their understanding, identify emerging patterns, and explore unexpected findings.
- ***Methodological Plurality:***
  SAGE publications encourage the use of multiple qualitative methods – such as interviews, focus groups, ethnography, observations, narrative analyses, or document reviews – to capture rich, multifaceted data. Researchers select and combine methods based on the research question and the data's evolving nature, leading to a more holistic understanding of the phenomenon under study.
- ***Credibility and Trustworthiness:***
  While flexible, qualitative research design is not devoid of rigor. SAGE emphasizes strategies for ensuring trustworthiness – such as triangulation of data sources, member checking, and thick description – to enhance the credibility, transferability, dependability, and confirmability of the findings.

In summary, from a SAGE standpoint, qualitative research design is best viewed as a dynamic, interpretive, and context-driven process. It prioritizes depth over breadth, embraces complexity, and adapts continually as the researcher learns from the data and the research context. This fluid, responsive approach enables a more nuanced understanding of social realities and human experiences.

Data Collection Methods in Qualitative Research

Qualitative research employs a variety of data collection methods aimed at capturing rich, contextualized, and detailed information about participants' perspectives, experiences, and social environments. These methods are often flexible and iterative, allowing the researcher to refine approaches as insights emerge. Common qualitative data collection methods include:

In-Depth Interviews

In-depth interviews are one-on-one conversations between a researcher and a participant that seek to explore personal experiences, perceptions, and meaning-making processes. These interviews can be semi-structured, guided by a list of open-ended questions while allowing flexibility to pursue emergent topics, or unstructured, more akin to a natural conversation. This method is particularly useful when exploring complex or sensitive topics where depth of insight is more important than breadth. In IS research, in-depth interviews are frequently used to explore topics such as user resistance to new enterprise systems, IT leadership experiences during digital transformation, or the lived experiences of remote workers adapting to virtual collaboration tools. For example, a study investigating how IT professionals adapt to the pressures of 24/7 connectivity might employ in-depth interviews to uncover stressors, coping strategies, and perceptions of work-life boundaries. The strength of this method lies in its ability to elicit rich, contextualized narratives that reveal not just what participants do, but *why* they do it and how they feel about it.

Focus Groups

Focus groups bring together a small group of participants to discuss a specific topic, moderated by a researcher who facilitates the conversation. The power of this method lies in its ability to capture social interaction, group dynamics, and collective views. Participants can react to each other's ideas, challenge assumptions, or build consensus, making focus groups particularly effective when studying shared cultural norms or contested issues. In the IT and IS domain, focus groups might be used to explore user opinions on newly introduced technologies, such as a university adopting a learning management system (LMS) or a company piloting a new cybersecurity awareness program. For example, a focus group of employees could reveal varying attitudes toward adopting biometric authentication systems, from enthusiasm about convenience to concerns over privacy. This method is especially helpful when researchers want to understand how opinions are socially constructed, reinforced, or challenged within a community or organization.

Participant Observation and Ethnography

Participant observation and ethnographic methods involve immersing oneself in a natural setting to observe social interactions, behaviors, and cultural practices. The researcher may assume an observer role or participate actively in the setting, depending on the goals and ethical boundaries of the study. Data are typically collected through detailed field notes, audio-visual recordings, or reflective journals. In IS research, ethnography has been used to understand how IT teams collaborate in agile development environments, how helpdesk staff interact with users, or how knowledge is shared in co-located versus remote workspaces. For instance, an ethnographic study of a hospital's IT department during an electronic health record (EHR) rollout could uncover unspoken norms, informal workarounds, and power dynamics not easily captured through surveys or interviews. This method excels in revealing the "real-world" use of technology in context, what people *actually do*, not just what they say they do.

Document and Content Analysis

Document and content analysis involve systematic examination of texts, images, videos, or digital artifacts to identify patterns, meanings, and themes. This method is ideal for examining organizational policies, training manuals, meeting transcripts, social media discussions, or digital user reviews. Depending on the analytical focus, researchers may use thematic analysis, discourse analysis, or narrative analysis to interpret the data. In the field of IT, content analysis could be applied to internal IT policy documents to examine how security is framed within an organization, or to tech blogs and forums to understand community discourse around open-source development. Another example includes analyzing job postings for IT roles to identify emerging skill requirements and industry trends. The strength of this method lies in its unobtrusiveness and its ability to provide historical and contextual insights, especially when participant access is limited or when triangulating with other data sources.

Audio-Visual and Visual Methods

Visual and audio-visual methods involve the use of images, videos, and other visual artifacts as either data or elicitation tools. Researchers might analyze existing media (e.g., corporate training videos, product demo reels) or invite participants to create visual materials (e.g., drawings, diaries) that express their experiences. In IS research, this could include recording screen-sharing sessions during user testing of a new mobile app, or asking IT users to create visual representations of their experience navigating a complex interface. For instance, video recordings of team meetings in a software development firm can be analyzed to understand decision-making processes or power dynamics in agile teams. These methods provide access to non-verbal cues and embodied interactions that might otherwise go unnoticed in verbal accounts.

Diaries and Journals

Diary and journal methods involve participants documenting their own experiences, reflections, and emotions over time. These records may take the form of handwritten notes, digital logs, or voice memos, and can be structured or unstructured depending on the research design. This approach is particularly useful for studying processes or changes over time such as how perceptions of a new IT system evolve during a training period, or how remote workers' productivity and well-being fluctuate across weeks. For example, an IS researcher might ask participants in a digital transformation project to maintain weekly journals about their engagement with new tools, organizational communication, and stress levels. These longitudinal insights are invaluable for capturing temporal dynamics and for exploring personal experiences that might be difficult to articulate face-to-face.

Online and Digital Methods

As digital technologies transform how people communicate and work, qualitative research has adapted to virtual environments. Online and digital methods encompass a range of approaches, including virtual interviews, online focus groups, social media analysis, and digital ethnography. These methods allow researchers to access geographically dispersed participants and study digital interactions in real-time. In the IT and IS field, researchers have used these methods to study user communities on GitHub, social media debates around data privacy, or collaboration patterns on platforms like Slack and Microsoft Teams. A study might involve analyzing Reddit threads to understand public sentiment around a tech company's data practices, or observing online gaming forums to explore virtual identity and community building. These methods are particularly well-suited for investigating emerging digital cultures and for reaching participants who may be otherwise difficult to engage through traditional means.

Qualitative data collection methods are diverse and can be mixed and matched to suit the research question, context, and participants. By choosing appropriate methods and remaining flexible and responsive as the study progresses, qualitative researchers can gather nuanced, contextualized data that leads to a richer understanding of human experiences, social phenomena, and cultural meaning-making (Table 7.6).

Data Analysis Techniques in Qualitative Studies

QDA is an iterative, interpretive process aimed at making sense of complex, nuanced, and context-specific information. Rather than relying on statistical formulas or standardized tests, qualitative analysis focuses on identifying patterns, themes, and meanings within rich, detailed data sources such as interview transcripts, field notes, images, and documents. The process often evolves alongside data collection and involves constant reflection, refinement, and interpretation. Below is an overview of key steps, principles, and common techniques employed in QDA.

The Analysis Process

Data Familiarization

The first step in qualitative analysis is becoming intimately familiar with the data. This involves reading and rereading transcripts, listening to recordings, reviewing field notes, and jotting down early impressions. During this phase, researchers begin to notice recurring ideas, emotional tones, or unexpected details that may warrant closer attention later. Familiarization builds the foundation for deeper analytical work by allowing the researcher to understand the "big picture" before narrowing in on specific parts.

Table 7.6 Advantages and Disadvantages of Different Qualitative Methods

Method	*Advantages*	*Disadvantages*
In-Depth Interviews	• Elicits rich, personal insights and deep understanding of individual experiences • Flexible and responsive to emerging themes • Allows exploration of sensitive or complex issues	• Time-consuming to conduct and analyze • Requires skilled interview-ing- Data may be difficult to compare across participants
Focus Groups	• Reveals group dynamics and social influences on opinions • Efficient way to gather diverse views at once • Encourages participants to build on each other's ideas	• Risk of groupthink or domi-nance by strong voices • Less depth per individual • Managing dynamics can be challenging
Participant Observation & Ethnography	• Captures real-life behavior in natural context • Provides cultural and social insights often missed in interviews • Allows understanding of non-verbal cues and routines	• Very time-intensive and may require long immersion • Researcher bias and influ-ence on the setting • Access to field sites may be restricted
Document and Content Analysis	• Non-intrusive; use existing materials • Good for historical or contextual data • Useful when participant access is limited	• Limited to what's recorded or published • Interpretation can be subjective • Cannot probe for clarification or intent
Audio-Visual and Visual Methods	• Captures non-verbal and spatial data • Enables creative participant expression • Useful for exploring unarticulated or tacit knowledge	• Data analysis can be com-plex- Requires technical equipment and skills • Some participants may be uncomfortable with visual tasks
Diaries and Journals	• Supports longitudinal data collection • Allows for personal and reflective accounts • Less intrusive and can be done privately	• Inconsistent participation or detail • Relies on participant motivation • Hard to verify or clarify entries
Online and Digital Methods	• Access to dispersed or hard-to-reach populations • Captures digital culture and online behavior • Cost-effective and scalable	• Digital divide may limit participation • Ethical concerns around privacy in online spaces • Interpreting online behavior may lack context

Data Management and Organization

Qualitative data can quickly become overwhelming due to its volume and unstructured nature. Organizing the data in a systematic way – through consistent file naming, careful transcription, and the use of QDA software (e.g., NVivo, MAXQDA, ATLAS.ti) is essential. These tools help researchers categorize, retrieve, and visualize coded data, making analysis more efficient and rigorous.

Coding the Data

Coding is the heart of qualitative analysis. It involves assigning meaningful labels called *codes* to segments of data that capture key ideas, actions, or sentiments. Coding typically unfolds in several stages:

- **Open Coding**: Initial labeling of data without imposing a predefined framework. The researcher identifies concepts that emerge naturally from the text.
- **Axial Coding**: This step links related codes, explores relationships between categories, and begins to build a structure around emerging themes.
- **Selective Coding**: Researchers identify core categories that serve as the central focus of the analysis. These themes are refined and integrated into broader narratives or theoretical constructs.

Throughout the coding process, researchers revisit the data repeatedly to revise codes and ensure alignment with the research questions.

Theme Development

After coding, the next step is to identify and refine themes, recurring patterns, or ideas that provide insight into the phenomenon under investigation. A good theme is both analytically significant and grounded in the data. Researchers test emerging themes by comparing them across cases or data sources, ensuring they are coherent, well-supported, and clearly distinguishable from one another.

Iterative Analysis and Reflexivity

Qualitative analysis is rarely linear. Researchers often cycle back to earlier steps as new insights arise. This iterative nature helps ensure that the findings are robust and deeply rooted in the data. At the same time, reflexivity plays a critical role: researchers must continually reflect on how their own backgrounds, assumptions, and positions influence their interpretations. Keeping a reflexive journal or memo can support this practice.

Triangulation and Verification

To ensure trustworthiness, researchers use strategies such as:

- **Triangulation**: Comparing data from different sources (e.g., interviews, observations, documents) or involving multiple analysts to validate interpretations.
- **Member Checks**: Sharing preliminary findings with participants to confirm accuracy and resonance.
- **Peer Debriefing**: Discussing emerging themes and interpretations with colleagues to reduce bias.
- **Audit Trails**: Keeping detailed records of decisions made throughout the analysis process to support transparency and credibility.

Interpretation and Reporting

The final stage of qualitative analysis involves weaving together the themes, patterns, and insights into a compelling narrative or conceptual framework. Researchers present their findings using rich, illustrative quotes, stories, or examples that reflect the complexity and nuance of participants' experiences. Interpretation goes beyond surface-level description, aiming to explain the underlying meaning of the data and connect it to theoretical perspectives and the research questions.

Common Techniques in Qualitative Data Analysis

QDA encompasses a range of interpretive approaches, each grounded in different philosophical traditions and suited to different types of research questions. These techniques help researchers uncover patterns, meanings, and structures within complex data sets such as interviews, observations, narratives, and visual materials. Below are several widely used qualitative analysis techniques in the fields of IS and IT.

Thematic Analysis

Thematic analysis is one of the most widely used and accessible methods in qualitative research. It involves identifying, analyzing, and interpreting patterns or *themes* within qualitative data. This approach is highly flexible and can be adapted to various theoretical frameworks, making it suitable for both novice and experienced researchers. Researchers begin by coding the data line by line, tagging relevant phrases or passages. Codes are then clustered into broader categories and ultimately developed into themes that reflect significant ideas related to the research question. In IT or IS studies, thematic analysis might be used to analyze users' responses to a new software interface, categorizing feedback into themes like usability, trust, or privacy concerns.

Grounded Theory Analysis

Grounded theory is a systematic method designed to generate theory from data, rather than to test existing theories. It is particularly useful when studying underexplored phenomena or when the goal is to build new conceptual frameworks. Throughout, researchers engage in constant comparison, systematically comparing data segments to refine categories. In the IS field, grounded theory might be applied to develop a theory of user resistance to IT change, based on interviews with employees across multiple organizations.

Narrative Analysis

Narrative analysis focuses on the stories people tell and how they make sense of their experiences through narrative structures. It is especially effective when research aims to explore personal or organizational change, identity construction, or sense-making processes. Researchers pay attention to plot development, turning points, character roles, and the cultural or organizational context in which the story is told. In IT research, narrative analysis might be used to explore how developers recount their experience with a failed project, revealing how they attribute causes, assign responsibility, and make sense of failure.

Discourse Analysis

Discourse analysis examines how language shapes social realities and power dynamics. It explores how individuals or groups use language to construct meaning, define identities, and legitimize actions or ideologies. Researchers analyze spoken or written texts such as interviews, emails, policy documents, or software manuals, looking at word choice, metaphors, rhetorical strategies, and interactional patterns. In an IS context, discourse analysis could uncover how organizations frame "digital transformation" and how that discourse influences employee expectations and behavior.

Content Analysis

Content analysis involves a systematic examination of textual, visual, or audio materials to identify recurring themes, categories, and meanings. While it can be quantitative or qualitative, qualitative content analysis focuses on interpreting underlying meanings rather than counting occurrences. Researchers may start with predefined categories (deductive) or allow themes to emerge from the data (inductive). This method is particularly useful for analyzing corporate reports, user feedback, or social media posts. For example, a researcher might examine forum posts to identify how users describe trust in cloud-based systems.

Phenomenological Analysis

Phenomenological analysis aims to capture the essence of lived experiences from the perspective of participants. This method emphasizes understanding how individuals experience, interpret, and find meaning in specific phenomena. Researchers begin by *bracketing* their own assumptions to stay close to participants' accounts. The focus is on detailed descriptions and reflective analysis. In IT research, phenomenology might be used to understand the experience of remote workers adjusting to virtual collaboration platforms, exploring their perceptions of isolation, productivity, and digital fatigue.

QDA is not a fixed procedure but an evolving and reflective journey. Unlike statistical models, qualitative techniques invite the researcher to engage deeply with the data, interpreting nuance, tracing connections, and uncovering rich contextual insights. Whether through thematic analysis, grounded theory, narrative inquiry, or other approaches, qualitative researchers strive to construct interpretations that are both empirically grounded and theoretically meaningful. These methods are especially valuable in the fields of IT and IS, where human experience, organizational context, and technological change often intersect in complex and unpredictable ways.

Qualitative Research Approaches and Modes

Qualitative research comprises a diverse set of methodologies, each underpinned by unique philosophical assumptions and tailored to specific types of research questions. While all qualitative methods aim to gain a deep understanding of human experiences and social processes, they differ in focus, data collection strategies, and analytic approaches. Below is an overview of commonly used qualitative research methods and their defining characteristics:

Ethnography

- **Purpose:** To understand cultures, communities, or social groups from an insider's perspective.
- **Approach:** Ethnographers immerse themselves in the setting under study, often for extended periods. They observe routines, rituals, communication styles, values, and power dynamics.
- **Data Collection:** Participant observation, field notes, informal interviews, cultural artifacts.
- **Outcome:** Rich, contextualized descriptions of social life that reveal how members make sense of their world.

Case Study

- **Purpose:** To conduct an in-depth examination of a single case (or a small number of cases) within its real-life context.

- **Approach:** The case is studied holistically, including its historical background, environment, and internal dynamics.
- **Data Collection:** Interviews, observations, documents, archival records; may include quantitative data for triangulation.
- **Outcome:** A nuanced understanding of the specific case, generating insights applicable to similar settings or theoretical propositions.

Phenomenology

- **Purpose:** To explore and describe the *essence* of lived experiences related to a specific phenomenon.
- **Approach:** Researchers focus on participants' subjective accounts, using *bracketing* to set aside personal biases and assumptions.
- **Data Collection:** In-depth, semi-structured interviews; written or verbal first-person narratives.
- **Outcome:** A synthesized description of the core structures and meanings shared across individual experiences.

Grounded Theory

- **Purpose:** To develop theory directly from empirical data rather than starting with a predefined framework.
- **Approach:** Employs iterative data collection and analysis, emphasizing constant comparison and theoretical sampling.
- **Data Collection:** Interviews, observations, documents; new data sources are selected based on emerging concepts.
- **Outcome:** A data-driven, mid-range theory explaining patterns, social processes, or interactions.

Narrative Inquiry

- **Purpose:** To understand how individuals make sense of their lives and experiences through storytelling.
- **Approach:** Emphasizes the structure, content, and context of personal narratives; attends to the temporal and relational aspects of stories.
- **Data Collection:** Interviews, oral histories, autobiographies, diaries, and personal documents.
- **Outcome:** Interpretive accounts that reveal identity construction, sensemaking, and life trajectories.

Action Research (Participatory or Practitioner Research)

- **Purpose:** To generate change or improvement in a particular setting (e.g., classroom, organization) through collaborative inquiry.

- **Approach:** Cyclical process of identifying issues, planning action, implementing change, observing results, and reflecting on outcomes.
- **Data Collection:** Multi-method: interviews, focus groups, observations, surveys – based on the context and goals of the intervention.
- **Outcome:** Locally relevant solutions and insights into change processes; empowers participants as co-researchers.

Discourse Analysis

- **Purpose:** To examine how language constructs meaning, identity, power, and social realities.
- **Approach:** Analyzes written, spoken, or visual texts, focusing on word choice, framing, and the sociocultural functions of language.
- **Data Collection:** Interview transcripts, documents, media content, online forums, policy texts.
- **Outcome:** Unveiling of hidden assumptions, ideological undercurrents, and power relations embedded in communication.

Interpretive Description (Common in Applied Disciplines)

- **Purpose:** To generate practically useful knowledge in applied fields such as nursing, education, or social work.
- **Approach:** Integrates elements from multiple qualitative traditions while maintaining methodological flexibility; rooted in real-world contexts.
- **Data Collection:** Interviews, observations, and context-sensitive methods aligned with professional practice.
- **Outcome:** Conceptual models or insights that inform policy, intervention design, and professional decision-making.

Each qualitative method provides a distinct epistemological and methodological lens through which researchers can explore complex human and organizational phenomena. The choice of method should align with the research question, context, and desired level of abstraction. When thoughtfully applied, qualitative methods offer deep, context-sensitive insights that are often inaccessible through quantitative approaches alone.

Structure and Organization of Qualitative Research Reports

The structure and organization of qualitative research reports can vary depending on the methodological tradition, disciplinary norms, and the intended audience. However, most qualitative reports adhere to a logical, transparent format that guides readers through the research process, the findings, and their significance. Below are common elements and a typical organizational flow:

Introduction

The introduction sets the stage for the study. It introduces the research problem, provides background context, and articulates the research purpose, aims, or questions. The rationale for why the study is important, timely, or unique is also presented here. Some researchers may discuss their personal or professional motivation for undertaking the research, establishing a foundation for reflexivity.

Research Questions and Objectives

The introduction usually culminates by stating the central research questions or objectives that guide the inquiry.

Literature Review and Theoretical Framework

Review of Existing Knowledge

This section synthesizes relevant literature to highlight what is known about the topic and where knowledge gaps or controversies exist. Unlike quantitative studies, the literature review in qualitative research may be more flexible and can sometimes be revisited and refined after initial data analysis if using certain emergent designs like grounded theory.

Conceptual or Theoretical Framework

If applicable, the researcher explains the conceptual lens or theoretical perspective guiding the study. This might be a particular theory, model, or philosophical stance (e.g., constructivism, phenomenology, critical theory) that influences how the data is interpreted.

Methodology

- **Research Design and Approach**: The researcher clearly states the qualitative approach or tradition employed (e.g., ethnography, phenomenology, grounded theory, narrative inquiry) and justifies why this approach is appropriate for the research question.
- **Role of the Researcher and Reflexivity**: Qualitative reports often include a discussion of the researcher's positionality, acknowledging how their background, assumptions, and perspectives may influence data collection, analysis, and interpretation.
- **Sampling and Recruitment**: This part outlines how participants, sites, or documents were selected, as well as the sample size and rationale. Transparency about inclusion and exclusion criteria and any ethical considerations is essential.

- **Data Collection Methods**: The chosen methods – interviews, focus groups, participant observation, document analysis – are described in detail. The researcher explains how data were recorded (e.g., audio-recordings, field notes, transcripts) and any protocols or guides used.
- **Data Analysis Procedures**: Here, the researcher details how the data were organized, coded, and interpreted. This could involve describing the iterative coding process, thematic analysis steps, use of QDA software, or techniques such as constant comparison in grounded theory.
- **Ensuring Trustworthiness**: Qualitative reports often address criteria for rigor and credibility (e.g., member checking, triangulation, peer debriefing, thick description, audit trails). This section explains how the researcher ensured the integrity and reliability of the findings.

Findings or Results

- **Presentation of Themes, Categories, or Narratives**: The findings section is the core of a qualitative report. Rather than just listing results, qualitative researchers interpret and present meaningful patterns, themes, or categories that emerged from the data.
- **Use of Exemplary Quotes and Evidence**: Verbatim participant quotes, excerpts from field notes, or visual materials are included to illustrate the themes and ground the analysis in participants' own words. The researcher's interpretations are woven with the data, demonstrating how conclusions are supported by evidence.
- **Organization by Key Themes**: Findings may be structured around major thematic headings, each accompanied by illustrative data and explanatory commentary. Subthemes may be presented to refine or elaborate upon broader categories.

Discussion

- **Connecting Findings to Literature and Theory**: In the discussion, the researcher situates the findings in relation to existing research and theoretical frameworks identified in the literature review. Points of convergence, divergence, or innovation are highlighted.
- **Interpretation of Meanings and Implications**: The researcher goes beyond describing what was found to consider why it matters. This may involve exploring the significance of the findings, their implications for practice, policy, or theory, and the questions they raise for future research.
- **Strengths, Limitations, and Boundaries of the Study**: A transparent discussion of the study's limitations – such as sample size, context-specific nature of findings, or researcher bias – is included. This honesty aids readers in understanding the scope and applicability of the study's conclusions.

Conclusion

- **Summation of Key Insights**: The conclusion recaps the essential findings and interprets their broader relevance. It may restate how the research question was addressed and highlight the study's primary contributions to knowledge.
- **Future Directions**: Many qualitative reports end by suggesting areas for further research, noting lingering questions or topics that emerged during analysis but were not fully explored.
- **References:** All sources cited throughout the report are listed according to the appropriate citation style, ensuring readers can locate and verify referenced materials.

Appendices (If Needed)

Supplementary Materials: Appendices might include interview guides, observation protocols, coding frameworks, consent forms, or other documents that provide transparency and allow readers to understand the methodological details more fully.

A qualitative research report typically progresses from a broad introduction of the research problem, through a theoretical and methodological foundation, into a richly evidenced presentation of findings, and closes with interpretative insights and conclusions. Throughout, the emphasis is on clarity, transparency, and reflexivity, ensuring readers can trace the analytical journey and judge the credibility and relevance of the study's outcomes.

Future Trends and Innovations in Qualitative Research for Information Systems

Qualitative research in the field of IS is poised to evolve in response to emerging technologies, changing organizational environments, and the increasing complexity of digital ecosystems. As researchers grapple with dynamic sociotechnical landscapes, several key trends and innovations are shaping the future direction of qualitative methods in IS Research:

Integration of Digital and Virtual Ethnographies

Trend: With the proliferation of online communities, social media platforms, and virtual workplaces, researchers are turning to digital ethnography to understand how people interact with technologies and each other in virtual spaces.

Innovation: Techniques such as "netnography" and virtual participant observation enable scholars to capture naturally occurring digital interactions, user-generated content, and real-time discussions, providing richer insights into emerging online behaviors and norms.

Advanced Qualitative Data Analysis Tools

Trend: The volume and complexity of data in IS research have grown exponentially, with diverse sources ranging from text-based documents and chat logs to audio-visual recordings and data from Internet of Things (IoT) devices.

Innovation: Natural language processing (NLP), machine learning, and AI-driven QDA tools are increasingly integrated into the research workflow. These tools can assist in pattern detection, coding support, sentiment analysis, and thematic extractions, helping researchers handle large data sets more efficiently while maintaining interpretive rigor.

Mixed Methods and Methodological Hybrids

Trend: As IS research questions become more complex, single-method approaches may not fully capture the multifaceted nature of digital transformation.

Innovation: Researchers are experimenting with combining qualitative approaches – like ethnographic fieldwork or semi-structured interviews – with quantitative data analytics and computational social science techniques. This blending provides multi-level insights: rich contextual understanding from qualitative methods and generalizable patterns from quantitative or computational data.

Real-Time and Rapid Qualitative Approaches

Trend: IS environments change rapidly due to iterative software development, agile project management, and evolving user expectations. Traditional qualitative methods, which can be time-consuming, may struggle to keep pace.

Innovation: Rapid qualitative inquiry methods and real-time data capture tools (such as digital diaries, instant messaging interviews, or live document annotation) are emerging. These allow researchers to capture evolving phenomena as they unfold, enabling more timely insights and interventions.

Greater Emphasis on Reflexivity and Ethical Considerations

Trend: As data collection moves into digitally mediated spaces, issues of privacy, consent, and data ownership become increasingly complex. Researchers also face new ethical dilemmas when analyzing online behavior and proprietary data.

Innovation: Future qualitative IS research will likely incorporate more robust ethical frameworks, ongoing reflexivity, and transparency about researcher positionality. Interactive consent processes, anonymization techniques, and involvement of community stakeholders will play larger roles in designing ethically sound studies.

Visual, Sensory, and Multimodal Methods

Trend: IS no longer reside solely in text-based interfaces; they encompass voice assistants, augmented reality (AR), virtual reality (VR), and multisensory experiences.

Innovation: Qualitative researchers are exploring multimodal approaches that integrate video ethnographies, digital storytelling, and immersive simulations. Such innovations capture non-verbal cues, embodied interactions, and spatial dimensions of IS use, offering deeper insights into user experiences and organizational change processes.

Longitudinal and Process-Oriented Studies

Trend: Many IS phenomena – digital transformation initiatives, technology adoption lifecycles, or platform ecosystem evolution – unfold over time. Traditional snapshots of data may not capture dynamic changes and cumulative effects.

Innovation: Future qualitative studies will emphasize longitudinal designs, facilitated by digital tools that track and record interactions continuously. Techniques like qualitative longitudinal analysis and process tracing will provide more nuanced understandings of how technologies evolve, integrate, or disrupt organizational practices over extended periods.

Participatory and Co-Creation Approaches

Trend: As stakeholders (e.g., users, managers, designers, policymakers) become more engaged in shaping IS, their involvement in the research process itself is increasing.

Innovation: Participatory action research, design thinking workshops, and co-creation sessions will grow in popularity, allowing participants to collaborate in the study design, data interpretation, and solution development. This approach ensures that research outcomes are more relevant, actionable, and aligned with user needs.

In addition to the trends already mentioned, AI is poised to significantly influence and enhance qualitative research processes, particularly in IS research. As machine learning algorithms, NLP, and large language models (LLMs) continue to mature, they are creating new possibilities for how qualitative data can be collected, analyzed, and interpreted:

Intelligent Transcription and Pre-Processing

Modern AI tools can automatically transcribe interviews, focus groups, and user-generated content with increasing accuracy, saving researchers substantial time. Beyond transcription, AI can perform preliminary cleaning and organization of qualitative data, such as identifying speaker turns, translating languages, or flagging low-quality data segments for human review.

Augmented Coding and Thematic Analysis

AI-driven QDA tools can assist in the coding process by suggesting preliminary codes and identifying potential themes or patterns within large datasets. These tools can highlight frequently occurring concepts, semantic relationships, or sentiment shifts, enabling researchers to navigate extensive corpora more efficiently. While human analysts will still provide the interpretive lens, AI can streamline initial analytical steps, making the iterative coding process more manageable.

Pattern Recognition in Multimodal Data

As qualitative data increasingly incorporates video, images, audio, and other non-textual formats, advanced machine learning models can help identify patterns across multiple modalities. AI might detect facial expressions, gestures, or tone of voice and correlate these with textual data, adding dimensionality to qualitative insights. This multimodal capability allows a more holistic understanding of user experiences and behavior in digital contexts.

Real-Time Analytics and Adaptive Inquiry

AI can enable real-time analysis of ongoing qualitative data collection, such as live interviews or online community discussions. Researchers can receive immediate feedback on emerging themes or anomalies, guiding the direction of subsequent questioning or data gathering. This adaptive approach helps investigators dynamically refine their inquiry in light of incoming findings, making the research process more responsive and iterative.

Scaling Qualitative Research

AI can help scale up qualitative approaches from small, in-depth studies to larger, more diverse data sets without losing interpretive depth. By efficiently coding large volumes of data, identifying rare phenomena, or segmenting subpopulations of interest, AI empowers researchers to generate more comprehensive insights from expansive and complex IS environments (e.g., global user bases of social platforms, enterprise system usage logs).

Enhanced Reflexivity and Researcher Transparency

While AI's speed and efficiency are appealing, qualitative researchers must be mindful of how algorithmic biases or model assumptions influence findings. Future trends include incorporating reflexive tools that allow researchers to inspect the AI's decision-making processes – understanding how certain codes or themes were suggested, and which parts of the data influenced them. Such transparency features can become integral to ensuring trustworthiness and ethical rigor in AI-assisted qualitative research.

Integration with Mixed Methods and Automated Insights

The integration of AI with quantitative and computational techniques paves the way for mixed-methods research at unprecedented scales. For instance, after automated qualitative coding identifies emerging themes, statistical or network analyses can quantify their prevalence or relationships, blending interpretive depth with empirical breadth. This synergy can produce more robust and actionable insights for IS researchers and practitioners.

Personalized and Contextual AI Assistants

In the future, domain-specific AI assistants could be trained on particular IS subfields – such as cybersecurity cultures, enterprise system adoption, or platform governance – and act as informed co-analysts. By learning from previous qualitative studies and continuously refining their models, these assistants can guide researchers toward literature, theory, or frameworks relevant to their emerging findings, thus enhancing both efficiency and conceptual sophistication.

The future of qualitative research in IS is marked by methodological agility, technological augmentation, and deeper integration of participants and technologies in the research process. By embracing digital ethnographies, advanced analysis tools, multimodal data, and participatory practices, IS researchers can generate richer, more context-sensitive insights. These innovations will help qualitative research keep pace with the evolving nature of IS, ensuring it remains a vital tool for understanding and shaping our digital futures. AI is set to transform qualitative research in IS by accelerating data handling, enhancing the depth and breadth of analysis, and fostering new forms of multimodal and mixed-method inquiry. While these advancements present ethical and epistemological considerations – such as ensuring interpretability, mitigating algorithmic bias, and maintaining reflexive rigor – they ultimately position qualitative researchers to engage more dynamically with complex digital ecosystems and provide richer, more impactful insights.

Mixed-Methods Research Approaches

Mixed methods research involves the deliberate integration of both quantitative and qualitative approaches within a single study or research program to capitalize on the strengths of each method while offsetting their individual limitations. By combining the depth and context-sensitive nature of qualitative inquiry with the breadth, measurement precision, and generalizability of quantitative analysis, mixed methods design offers a more comprehensive understanding of complex phenomena.

Key Principles of Mixed Methods Research

Complementary

Qualitative and quantitative methods are often combined so that one method can enrich or clarify findings generated by the other. For example, a survey might quantify attitudes toward a new information system, while follow-up interviews explore why users feel a certain way, adding interpretive depth.

Triangulation

Using different methods to study the same phenomenon can strengthen the credibility and validity of the results. If findings from multiple sources converge, researchers gain confidence that the results are robust and not artifacts of a single methodological approach.

Expansion

Mixed methods can broaden the scope of inquiry. A quantitative survey may measure the prevalence of an outcome, while qualitative data can identify unexpected factors, processes, or contextual nuances, expanding the original research framework.

Development

Insights from one method can guide the design or focus of another method. For example, initial qualitative findings from interviews can help refine survey questions or scales to ensure that quantitative measures address the most relevant aspects of the topic.

Initiation

When results from qualitative and quantitative approaches conflict, this discrepancy can spur new questions and theoretical insights. Contradictory findings may reveal hidden dimensions of the phenomenon or highlight areas that need methodological adjustments or further investigation.

Common Mixed Methods Designs

Mixed methods research designs offer a powerful way to explore complex phenomena in IS by integrating both qualitative and quantitative approaches. These designs are particularly valuable when a single methodological lens is insufficient to fully capture the richness and scope of a research problem – such as understanding user adoption, technology implementation, or the impact of digital transformation. Several established mixed methods designs are frequently used in IS research, each with its own logic and sequence.

Sequential Exploratory Design

In a sequential exploratory design, the researcher begins with a qualitative phase to gain an in-depth understanding and generate initial insights. These findings then inform a follow-up quantitative phase, often in the form of a survey or structured instrument, designed to test or measure the patterns identified in the qualitative data. For instance, an IS researcher might start by conducting in-depth interviews with employees at a company that recently implemented a new software platform, aiming to understand the social and organizational factors influencing adoption. Themes such as "peer support," "training quality," or "management communication" might emerge. These themes could then be used to construct a survey distributed to a broader employee population to assess how widespread these drivers are and how they relate statistically to adoption rates or satisfaction levels.

In contrast, a sequential explanatory design reverses this order. The study begins with a quantitative phase, often to detect relationships or patterns across a larger dataset. The qualitative phase follows and is used to dig deeper into the underlying reasons or contextual meanings behind those patterns. For example, a researcher might survey several hundred users of a mobile health application and find that younger users and those with higher digital literacy engage with the app more frequently. In the subsequent phase, the researcher might conduct focus groups with selected participants from different demographic groups to explore the motivations, barriers, or cultural perceptions that influence usage patterns. This design is particularly useful in IS for adding explanatory depth to broad patterns identified in usage data or satisfaction metrics.

Concurrent Triangulation Design

A concurrent triangulation design collects qualitative and quantitative data at the same time, aiming to corroborate or compare the results during interpretation. This approach is often used when time is constrained or when the researcher seeks to balance the strengths of both data types equally. For instance, an IS researcher evaluating the rollout of a new information system might distribute a survey measuring user satisfaction and system usability while simultaneously observing employees interacting with the system and conducting short interviews. The combination of statistical trends and real-time observations can lead to a more nuanced understanding, especially when findings from both strands either reinforce or challenge each other.

Concurrent Embedded Design

In a concurrent embedded design, one method – either qualitative or quantitative – takes center stage, while the other plays a secondary, supportive role. Both are conducted within the same research timeframe, but the embedded method provides contextual depth or clarification. For example, a study might primarily rely on a large-scale survey to assess user satisfaction with a university's new LMS. However, the survey could include a few open-ended questions or be supplemented by follow-up interviews with selected respondents to better understand specific concerns, such as interface issues or challenges in uploading assignments. This approach allows researchers to address specific questions more holistically without requiring a full two-phase design.

Transformative or Complex Mixed Methods Designs

Transformative or complex mixed methods designs involve multiple phases and iterative cycles of data collection, often guided by a particular theoretical lens or the need for practical intervention. These designs are particularly common in action research or design science research in IS, where researchers might iteratively test and refine a new system or intervention while collecting both qualitative and quantitative data throughout the process. For example, a project aiming to improve cybersecurity awareness in a government agency might involve repeated cycles of surveys, focus groups, pilot interventions, and behavioral tracking, all embedded within a participatory framework aligned with change management theory. These designs are more adaptive and often tailored to real-world problem-solving in complex socio-technical systems.

Benefits of Mixed Methods Research

- **Richer Insights**: By integrating contextual, narrative-rich qualitative data with statistically validated quantitative findings, researchers gain multifaceted perspectives on the topic at hand.
- **Enhanced Validity**: Multiple forms of evidence strengthen the trustworthiness and credibility of findings.
- **Relevance to Stakeholders**: Mixed methods provide actionable insights for practitioners, policymakers, and other stakeholders by addressing both "what is happening?" (quantitative) and "why is it happening?" (qualitative) questions.
- **Methodological Innovation**: Mixing methods can spark creativity and lead to new, integrative analytical frameworks that move beyond traditional boundaries.
- **Challenges and Considerations**
- **Complexity of Design and Implementation**: Managing different data types, timelines, and analytical procedures is more complex and can be time-consuming.
- **Skill Requirements**: Researchers need proficiency in both quantitative and qualitative methods, as well as expertise in how to integrate the findings effectively.

- **Interpretive Complexity**: Combining datasets requires careful consideration to ensure coherence and consistency, particularly when results conflict or point in different directions.
- **Resource Intensive**: Mixed methods projects often require greater resources – time, funding, and personnel – compared to single-method studies.

Mixed methods research transcends the boundaries of qualitative and quantitative paradigms, offering a fuller, more nuanced picture of complex phenomena. By strategically integrating both forms of data, researchers can address questions that neither approach could answer alone, ultimately leading to more robust, meaningful, and actionable findings.

Chapter Summary

Over the course of these discussions, qualitative research has evolved into a rich, dynamic paradigm that prioritizes depth, context, and meaning over purely numerical measures. Initially defined by its exploratory, participant-centered, and flexible nature, qualitative inquiry is especially valuable for understanding complex phenomena, human experiences, organizational contexts, and cultural systems. When guided by established frameworks and transparent methodological rigor, qualitative studies yield nuanced insights that can inform theory, practice, and policy.

Core to qualitative research are the diverse methods used to gather and interpret data – ranging from interviews, focus groups, and ethnography to content and narrative analyses – each chosen to align with specific research questions and contexts. These methods allow researchers to capture the richness of lived experiences, understand emerging patterns, and appreciate the interplay of social, cultural, and technological factors shaping behavior. The analysis process is iterative and interpretive, demanding reflexivity, ethical considerations, and consistent efforts to ensure trustworthiness and credibility.

Contemporary developments highlight the adaptability of qualitative research to the digital age. IS research, for instance, increasingly employs digital ethnographies, examines online communities, and integrates advanced software tools to handle large, multimodal data sets. The advent of sophisticated qualitative data analysis software (QDAS) and the incorporation of AI enable researchers to code, visualize, and interpret data more efficiently, while preserving the interpretive depth that characterizes qualitative inquiry. At the same time, researchers must remain vigilant about potential biases, ethical complexities, and issues of privacy associated with new digital and AI-driven methodologies.

Furthermore, a mixed methods approach, which combines qualitative and quantitative techniques, offers a richer, more comprehensive understanding of multifaceted phenomena. By blending the breadth and generalizability of quantitative findings with the depth and contextual sensitivity of qualitative insights, mixed methods designs can yield more robust and actionable conclusions.

In sum, qualitative research stands at the intersection of tradition and innovation. Its philosophical underpinnings and established methodological rigor provide a strong foundation, while evolving tools, interdisciplinary integrations, and emerging analytical techniques propel the field forward. As scholars continue to embrace these advancements, qualitative research will remain an indispensable approach for uncovering meaning, guiding informed decision-making, and responding thoughtfully to the complexity of our social and technological landscapes.

Review Questions

1 What are the key characteristics that distinguish qualitative research from quantitative research?
2 Why is reflexivity considered an important practice in qualitative research?
3 In what ways can qualitative research methods (such as interviews, ethnography, or narrative analysis) contribute to a deeper understanding of human experiences or organizational contexts?
4 How have advancements in QDAS and AI influenced the way qualitative data is managed and interpreted?
5 What benefits can a mixed methods approach bring to a study, and how does it enhance the insights gained from qualitative data alone?

References

Berger, P. L., & Luckmann, T. (1966). *The Social Construction of Reality: A Treatise in the Sociology of Knowledge*. Anchor Books.

Bryman, A. (2016). *Social Research Methods* (5th ed.). Oxford University Press.

Crotty, M. (1998). *The Foundations of Social Research: Meaning and Perspective in the Research Process*. SAGE.

Denzin, N. K.; & Lincoln, Y. S. (Eds.). (2011). *The SAGE Handbook of Qualitative Research* (4th eds.). SAGE.

Guba, E. G., & Lincoln, Y. S. (1994). Competing Paradigms in Qualitative Research. In N. K. Denzin & Y. S. Lincoln (Eds.), *Handbook of Qualitative Research* (pp. 105–117). SAGE.

Lincoln, Y. S., & Guba, E. G. (1985). *Naturalistic Inquiry*. SAGE.

Schwartz-Shea, P., & Yanow, D. (2012). *Interpretive Research Design: Concepts and Processes*. Routledge.

8 Grounded Theory Research in Information Systems

Chapter Objectives

After reading this chapter, readers should understand:

- The use of Grounded Theory in Information Systems Research
- The History and Origins of Grounded Theory
- The Process of Grounded Theory, Data Collection & Analysis, and Reporting Approaches
- Grounded Theory Challenges and Limitations

Grounded Theory in Information Systems Research

Grounded theory (GT) research is increasingly being utilized in the field of information systems (IS) to develop theories directly from data, rather than testing existing hypotheses. This methodology emphasizes the iterative process of data collection and analysis, allowing researchers to derive insights that are grounded in real-world observations. By engaging deeply with qualitative data, researchers can explore complex phenomena within IS, uncovering patterns and relationships that may not be evident through traditional research methods. GT's flexibility and inductive nature make it particularly suited for exploring new areas within the rapidly evolving landscape of information technology (IT).

Origins and Development of Grounded Theory

GT is a systematic methodology in the social sciences for constructing theory from data. It was developed by sociologists Barney Glaser and Anselm Strauss in the 1960s. The origins of GT are rooted in the qualitative research tradition, emphasizing inductive reasoning and the generation of theory from data rather than testing existing theories. The development of GT was significantly influenced by Glaser and Strauss's collaborative work on "Awareness of Dying," a study that looked at the interactions between dying patients and healthcare professionals. Dissatisfied

DOI: 10.4324/9781003545521-10

with the existing research methods, they sought a more flexible, data-driven approach that allowed theories to emerge directly from the data itself. It is designed to build theory directly from data, making it especially suitable for examining emerging or poorly understood phenomena in IS. Rather than beginning with pre-existing theoretical assumptions, GT adopts an inductive approach, allowing patterns, relationships, and concepts to surface organically from participants' experiences. This makes it a powerful tool for exploring complex socio-technical issues such as user resistance to new technologies, the dynamics of digital transformation, or the emergence of informal IT governance structures in organizations.

GT involves several key processes: data collection, coding, and analysis occur simultaneously, allowing patterns, concepts, and categories to emerge naturally. Researchers can then refine these categories through constant comparison, enabling a detailed and grounded understanding of the social phenomena under study. Over time, GT has evolved, with Glaser and Strauss diverging in their approaches. Glaser emphasized a more flexible and less structured methodology, while Strauss, along with Juliet Corbin, introduced a more systematic and structured approach in their later works. This divergence has led to the development of various approaches within GT, yet all maintain the core principle of deriving theory from data.

History of Grounded Theory in Social Sciences and Information Systems

GT is a research methodology that was developed by sociologists Barney Glaser and Anselm Strauss in the 1960s. It emerged as a response to the rigid structure of quantitative research methods in the social sciences, advocating for a more flexible approach to developing theories directly from data. In their seminal work, "*The Discovery of Grounded Theory*" (1967), Glaser and Strauss introduced this methodology, emphasizing the systematic gathering and analysis of qualitative data to generate theoretical frameworks. The process involves collecting data without a preconceived hypothesis, coding it into categories, and iteratively refining these categories into a cohesive theory. GT gained popularity in social sciences due to its ability to provide rich, contextual insights, often employed in sociology, psychology, and education research. It allows researchers to explore complex social phenomena and generate theories that are deeply rooted in empirical observations.

In IS, GT has become a valuable tool for understanding user behavior, system interactions, and technological impacts on society. Researchers in this field use GT to explore how IS are implemented, used, and integrated into organizational processes, providing a nuanced understanding of technology's role in social and organizational contexts. Overall, GT's adaptability and focus on real-world data have made it a crucial methodology in both social sciences and IS, offering a way to build theories that are closely aligned with the realities of human experience. In GT, the researcher is searching for a theoretical framework, or a theory that is grounded in the data of the research. The theory is the result of the GT research.

Theoretical Sampling and Data Collection

Theoretical sampling in GT is a process of data collection driven by concepts that emerge from the data itself, rather than being predetermined by a preconceived hypothesis. It involves selecting participants, situations, or data types based on their potential to contribute to the development or refinement of emerging categories. This iterative process continues until theoretical saturation is reached, meaning no new insights are being obtained. Data collection in GT is typically qualitative and can involve methods such as interviews, observations, and document analysis. The data is coded and categorized, with constant

Table 8.1 Advantages and Disadvantages of Grounded Theory Approach

Aspect	*Advantages*	*Disadvantages*
Theory Development	Enables theory generation directly from data, which is valuable when existing theories are inadequate. (Glaser & Strauss, 1967, Strauss & Corbin, 1994)	It can result in fragmented or overly narrow theories if not rigorously executed. (Myers, 2009)
Flexibility	Adaptable to diverse settings and research topics, especially useful in exploratory IS studies. (Charmaz, 2003; Denscombe, 2010)	The flexibility can lead to a lack of focus or inconsistent application if not carefully managed. (Denscombe, 2010)
Iterative Process	Allows for ongoing refinement of data collection and analysis based on emerging insights. (Charmaz, 2006)	Time-consuming and labor-intensive due to the continuous interplay between coding, sampling, and analysis. (Denscombe, 2010)
Relevance to Practice	Produces findings closely aligned with organizational or user realities, useful for IS practitioners. (Denscombe, 2010)	Findings may lack generalizability due to the typically small, context-specific samples. (Denscombe, 2010)
Emergent Design	Facilitates discovery of unexpected patterns or social processes not anticipated at the outset. (Charmaz,2006; Glazser, 1978)	Difficult to plan and manage, especially in structured or time-limited research projects. (Denscombe, 2010)
Theoretical Saturation	Ensures depth of understanding by continuing data collection until no new themes emerge. (Charmaz, 2006; Strauss & Corbin, 1990)	Determining when saturation is truly achieved can be subjective and unclear. (Denscombe, 2010)
Methodological Rigor	Encourages transparency through memo writing, coding audits, and constant comparison. (Charmaz, 2006; Urquhart et al., 2010)	Requires high methodological skill; novice researchers may struggle to maintain consistency and rigor. (Charmaz, 1989; Myers, 2009)

comparison used to identify patterns and relationships, allowing the theory to evolve throughout the research process. Researchers maintain flexibility, allowing the theory to guide further data collection and analysis (Table 8.1).

The Grounded Theory Research Process

GT is valued for its ability to generate new theories from data rather than relying on existing theoretical frameworks, making it particularly useful for exploring complex phenomena where little pre-existing theory exists. GT studies primarily focus on generating theories through the systematic collection and analysis of qualitative data.

The research design typically involves these stages.

Data Collection

The process begins with data collection, typically through qualitative methods such as in-depth interviews, participant observations, focus groups, or document analysis. Importantly, grounded theorists enter the field without a rigid theoretical framework, allowing for openness and discovery. For example, an IS researcher interested in understanding how remote employees adapt to new enterprise collaboration tools might begin by interviewing a small group of users without predefined assumptions, seeking to uncover their natural experiences, strategies, frustrations, and workarounds.

Coding and Analysis

Following data collection, the researcher engages in open coding, the first analytic step. During open coding, the data is broken down into discrete parts and examined line by line to identify key concepts or actions. These initial codes are often descriptive and closely tied to the language of participants. In an IS study, open codes might include "email overload," "shadow IT workarounds," "managerial monitoring," or "learning from peers." These codes are provisional and are constantly compared with new data to ensure consistency and relevance.

Once a substantial set of initial codes is developed, the researcher proceeds to axial coding, which involves identifying relationships among the categories generated during open coding. In this phase, categories are organized around central phenomena by exploring their conditions, actions/interactions, and consequences. For example, a study on digital transformation might find that "resistance to change" is linked to "lack of managerial communication," "unclear training resources," and "legacy system attachment." Axial coding helps to move the analysis from fragmentation toward integration by specifying how different concepts relate to one another in a meaningful structure.

Selective coding follows, during which the researcher identifies a central, or "core," category that represents the main theme of the study and integrates all other categories around it. This step is where the emerging theory begins to take shape. In an IS context, the core category might be something like "navigating uncertainty in digital adoption" or "crafting informal digital resilience." The researcher refines the surrounding categories to ensure they fit logically within the emerging theoretical framework and returns to earlier data as needed to ensure coherence.

Theoretical Sampling

Throughout the research, theoretical sampling is employed. This means that instead of gathering all data upfront, researchers collect, analyze, and then strategically seek out new participants or cases that help to clarify or extend emerging categories. If an IS study reveals that senior IT managers experience digital transformation differently from front-line users, the researcher might conduct follow-up interviews specifically with mid-level managers or external consultants to examine how those roles bridge gaps between strategic planning and daily practice. The process continues until theoretical saturation is reached, that is, when additional data no longer yield new insights about the emerging categories.

Memo Writing

A distinctive feature of GT is the use of memo writing, which occurs throughout the research process. Memos are reflective, analytic notes written by the researcher to document emerging ideas, explore connections among concepts, and trace theoretical development. In the context of IS research, memos might capture reflections on how power dynamics between IT departments and end users influence technology appropriation, or they may include tentative diagrams showing causal relationships among constructs. Memos function as the intellectual bridge between raw data and theoretical abstraction.

Constant Comparison

Another essential element of GT is constant comparison. This refers to the continuous process of comparing data with data, data with codes, codes with categories, and categories with other categories. For example, if one participant describes developing a workaround to bypass a restrictive company firewall, that instance is compared with other participants' workaround strategies to identify common patterns and variations. This recursive analytic process ensures that the theory remains deeply grounded in empirical observations and sensitive to variation across cases.

Theory Building and Reporting

As the analysis progresses and categories become more abstract and integrated, the researcher begins to construct the final GT. This theory should offer explanatory power, helping to make sense of the central phenomenon under investigation and providing insights that extend beyond the specific context. For instance, a GT might explain how "adaptive digital agency" emerges among non-technical employees as they creatively navigate IT-imposed constraints, offering implications for the design of more flexible enterprise systems and change management strategies. The final report includes rich descriptions, illustrative quotes, and a detailed presentation of the GT itself. A well-executed GT study in IS contributes not just by describing practice but by offering conceptual tools that can inform design, implementation, and policy in digital environments. Whether used to understand user behaviors, IT alignment processes, or the unintended consequences of artificial intelligence (AI) deployment, GT offers a robust, flexible approach to theory generation that is deeply rooted in real-world experiences.

When Is Grounded Theory Approach Appropriate

GT becomes necessary in research scenarios where existing models fail to adequately explain new developments such as the adoption of AI tools in sensitive processes, the emergence of shadow IT practices, or the evolving nature of digital transformation in traditional organizations. It is also particularly suited to contexts where participant experiences, processes, and meanings are central to understanding the phenomenon under study. Because IS phenomena often unfold in real time and are shaped by social, technical, and organizational factors, GT's iterative approach allows for the discovery of patterns and processes that might be missed by other methods. Table 8.2 shows some examples of various scenarios and why the GT approach would be appropriate.

Table 8.2 Examples

Scenario/Research Question	*Why Grounded Theory Is Appropriate*	*IS Example/Context*
How do users adapt to AI-based decision-support systems in high-stakes environments?	Little is known about user cognitive and behavioral adjustments to AI in complex, high-risk settings. Grounded theory allows the discovery of emergent patterns of adaptation.	Studying how emergency room staff use predictive analytics tools in real-time clinical decisions.
What processes do organizations follow to implement digital transformation in legacy systems?	The path to digital transformation is often nonlinear and context-dependent. Grounded theory helps build a process model from real-world narratives.	Exploring how traditional banks restructure workflows to integrate fintech platforms.

(Continued)

Table 8.2 (Continued)

Scenario/Research Question	*Why Grounded Theory Is Appropriate*	*IS Example/Context*
How do IT professionals experience burnout in agile development environments?	This complex phenomenon lacks a unified theory in the IS context. Grounded theory allows researchers to build a model of stress triggers and coping mechanisms.	Investigating the lived experiences of software engineers under continuous deployment pressure.
How does trust develop between humans and autonomous systems in workplace settings?	Trust in automation is multi-dimensional and context-sensitive. Grounded theory helps identify dimensions and sequences of trust formation from users' perspectives.	Analyzing employee interaction with autonomous delivery drones in a warehouse.
How do data governance practices emerge in data-driven organizations without formal policies?	Formalized models of data governance may not reflect evolving practices. Grounded theory captures the organic, bottom-up emergence of informal rules and roles.	Observing how departments self-regulate data sharing in a mid-sized healthcare analytics firm.
What are the decision-making processes behind shadow IT adoption by employees?	The phenomenon is emergent and under-theorized, especially in different organizational cultures. Grounded theory reveals user logic and risk-reward thinking.	Understanding why marketing staff use unauthorized SaaS tools instead of official IT-approved software.
How do knowledge workers integrate multiple digital platforms to construct their workflows?	This question involves complex social and technical interactions. Grounded theory helps generate conceptual categories for digital work practices.	Mapping how remote teams blend tools like Slack, Trello, and Dropbox into a coherent workflow.
What motivates ethical (or unethical) behavior in AI data labeling workforces?	This is a relatively novel topic with limited prior theory in IS. Grounded theory supports bottom-up understanding of worker perceptions and decision rationales.	Interviewing gig workers who label content for machine learning training datasets.
How do user expectations evolve during the implementation of an ERP system?	Expectation management during large-scale IS projects is dynamic. Grounded theory can track how perceptions shift through different implementation stages.	Following a university's faculty and staff through the rollout of a new ERP for HR and finance.

Data Collection in Grounded Theory

GT is a research methodology used primarily within the social sciences to develop theories through systematic data collection and analysis. In GT, data collection is an iterative process that involves simultaneous data collection and analysis to refine and evolve the emerging theory. Researchers typically begin with initial data collection through methods such as interviews, observations, or document reviews. As data is collected, researchers utilize a process called "coding" to break down the data into manageable segments and identify recurring themes or patterns. These codes are then organized into categories, which form the foundation for developing broader theoretical constructs. The researcher continuously compares new data with existing codes and categories, a process known as "constant comparison," to refine and elaborate on the emerging theory. The data collection process in GT is flexible and evolves as the research progresses, allowing the researcher to follow leads and insights that emerge during the analysis. This process continues until "theoretical saturation" is reached, meaning no new insights or categories are emerging from the data. GT emphasizes the importance of remaining open to new data and interpretations, allowing the theory to emerge from the data rather than imposing preconceived notions or hypotheses.

Writing and Reporting

GT research is a qualitative methodology that emphasizes the generation of theory from data systematically gathered and analyzed. The process begins with open-ended data collection, often through interviews or observations, without a preconceived hypothesis. Researchers identify patterns and themes through a constant comparative method, where data is continuously compared and contrasted. This process leads to the development of codes and categories that form the basis of an emergent theory. In writing and reporting GT, researchers focus on presenting a clear and logical narrative that reflects the iterative nature of the research process. They emphasize the context and experiences of participants and ensure the theory is grounded in the data gathered. A thorough discussion of the findings and their implications is included, often highlighting how the theory contributes to existing literature or practice.

Key Components of Grounded Theory Research

GT research involves several key components when writing and reporting, including:

1. **Introduction**: Introduce the research question and the significance of the study, explaining the rationale behind using GT.

2 **Literature Review**: Provide a brief review of existing literature to contextualize the study, emphasizing gaps that the research aims to address.
3 **Methodology**: Describe the GT methodology, explaining how data collection and analysis are conducted, including coding procedures, sampling strategies, and ensuring rigor.
4 **Data Collection**: Detail the methods used for gathering data, such as interviews, observations, or document analysis, and discuss how data saturation was achieved.
5 **Data Analysis**: Explain the process of coding, categorizing, and developing themes or concepts, leading to the construction of a GT.
6 **Findings**: Present the core categories or themes identified, supported by relevant data excerpts or quotes.
7 **Discussion**: Interpret the findings in the context of existing literature, highlighting the theoretical contributions and implications.
8 **Conclusion**: Summarize the study's contributions, limitations, and potential areas for further research.
9 **References**: Include a list of all sources cited in the study.

These components help ensure that GT research is thorough, transparent, and contributes meaningfully to the field.

Challenges and Limitations of Grounded Theory Approach

GT research, while a valuable qualitative method, presents several challenges and limitations. One major challenge is the potential for researcher bias, as the method involves extensive interpretation of data. Additionally, the process is time-consuming and labor-intensive, requiring continuous data collection and analysis, which can be overwhelming. Another limitation is the difficulty in achieving theoretical saturation, where no new information or themes emerge, necessitating careful judgment to determine when to stop data collection. Furthermore, GT's emphasis on generating theory from data can lead to questions about the generalizability and transferability of the findings, as the results are often highly context-specific. Despite these challenges, GT remains a powerful tool for uncovering deep insights into complex social phenomena.

Discussions on Objectivity vs. Subjectivity in Grounded Theory

GT research aims to generate a theory from the data systematically collected and analyzed. The interplay between objectivity and subjectivity is a critical part of GT research as it shapes the research process, findings, and credibility. Below are the roles of objectivity and subjectivity in GT research, and how researchers can navigate them.

Objectivity in Grounded Theory

Objectivity refers to the pursuit of impartial, unbiased, and replicable findings that reflect the data rather than the researcher's preconceptions. In GT, objectivity is emphasized through:

- Systematic procedures: GT employs structured methods like coding (open, axial, and selective), constant comparison, and memo-writing to ensure data-driven analysis. These steps aim to minimize researcher bias by grounding the findings in the data itself. Example: Constant comparison involves comparing data points to identify patterns, ensuring categories emerge from evidence (data) rather than assumptions.
- Emergence Principle: GT prioritizes letting concepts and theories emerge from the data without imposing preconceived hypotheses. This is an inductive approach which seeks to capture the reality of the participants' experiences objectively. Example: A researcher studying patient experiences in healthcare would avoid preconceived frameworks, allowing themes like "trust in providers" to emerge organically.
- Theoretical Sampling: In GT research, theoretical sampling is used to collect data based on evolving categories, ensuring the theory is comprehensive and grounded in diverse evidence, enhancing objectivity.
- Auditability: Detailed documentation (memos, coding trails) allows others to trace the research process, fostering transparency and reducing subjective influence.

Subjectivity in Grounded Research

Subjectivity acknowledges the researcher's role in interpreting data, shaped by their perspectives, experiences, and theoretical sensitivities. In GT, subjectivity is not only inevitable but also a valuable component.

- **Researcher as an Instrument**: GT researchers actively engage with the data, making interpretive decisions during the coding and theorizing. Their background, disciplinary knowledge, and insights influence how they perceive and categorize the data. Example: A researcher with an IS background might emphasize social and organizational behavior structures in their analysis, while a psychologist may focus on individual motivations.
- **Theoretical Sensitivity**: Glaser emphasizes that a researcher's theoretical sensitivity – awareness of concepts from prior knowledge enhances their abilities to identify meaningful patterns. This subjectivity helps generate nuanced theories but risks bias if unchecked. Example: A researcher familiar with feminist theory might be more attuned to gender dynamics in workplace data, enriching the analysis but potentially skewing the focus.
- **Reflexivity**: GT researchers are encouraged to reflect on their biases and assumptions through memo-writing or discussions with peers. Reflexivity

acknowledges subjectivity and aims to manage its impact. Example: A researcher may note in a memo how their cultural background shapes their interpretation of organizational behavior in a study.

- **Constructivist GT:** Charmaz's constructivist GT explicitly embraces subjectivity, viewing knowledge as co-constructed between researcher and participants. This approach views subjectivity as an integral component of understanding participants' subjective experiences over universal truths.

Balancing Objectivity and Subjectivity

The balance between objectivity and subjectivity in GT presents challenges:

Bias vs. Insight: While subjectivity fuels theoretical sensitivity, it can introduce bias if the research imposes personal assumptions. For instance, overemphasizing a familiar concept might obscure other patterns. GT researchers should use constant comparison and peer debriefing to challenge their interpretations and ensure data-driven conclusions.

Emergence vs. Preconception: The GT principle of emergence clashes with researchers' inevitable preconceptions. Even with systematic methods, prior knowledge can subtly change or shape coding or category formation. Researchers delay literature reviews (per Glaser) or explicitly address preconceptions in memos to preserve emergence.

Replicability vs. Uniqueness: Objectivity seeks replicable findings, but GT's interpretive nature means different researchers might produce varying theories from the same data. This subjectivity can undermine perceived rigor. Detailed audit trails and clear methodological descriptions enhance trustworthiness, even if exact replication is not feasible.

Philosophical Divide: Classic GT (Glaser) leans toward objectivity, aiming for theories that reflect external realities. Constructivist GT (Charmaz) embraces subjectivity, viewing theories as interpretive constructions. Researchers must navigate these paradigms, which can create methodological confusion.

Example: A classic GT study might seek a generalizable theory of workplace stress, while a constructivist approach might focus on workers' subjective meanings of stress.

Navigating Objectivity and Subjectivity

To navigate objectivity and subjectivity, GT researchers employ strategies to provide a balance between the two ensuring rigorous yet insightful findings:

- **Triangulation**: Using multiple data sources (e.g., interviews, observations) or perspectives (e.g., participants, literature) strengthens objectivity by cross-validating findings.

- **Member Checking**: Sharing findings with participants ensures interpretations align with their realities, blending subjective insights with objective validation.
- **Peer Review**: Colleagues or research teams review coding and interpretations to challenge subjective biases and enhance credibility.
- **Reflexive Practices**: Regular memo-writing and journaling help researchers identify and manage their subjective influences, fostering transparency.
- **Clear Methodological Choices**: Researchers articulate their GT approach (e.g., classic, Straussian, constructivist) to clarify how they handle objectivity and subjectivity, aligning methods with philosophical assumptions.

In GT research, objectivity and subjectivity are not mutually exclusive but interwoven elements that shape the research process. Objectivity is pursued through systematic, data-driven methods and transparency, while subjectivity enriches analysis through the researcher's interpretive lens and theoretical sensitivity. The challenge lies in balancing these forces to produce credible, meaningful theories. By employing strategies like reflexivity, triangulation, and clear documentation, GT researchers can navigate this tension, leveraging both objectivity and subjectivity to generate robust, grounded theories that reflect participants' realities while acknowledging the researcher's role in knowledge construction.

Alternative Approaches to Theory Building in Information Systems Qualitative Research (IS)

In IS qualitative research, GT is a widely used method for building theory, but several alternative approaches can also generate robust, data-driven theories. These alternatives vary in their philosophical underpinnings, processes, and applications, offering flexibility to suit different research contexts, questions, and data types. In IS research, GT is a widely used method for building theory, but several alternative approaches can also generate robust, data-driven theories. These alternatives vary in their philosophical underpinnings, processes, and applications, offering flexibility to suit different research contexts, questions, and data types. Key alternative methods include case study research, which involves in-depth contextual analysis of one or more cases to develop theoretical insights, and narrative analysis, which focuses on stories or accounts to construct theories about sensemaking in IS contexts. When selecting a method, researchers should match it to the *research question*, such as using phenomenology for exploring user experiences or process research for examining change over time. The *philosophical stance* of the study is also critical, as it may lean interpretive, as seen in narrative or phenomenological approaches, critical, as in critical discourse analysis (CDA), or pragmatic, as in action research. Additionally, the method must suit the *data type*, with ethnography being appropriate for observational data and CDA for textual data. The IS context should guide *method selection*, with case studies fitting organizational settings and ethnography aligning with community-based studies. Finally, researchers must *assess available resources*, including time, access, and expertise, since methods like ethnography require prolonged fieldwork, while action research demands stakeholder collaboration.

Below, I outline key alternative methods for theory building in IS qualitative research, focusing on their core principles, processes, and relevance to IS. Each method is compared briefly to GT to highlight distinctions.

Case Study Research

Case study research involves an in-depth, contextual analysis of one or more cases (e.g., organizations, projects, or systems) to develop theoretical insights. It is particularly suited for exploring complex IS phenomena in real-world settings.

Process:

- Select case(s) based on theoretical or purposive sampling (e.g., a firm implementing a new ERP system).
- Collect data through multiple sources (e.g., interviews, observations, documents) for triangulation.
- Analyze data using thematic analysis, pattern matching, or cross-case synthesis to identify theoretical constructs.
- Develop propositions or a conceptual framework based on case findings.
- Iterate between data and literature to refine theory.

Relevance to IS: Ideal for studying technology adoption, IT implementation, or digital transformation in organizational contexts (e.g., how firms adopt AI systems).

Comparison to GT: Unlike GT's emergent, inductive approach, case studies often use existing frameworks or theories to guide analysis, though they can be exploratory. Case studies emphasize contextual depth over GT's systematic coding and category development.

Example: Yin's case study approach to explore how blockchain implementation affects supply chain transparency, leading to a model of trust dynamics.

Narrative Analysis

Narrative analysis focuses on stories or accounts (e.g., user experiences, organizational histories) to construct theories about how individuals or groups make sense of IS phenomena.

Process:

- Collect narrative data (e.g., interviews, diaries, or organizational reports) about experiences with technology.
- Analyze narratives for structure (e.g., plot, characters), themes, or temporal sequences.
- Identify recurring patterns or archetypes to build theoretical insights (e.g., user resistance narratives).
- Develop a theory that explains how narratives shape IS phenomena.

Relevance to IS: Useful for studying user experiences with technology, such as sensemaking in IT failures or adoption of wearable devices.

Comparison to GT: Narrative analysis emphasizes subjective, storied accounts and interpretive depth, while GT focuses on systematic coding and abstraction. Narrative analysis is less structured and more focused on meaning-making.

Example: Analyzing IT managers' stories of cybersecurity breaches to theorize how narrative framing influences organizational learning.

Ethnography

Ethnography involves immersive observation and participation in a social setting to understand IS phenomena from the participants' perspective, leading to context-rich theories.

Process:

- Engage in prolonged fieldwork (e.g., observing a software development team).
- Collect data through participant observation, interviews, and artifacts.
- Analyze data using thick description, coding, or thematic analysis to identify cultural or social patterns.
- Develop theories grounded in the lived experiences of the setting.

Relevance to IS: Suited for studying technology use in naturalistic settings, such as agile development teams or online communities.

Comparison to GT: Ethnography prioritizes holistic, contextual understanding over GT's focus on abstract categories. It is less systematic but richer in cultural detail.

Example: An ethnographic study of a DevOps team to theorize how collaboration tools shape team dynamics and innovation.

Action Research

Action research combines theory building with practical problem-solving, involving collaboration with participants to address IS issues and develop theoretical insights.

Process:

- Identify a practical IS problem (e.g., improving user adoption of a system).
- Collaborate with stakeholders to design and implement interventions.
- Collect data on intervention outcomes (e.g., via surveys, logs, or interviews).
- Analyze data iteratively to refine interventions and develop theoretical insights.
- Generate a theory that links actions to outcomes.

Relevance to IS: Effective for studying participatory design, system implementation, or organizational change driven by IT.

Comparison to GT: Action research is intervention-oriented and collaborative, while GT is purely observational and inductive. Action research balances practical and theoretical outcomes, whereas GT prioritizes theoretical abstraction.

Example: Collaborating with a firm to improve a CRM system, leading to a theory of user engagement in system design.

Phenomenology

Phenomenology explores the lived experiences of individuals interacting with IS phenomena to uncover their subjective meanings and develop theories.

Process:

- Collect data through in-depth interviews or reflective accounts from participants (e.g., users of a mobile app).
- Analyze data using phenomenological reduction to identify essential themes or structures of experience.
- Develop a theory that captures the essence of the phenomenon.

Relevance to IS: Useful for studying user experiences, such as emotions in technology adoption or perceptions of AI ethics.

Comparison to GT: Phenomenology focuses on subjective, lived experiences and descriptive depth, while GT seeks abstract, generalizable categories. Phenomenology is less systematic and more interpretive.

Example: Studying developers' experiences with AI coding tools to theorize trust in automation.

Critical Discourse Analysis (CDA)

CDA examines language, texts, and communication in IS contexts to uncover power dynamics, ideologies, or social structures, leading to critical theories.

Process:

- Collect textual data (e.g., IT policy documents, social media posts, or meeting transcripts).

- Analyze discourse for themes, power relations, or ideological assumptions
- Develop a theory that explains how discourse shapes IS phenomena.

Relevance to IS: Ideal for studying power dynamics in IT governance, digital inequality, or technology-driven social change.

Comparison to GT: CDA is explicitly critical and focused on language, while GT is neutral and data-driven. CDA emphasizes social critique over GT's focus on emergent theory.

Example: Analyzing corporate IT strategy documents to theorize how discourse shapes digital transformation priorities.

Process Research

Process research examines sequences of events or changes over time in IS contexts to build theories about how and why phenomena evolve.

Process:

- Collect longitudinal data (e.g., project timelines, system logs, or repeated interviews).
- Analyze data using temporal coding, event sequencing, or process mapping to identify patterns.
- Develop a process theory that explains stages, transitions, or mechanisms of change.

Relevance to IS: Suited for studying IT project lifecycles, technology adoption processes, or digital innovation trajectories.

Comparison to GT: Process research focuses on temporal dynamics and sequences, while GT emphasizes static categories and relationships. Process research may use deductive elements, unlike GT's purely inductive approach.

Example: Mapping the stages of cloud migration to theorize barriers and facilitators of adoption.

Practice Lab 8.1: Grounded Theory in Practice

Objective

To develop your ability to identify GT research in IS and critically engage with published studies to understand their methodological choices, contributions, and limitations.

Task Description

You are required to locate and analyze a peer-reviewed academic article in the IS field that uses **GT** as its primary research methodology.

Your assignment is to write a **2–3 page report** (approx. 1000–1200 words) that includes the following components:

Part 1: Article Summary

Provide a concise overview of the article

Part 2: Critique

Evaluate the article in terms of:

- **Clarity and transparency** in explaining the GT process
- **Suitability of GT** for the research problem
- **Depth of theory development** (Did they really generate a theory or just describe themes?)
- **Credibility and trustworthiness** of the study (e.g., use of member checking, theoretical sampling, saturation)

Part 3: Lessons Learned

Reflect on your insights from this article:

- What did you learn about the GT process?
- What would you do similarly or differently if you were conducting a GT study?
- How could the findings from this article inform practice or future research in IS?

Submission Guidelines

- Format: PDF or Word
- Length: 2–3 pages, double-spaced

Grounded Theory Research Checklist

This checklist provides a structured guide for conducting GT research, ensuring systematic, rigorous, and data-driven theory development. It is applicable to classic, Straussian, and constructivist GT approaches.

Preparation Phase

Define Research Problem

- Identify a broad research area or problem suitable for GT (exploratory, no preconceived hypotheses).
- Ensure the problem allows for emergent, data-driven insights.

Select GT Approach

- Choose a GT paradigm (e.g., Glaser's classic, Strauss and Corbin's systematic, or Charmaz's constructivist).
- Justify the choice based on research goals and philosophical stance (e.g., objective vs. interpretive focus).

Conduct Initial Literature Review (Optional)

- For Glaserian GT, delay the extensive literature review to avoid preconceptions.
- For Straussian/constructivist GT, conduct a preliminary review to contextualize the study but avoid imposing frameworks.

Develop Research Questions

- Frame open-ended, exploratory questions to guide data collection (e.g., "How do participants experience X?").

Plan Ethical Considerations

- Obtain ethical approval from an institutional review board (if applicable).
- Prepare informed consent forms, ensuring participants understand the study's purpose and their rights.
- Plan for confidentiality and secure data storage.

Data Collection Phase

Select Initial Participants/Sites

- Identify initial participants or data sources (e.g., interviews, observations, documents) relevant to the research problem.
- Use purposive sampling to select information-rich cases.

Collect Initial Data

- Conduct interviews, observations, or document analysis, ensuring flexibility to capture participants' perspectives.
- Use open-ended questions or unstructured methods to allow emergent themes.

Begin Theoretical Sampling

- After initial coding, identify gaps in emerging categories and collect additional data to refine them.
- Adjust sampling based on evolving theoretical insights (e.g., new participant groups or contexts).

Document Data Collection

- Record interviews (with consent) or take detailed field notes.
- Maintain a clear log of data sources, dates, and contexts for auditability.

Data Analysis Phase

Open Coding

- Code initial data line-by-line or incident-by-incident to identify concepts and categories.
- Stay close to the data, using in-vivo codes (participants' words) where possible.

Constant Comparison

- Compare data within and across cases to refine categories and identify patterns.
- Ensure codes and categories are grounded in data, not preconceptions.

Axial Coding (Straussian/Constructivist GT)

- Relate categories to subcategories, identifying relationships (e.g., causes, contexts, consequences).
- Develop a coding paradigm if using Strauss and Corbin's approach.

Selective Coding

- Identify a core category that integrates all other categories.
- Refine the emerging theory around the core category.

Memo-Writing

- Write analytical memos to document insights, hypotheses, and reflections.
- Use memos to track theoretical development and researcher reflexivity.

Theoretical Saturation

- Continue data collection and analysis until no new categories or insights emerge.
- Verify saturation through constant comparison and theoretical sampling.

Reflexivity and Bias Management

Reflect on Researcher Role

- Document personal assumptions, biases, and theoretical sensitivities in memos.
- Use reflexivity to manage subjectivity and ensure data-driven findings.

Engage in Peer Debriefing

- Share coding and interpretations with colleagues or advisors to challenge biases.
- Incorporate feedback to enhance objectivity.

Conduct Member Checking (Optional)

- Share preliminary findings with participants to validate interpretations (especially in constructivist GT).
- Adjust findings based on participant feedback, if applicable.

Theory Development

Construct the Theory

- Articulate a substantive or formal theory based on the core category and relationships.
- Ensure the theory is grounded in data and addresses the research problem.

Validate Theoretical Integration

- Check that all categories are linked to the core category and supported by data.
- Use diagrams or models to visualize relationships (if applicable).

Compare with Existing Literature

- Conduct a full literature review to position the theory within existing knowledge.
- Highlight how the theory extends, challenges, or complements prior work.

Reporting and Dissemination

Document the Research Process

- Provide a clear audit trail (e.g., coding examples, memos, sampling decisions) for transparency.
- Describe the GT approach and methodological choices in detail.

Write the Research Report

- Structure the report to include background, methods, findings (with data excerpts), and the emergent theory.
- Discuss the role of subjectivity and objectivity in the analysis.

Ensure Trustworthiness

- Address credibility (e.g., triangulation, member checking), transferability (e.g., thick description), dependability (e.g., audit trail), and confirmability (e.g., reflexivity).

Disseminate Findings

- Prepare findings for publication, presentation, or practical application.
- Tailor the report to the audience (e.g., academic, practitioner, community).

Additional Considerations

Triangulation (Optional)

- Use multiple data sources or methods to enhance the credibility and robustness of findings.

Software Use (Optional)

- Consider qualitative data analysis software (e.g., NVivo, MAXQDA) for coding and organization, but ensure it supports, not drives, the analysis.

Address Philosophical Alignment

- Ensure methodological choices align with the chosen GT paradigm (e.g., objective focus in classic GT, interpretive focus in constructivist GT).

Monitor Time and Resources

- Plan for iterative data collection and analysis, which may be time-intensive.
- Secure resources for transcription, travel, or software as needed.
- This checklist is a flexible guide. Adapt it to your specific GT approach, research context, and disciplinary requirements while maintaining the core principles of GT.

Chapter Summary

GT remains a cornerstone of qualitative research in IS, offering a robust framework for developing theories that are deeply rooted in empirical data. Its inductive, iterative approach enables researchers to explore the dynamic interplay between technology, users, and organizations, generating insights that are both contextually rich and theoretically significant. Despite challenges such as managing researcher subjectivity and achieving theoretical saturation, GT's systematic processes – coding, constant comparison, and theoretical sampling – ensure rigor and transparency. By balancing objectivity and subjectivity through strategies like triangulation and reflexivity, GT produces credible theories that reflect real-world IS phenomena. The chapter's exploration of alternative methods, such as case studies and phenomenology, underscores GT's unique strengths while highlighting complementary approaches for diverse IS research questions. The provided checklist equips researchers with a practical guide to navigate GT's complexities, fostering rigorous and impactful contributions to IS scholarship. As IS continue to evolve, GT's adaptability positions it as a vital methodology for uncovering new theoretical insights and advancing the field.

Review Questions

1 What are the origins of GT, and how did Barney Glaser and Anselm Strauss's collaboration on "Awareness of Dying" shape its development? Discuss how their differing approaches (classic vs. Straussian) influence GT's application in IS research.

2. Explain the core processes of GT (open coding, axial coding, selective coding, constant comparison, and theoretical sampling). How do these processes ensure that theories are grounded in data, and why are they particularly suited for exploring complex IS phenomena?
3. Describe the role of theoretical saturation in GT research. What challenges might IS researchers face in determining when saturation has been achieved, and how can they address these challenges?
4. GT emphasizes both objectivity and subjectivity. Discuss how systematic procedures (e.g., coding, constant comparison) promote objectivity, while theoretical sensitivity and reflexivity incorporate subjectivity. Provide an example of how an IS researcher might balance these in a study of user adoption of a new technology.
5. Compare and contrast GT with one alternative theory-building method (e.g., case study research, phenomenology, or CDA) in the context of IS research. How do their philosophical underpinnings and processes differ, and when might the alternative method be more appropriate?
6. What are some key challenges and limitations of GT in IS research? How can researchers mitigate issues such as researcher bias or the time-intensive nature of the methodology?
7. Using the provided GT research checklist, outline the steps you would take to design a GT study exploring how employees adapt to a new enterprise system. Specify how you would address ethical considerations and ensure rigor.
8. How does GT's inductive approach differ from deductive approaches commonly used in quantitative IS research? Provide an example of an IS research question that is better suited to GT than a deductive approach, and justify your choice.
9. Discuss the role of memo-writing in GT research. How does it contribute to theory development and researcher reflexivity, and why is it critical for maintaining transparency in IS studies?
10. Consider an IS research topic, such as the impact of AI on organizational decision-making. How would you apply GT to study this topic, and how might an alternative method (e.g., process research or ethnography) offer a different perspective on the same topic?

References

Bryant, A., & Charmaz, K. (Eds.). (2007). *The SAGE Handbook of Grounded Theory*. SAGE Publications.

Charmaz, K. (2006). *Constructing Grounded Theory. A Practical Guide Through Qualitative Analysis*. SAGE Publications.

Corbin, J., & Strauss, A. (2015). *Basics of Qualitative Research: Techniques and Procedures for Developing Grounded Theory* (4th ed.). SAGE Publications.

Denscombe, M (2010). *The Good Research Guide for Small-Scale Social Research Projects* (4th ed.) Open University Press.

Glaser, B. G. (1992). *Basics of Grounded Theory Analysis: Emergence vs Forcing*. Sociology Press.

Glaser, B. G., & Strauss, A. L. (1967). *The Discovery of Grounded Theory: Strategies for Qualitative Research*. Aldine Publishing.

Myers, M. D. (2009). *Qualitative Research in Business & Management*. Sage Publications.

Myers, M. D. (2013). *Qualitative Research in Business and Management* (2nd ed.). SAGE Publications.

Orlikowski, W. J. (1993). CASE tools as organizational change: Investigating incremental and radical changes in systems development. *MIS Quarterly, 17*(3), 309–340. https://doi.org/10.2307/249774

Suddaby, R. (2006). From the editors: What grounded theory is not. *Academy of Management Journal, 49*(4), 633–642. https://doi.org/10.5465/amj.2006.22083020

Urquhart, C. (2013). *Grounded Theory for Qualitative Research: A Practical Guide*. SAGE Publications.

Urquhart, C., Lehmann, H., & Myers, M. D. (2010). Putting the 'theory' back into grounded theory: Guidelines for grounded theory studies in information systems. *Information Systems Journal, 20*(4), 357–381. https://doi.org/10.1111/j.1365-2575.2009.00328.x

Walsham, G. (1995). Interpretive case studies in IS research: Nature and method. *European Journal of Information Systems, 4*(2), 74–81. https://doi.org/10.1057/ejis.1995.9

Yin, R. K. (2018). *Case Study Research and Applications: Design and Methods* (6th ed.). SAGE Publications.

9 Interview Research in IS

Chapter Objectives

After reading this chapter, readers should understand:

- Interview Research
- Importance of Interview Research in IS
- Modes of Interview Research
- Recruitment Strategies

Interview Research in the Digital Age

In the digital age, interview research in information systems (IS) and information technology (IT) has undergone a significant transformation, leveraging emerging technologies to enhance both the reach and depth of qualitative inquiry. Online platforms such as Zoom, Microsoft Teams, and Skype have become standard tools for conducting semi-structured and unstructured interviews with participants across geographic and organizational boundaries. This shift not only reduces travel costs and logistical constraints but also allows researchers to engage with diverse stakeholders in real-time, including remote workers, IT consultants, and software developers across different time zones. For instance, in a study exploring the implementation challenges of Enterprise Resource Planning (ERP) – refers to the integrated software systems that organizations use to manage and streamline core business processes across all departments like human resources, finance, supply chain, customer relationship management, and so on. ERP systems centralize data, automate tasks and provide real-time data to improve decision-making – systems, researchers used Microsoft Teams to interview IT managers and system users in multinational firms, enabling them to collect cross-cultural insights on user resistance and system customization practices.

DOI: 10.4324/9781003545521-11

Interview research remains a cornerstone of qualitative research in IS, offering rich, contextual insights into user experiences, organizational processes, and technological impacts (Myers, 2013). The digital age has transformed interview methodologies, integrating advanced technologies that enhance accessibility, flexibility, and efficiency. This chapter explores interview research methodologies, their importance in IS, the role of digital technologies, and comparisons between traditional and digital interview methods. It also provides practical guidance on leveraging digital tools, designing digital interviews, and recruiting participants, addressing both opportunities and challenges in this evolving landscape.

Moreover, digital interviews allow the integration of screen-sharing, live demonstrations, and digital artifacts into the interview process, offering richer contextual data. In research examining the usability of healthcare IS, interviewees can walk researchers through electronic health record interfaces or patient portal dashboards during the conversation. This hybrid of interview and observation, facilitated by digital tools, enables a deeper understanding of user interaction and cognitive processes behind system navigation and decision-making. Additionally, automated transcription tools like Otter.ai or built-in Zoom transcription features streamline post-interview analysis by providing time-stamped transcripts, which can be directly imported into qualitative analysis software such as NVivo or MAXQDA for coding and thematic mapping. These innovations collectively enhance the methodological rigor and analytical potential of interview research in the IS and IT fields, while also introducing new challenges related to privacy, data security, and digital accessibility. Table 9.1 highlights how digital technologies have transformed traditional research methods, with a focus on interview-based research and other commonly used methods in IS.

Interview Research Methodology

Interview research in IS involves systematically collecting qualitative data through structured, semi-structured, or unstructured conversations with participants to explore their perspectives on technology-related phenomena (Kvale & Brinkmann, 2015). Structured interviews use predefined questions to ensure consistency, while semi-structured interviews allow flexibility to probe emergent themes, aligning well with inductive approaches like grounded theory (Charmaz, 2014). Unstructured interviews prioritize open-ended exploration, suitable for deeply interpretive studies. The methodology emphasizes iterative data collection and analysis, often involving transcription, coding, and thematic analysis to generate insights (Myers, 2013). In IS, interviews are particularly valuable for capturing nuanced user experiences, such as perceptions of system usability or organizational adoption challenges, which quantitative methods may overlook (Walsham, 1995).

Table 9.1 Impact of Digital Technologies

Research Method	*Before Digital Technologies*	*After Digital Technologies*
Interviews (Qualitative)	Conducted face-to-face; limited to local participants; required travel and scheduling logistics (Kvale & Brinkman, 2015; Myers, 2009)	Conducted via Zoom/Teams/ Skype; global reach; recorded easily; screen-sharing enables contextual walkthroughs (Salmons, 2015; Deakin & Wakefield, 2014)
Focus Groups	In-person group meetings; dependent on physical space; difficult to coordinate across locations (Kvale & Brinkman, 2015)	Virtual focus groups using breakout rooms; higher flexibility; real-time polling and chat enhance engagement (Salmons, 2015)
Surveys (Quantitative)	Paper-based or telephone surveys; slower data collection; manual data entry (Denscombe, 2010)	Online surveys (e.g., Qualtrics, Google Forms); automated collection and analytics; broader respondent base (Salmons, 2015)
Ethnographic Observation	Researcher physically embedded in setting; extensive note-taking (Myers, 2009)	Digital ethnography in online communities or platforms (e.g., GitHub, Reddit); screen capture for context (Charmaz, 2014; Myers & Newman, 2007)
Usability Testing	On-site labs with video recording and direct observation (Myers, 2009)	Remote usability testing using screen-sharing, mouse-tracking, and automated feedback tools (e.g., UserTesting)
Case Studies	Relied on physical document collection and in-person interviews (Myers, 2009; Urquhart et al., 2013)	Access to digital logs, email archives, and digital communications; hybrid data sources improve triangulation (Myers & Newman, 2007; Charmaz, 2013)
Transcription and Coding	Manual transcription; time-consuming; physical notes (Kvale & Brinkman, 2015)	Automated transcription (e.g., Otter.ai); direct import into NVivo, MAXQDA; faster coding with AI assistance (Salmons, 2015; Deakin & Wakefield, 2014)
Diary Studies	Participants kept physical journals or logs; prone to loss or incomplete entries (Denscombe, 2010)	Mobile diary apps and digital prompts (e.g., Dscout); real-time data capture; multimedia entries supported (Salmons, 2015)

Importance of Interviews in Information Systems Research

Interviews are critical in IS research due to their ability to uncover complex, context-specific insights into how individuals and organizations interact with technology (Urquhart, 2013). They enable researchers to explore user behaviors, motivations, and barriers in contexts like system implementation, digital transformation, or cybersecurity adoption. For example, Orlikowski (1993) used interviews to study how CASE tools influence organizational change, revealing emergent patterns that informed theory development. Interviews also support exploratory research in rapidly evolving IS domains, such as artificial intelligence (AI) or blockchain, where pre-existing theories may be limited (Myers & Newman, 2007). By providing rich, qualitative data, interviews complement other methods like surveys or observations, enhancing the depth and validity of IS findings through triangulation (Yin, 2018).

Integration of Digital Technologies in Interview Studies

Digital technologies have revolutionized interview research by enabling remote data collection, real-time interaction, and scalable participant recruitment. Tools like video conferencing platforms, online survey systems, and social media have expanded the scope and accessibility of interviews (Deakin & Wakefield, 2014). These technologies facilitate global reach, allowing researchers to engage diverse participants without geographic constraints. They also support asynchronous data collection (e.g., via email or messaging apps) and real-time transcription or recording, streamlining analysis (Salmons, 2015). However, digital integration introduces challenges, such as ensuring data security, managing technical issues, and maintaining participant engagement in virtual settings, which require careful methodological consideration (Kvale & Brinkmann, 2015).

Traditional vs. Digital Interviews

Comparison of Face-to-Face, Telephone, and Online Interviews

Traditional face-to-face interviews involve in-person interactions, offering rich nonverbal cues (e.g., body language) and a personal connection that fosters rapport (Kvale & Brinkmann, 2015). They are ideal for sensitive topics or complex IS phenomena, such as user resistance to new systems, but are resource-intensive and geographically limited. Telephone interviews provide a cost-effective alternative, maintaining vocal cues but lacking visual context, which can limit depth in interpretive studies (Deakin & Wakefield, 2014). Online interviews, conducted via video conferencing (e.g., Zoom) or text-based platforms (e.g., email), offer flexibility and global reach but may face challenges like technical disruptions or reduced nonverbal communication (Salmons, 2015). For example, a study on remote work software adoption might use online interviews to access distributed participants, but risk losing nuanced emotional cues compared to face-to-face settings.

Advantages and Limitations of Digital Interviews

Digital interviews offer several advantages: cost-efficiency, accessibility to diverse or remote participants, and the ability to record or transcribe directly, aiding analysis (Deakin & Wakefield, 2014). They are particularly suited for IS research involving global teams or virtual communities, such as studies of open-source software development. However, limitations include potential technical issues (e.g., poor internet connectivity), reduced rapport due to virtual settings, and privacy concerns related to data storage (Salmons, 2015). Additionally, digital interviews may exclude participants with limited digital literacy or access, introducing sampling bias (Myers & Newman, 2007). Researchers must weigh these factors when choosing interview modes, aligning them with research objectives and participant needs.

Digital Tools and Platforms for Conducting Interviews

Video Conferencing Software

Video conferencing tools like Zoom, Skype, and Microsoft Teams have become integral to digital interview research. These platforms support real-time, face-to-face-like interactions, preserving some nonverbal cues and enabling screen-sharing for discussing IS artifacts (e.g., software interfaces) (Deakin & Wakefield, 2014). Zoom, for instance, offers recording and transcription features, streamlining data capture. However, researchers must ensure secure data handling and test technology in advance to avoid disruptions (Salmons, 2015).

Online Survey and Interview Platforms

Platforms like Qualtrics and SurveyMonkey support asynchronous interviews by integrating open-ended questions into online surveys, allowing participants to respond at their convenience (Couper, 2011). These tools are useful for large-scale IS studies, such as gathering user feedback on system usability across multiple organizations. They offer data export features for analysis, but may limit probing compared to live interviews (Myers, 2013).

Social Media and Messaging Apps for Interview Recruitment

Social media platforms (e.g., LinkedIn, X (Twitter)) and messaging apps (e.g., WhatsApp, Slack) facilitate participant recruitment by targeting specific IS communities, such as IT professionals or user groups (Deakin & Wakefield, 2014). For example, LinkedIn can be used to recruit CIOs for a study on cloud adoption. These tools enable rapid, targeted outreach but require ethical considerations, such as transparency about research purposes and consent (Salmons, 2015).

Planning and Designing Digital Interviews

Determining Research Objectives and Interview Questions

In the digital age, the foundation of any successful interview-based study in the field of IS lies in the thoughtful articulation of research objectives and the strategic formulation of interview questions. Clear, well-defined research objectives serve not only to guide the flow and scope of the digital interview but also to ensure alignment with the theoretical and empirical goals of the study (Myers & Newman, 2007). For instance, in a study examining the implementation of cloud-based enterprise systems in multinational corporations, researchers might set objectives aimed at understanding both user adoption behaviors and organizational resistance. Such clarity in objectives enables the researcher to tailor their questions with precision and relevance.

Interview questions in digital settings, particularly in semi-structured or unstructured formats, must be open-ended and adaptable, while also accounting for the cognitive load and attentional span typical in virtual environments. Scholars such as Kvale and Brinkmann (2015) emphasize that questions should be not only exploratory but also concise to maintain participant engagement – an especially crucial consideration in remote or asynchronous interviews. For example, rather than asking a broad and potentially vague question like "What do you think about AI in the workplace?," a more focused digital interview might include: "How do AI-driven recommendation systems influence your decision-making processes during client interactions?" or "What ethical considerations arise when using predictive analytics in employee performance evaluations?" These questions are context-sensitive, grounded in digital practice, and conducive to eliciting nuanced responses.

Moreover, digital interviews allow for innovative question sequencing, use of screen sharing (e.g., to discuss system interfaces), and integration of digital artifacts (e.g., screenshots, dashboards, or audit logs), thereby enriching the dialogue. In a study exploring IT governance practices in decentralized organizations, for instance, researchers might first pose questions about individual roles and responsibilities, then present visual prompts such as RACI charts or Gantt timelines to stimulate deeper reflections on coordination challenges. This multimodal approach is unique to digital interviewing and offers new avenues for engagement and insight that traditional, in-person methods often lack. Ultimately, the digital transformation of the interview process demands a reconsideration of not only what we ask, but how we ask it. Researchers in IS and IT must therefore develop interview guides that are methodologically rigorous yet technologically responsive that reflect the complexity of digital environments in which their participants operate.

Here is a comprehensive checklist for planning digital interview questions in the context of IS and IT research. It includes tasks, explanations, and examples to ensure methodological rigor and alignment with digital interview practices (Table 9.2).

Table 9.2 Checklist for Planning Digital Interview Questions

Task	*Explanation*	*Example in IS Research*
1. Define Research Objectives	Establish the overarching purpose of the study to guide question development.(Myers, 2007; Kvale & Brinkmann, 2015)	Objective: Understand user trust in a new fintech app's AI-powered features.
2. Identify Target Participants	Determine who will be interviewed based on relevance to research objectives.(Myers & Newman, 2007, Charmaz, 2014)	CIOs and IT managers in organizations using blockchain for supply chain management.
3. Choose Interview Type	Decide between structured, semi-structured, or unstructured formats based on the level of control and flexibility required. (Kvale & Brinkman, 2015; Myers, 2007)	Semi-structured interview to explore both known and emerging cybersecurity practices.
4. Develop Open-Ended Questions	Craft questions that prompt detailed, reflective responses and avoid yes/no answers. (Rubin & Rubin, 2012, Kvale & Brinkmann, 2015)	"Can you describe a situation where automated decision-making improved your workflow?"
5. Adapt Questions for Digital Format	Shorten complex questions to maintain attention in virtual environments; consider digital fatigue. (Salmons, 2015; Deakin & Wakefield, 2014)	Instead of long multi-part questions, break them into simpler, follow-up prompts.
6. Integrate Contextual Prompts	Use screen sharing or digital artifacts to contextualize questions and stimulate richer dialogue. (Salmons, 2015; Myers & Newmann, 2007)	Ask users to describe their experience while showing a screenshot of an ERP dashboard.
7. Pilot Test Questions	Conduct a test run with a colleague or participant to assess clarity, pacing, and technical feasibility.(Kvale & Brinkmann, 2015; Rubin & Rubin, 2012)	Pilot with a colleague to test question flow in Microsoft Teams or Zoom.
8. Account for Technological Constraints	Ensure questions are understandable even with poor connectivity or lack of non-verbal cues.(Salmons, 2015), Deaking & Wakefield, 2014)	Avoid jargon or overly complex phrasing that may be misinterpreted in low-bandwidth environments.
9. Ensure Ethical Compliance	Confirm questions do not infringe on privacy or confidentiality, especially in recorded sessions. (Myers, 2009; Kvale & Brinkmann, 2015)	Avoid questions that request identification of specific clients or internal proprietary data.

(Continued)

Table 9.2 (Continued)

Task	*Explanation*	*Example in IS Research*
10. Sequence Questions Logically	Structure from general to specific to help participants ease into the conversation. (Myers & Newmann, 2007)	Start with "Tell me about your role," before asking "How have you applied agile methods in system deployment?"
11. Plan for Follow-Up Probes	Prepare flexible prompts to encourage elaboration or clarification. (Charmaz, 2014)	"Can you give an example of when that challenge occurred?" or "How did your team respond?"
12. Align with Theoretical Framework	Ensure questions are rooted in or map to key constructs of your theoretical lens. (Myers 2013)	Using TAM (Technology Acceptance Model), include questions on perceived usefulness and ease of use.

Structuring the Interview Protocol for Digital Settings

Developing a robust and flexible interview protocol is essential when conducting interviews in digital environments. The protocol must accommodate both methodological rigor and the unique affordances and limitations of virtual communication tools. At the outset, the protocol should include a detailed introduction that outlines the study's objectives, the role of the participant, and what will be expected during the session. This includes reviewing informed consent procedures (now often delivered electronically) and providing clear technical instructions, such as how to log in to the interview platform, how to enable audio/video, and how to use the chat function or virtual background if privacy is a concern (Salmons, 2015). For example, in a study on cloud migration strategies in mid-sized enterprises, participants may be asked to share their screen to demonstrate architectural choices, so the protocol must include permissions and instructions for this activity.

The protocol should carefully sequence interview questions, beginning with broad, rapport-building questions before narrowing the focus to more specific themes relevant to the research. For instance, an IT researcher investigating agile transformation might begin with, "Can you tell me about your role in your organization's digital projects?" before transitioning to more specific questions like, "How has agile impacted your team's collaboration in virtual environments?" This approach not only sets participants at ease but also provides contextual grounding for later responses. It is also critical to build in probes and prompts that can be used to deepen the conversation. These can be both pre-planned and emergent, especially in semi-structured formats aligned with constructivist grounded theory (Charmaz, 2014). Probes such as "Can you give an example of that situation?" or "What do you think caused that challenge?" help surface nuanced insights and can reveal themes not anticipated in the initial research design. For instance, in a digital ethnography of DevOps adoption, unexpected issues like remote team miscommunication or tool fatigue may emerge and require additional exploration.

A pilot test of the protocol is a crucial step, allowing researchers to identify issues related to question clarity, pacing, and technical reliability. During the pilot, researchers may find that a question such as "What are your views on digital governance?" is too abstract for remote participants and may need to be rephrased as "Can you describe a recent policy or practice that guided your digital transformation efforts?" Feedback from the pilot can also highlight logistical issues, such as time zone confusion, platform incompatibility, or interruptions caused by background noise – prompting adjustments in scheduling, platform choice, or participant preparation.

Additional considerations for the digital protocol include:

- Setting expectations for digital etiquette (e.g., muting when not speaking, avoiding distractions).
- Contingency plans for technical disruptions, such as backup platforms or phone call alternatives.
- Time management, ensuring that each section of the interview is time-bounded while allowing room for flexibility if rich discussions unfold.
- Post-interview follow-up procedures, including sending a transcript or summary for participant verification, which is particularly important for ensuring member checking in virtual contexts.

Structuring an interview protocol for digital settings requires deliberate planning that integrates ethical, technical, and methodological elements. By grounding the protocol in established qualitative research principles while adapting to digital realities, IS researchers can ensure high-quality, context-sensitive data collection in online environments. To enhance comfort, researchers should create a welcoming virtual environment, such as using neutral backgrounds and clear audio (Deakin & Wakefield, 2014). Engagement can be maintained through active listening, empathetic responses, and flexible pacing to accommodate participant needs. Offering technical support (e.g., troubleshooting Zoom) and ensuring privacy (e.g., secure platforms) are critical for trust (Salmons, 2015).

Online Recruitment Strategies

Online recruitment leverages social media advertising, online forums, and professional networks to reach IS-relevant populations (Deakin & Wakefield, 2014). For example, Reddit forums like r/technology can recruit participants for a study on user-generated content platforms. Strategies include posting targeted ads, engaging with community moderators, or using snowball sampling

Table 9.3 Online Recruitment Strategies for Digital Interviews

Recruitment Strategy	*Advantages*	*Examples in IS Research*
Email Invitations	Direct, personalized, professional; good response rate from known contacts (Kvale & Brinkman, 2015; Myers, 2013)	Recruiting IT managers from previous industry contacts for interviews on IT governance (Salmons, 2015; Deakin & Wakefield, 2014)
Social Media Outreach	Broad reach, cost-effective, fast dissemination	Posting calls for participants on LinkedIn to study digital transformation initiatives
Online Communities and Forums	Access to niche or expert groups; voluntary engagement	Recruiting software developers from Reddit for a study on agile tool adoption
Snowball Sampling	Useful for hard-to-reach or specialized populations	Asking blockchain researchers to refer peers for an interview study on blockchain adoption
Survey Screener Links	Efficient filtering; integrates with broader quantitative methods	Embedding an interview sign-up at the end of a tech adoption survey in a university setting
Institutional Participant Pools	Access to diverse, pre-consented participants	Using university student pools to study app usability or tech acceptance
Crowdsourcing Platforms	Fast recruitment, scalable, built-in consent mechanisms	Using Prolific to recruit remote workers for interviews about online collaboration tools
Website or Blog Announcements	Leverages personal/ professional networks; low-cost	Posting an interview call on a research lab's blog for a project on AI ethics in IS

via existing participants. Ethical recruitment requires clear communication of study goals, voluntary participation, and data protection measures (Myers & Newman, 2007) (Table 9.3).

Sampling Techniques

Digital interview studies often use purposive sampling to select participants with relevant IS experience, such as IT managers for a study on system implementation (Yin, 2018). Theoretical sampling, inspired by GT, can guide recruitment as emergent themes suggest new participant types (Charmaz, 2014). Snowball sampling is effective in digital contexts, leveraging referrals to access hard-to-reach groups, such as niche open-source developers. Researchers must balance inclusivity with representativeness to avoid bias, particularly in digital-only samples (Couper, 2011) (Table 9.4).

Table 9.4 Challenges and Solutions in Online Recruitment for Digital Interviews

Strategy	*Challenges*	*How to Address the Challenges*
Email Invitations (Couper, 2011)	Low response rate; outdated contact lists.	Use personalized, well-crafted emails; verify contact lists; send follow-up reminders.
Social Media Outreach (Charmaz, 2014)	Attracting unqualified participants; privacy concerns.	Use eligibility screening forms; include clear consent info; use targeted posts or ads.
Online Communities and Forums (Yin, 2018)	May be flagged as spam; community resistance.	Engage genuinely with the community; get moderator approval before posting.
Snowball Sampling (Charmaz, 2014)	Potential sampling bias; limited control over referrals.	Provide clear criteria to participants; track referral paths for transparency.
Survey Screener Links (Couper, 2011)	Low completion rates; drop-offs before scheduling.	Keep forms short; use progress indicators; offer small incentives for form completion.
Institutional Participant Pools (Yin, 2018)	Limited diversity; IRB constraints.	Supplement with external recruitment; design studies to appeal to various student demographics.
Crowdsourcing Platforms (Couper, 2011)	Quality and attention issues; participants may rush.	Use attention checks; filter by platform-reputation score; offer fair compensation.
Website or Blog Announcements (Yin, 2018)	Limited traffic; hard to reach target population.	Promote posts via email newsletters and social media; ensure SEO optimization for visibility.

Practice Lab 9.1: Designing a Social Media Strategy for Recruiting Research Respondents

Title

Designing a Social Media Recruitment Strategy for Digital Interviews

Objective

Students will develop and justify a social media strategy to recruit participants for a study involving digital interviews.

Instructions

Step 1: Define Your Research Context

- Choose a **topic** relevant to IS (e.g., cybersecurity behavior, AI adoption, digital health).

- Define:
    - Your **target population** (e.g., IT professionals, students, remote workers).
    - The **type of interview** you will conduct (e.g., semi-structured via Zoom).
    - The **inclusion criteria** for your participants.

Step 2: Select Platforms

- Choose **two social media platforms** (e.g., LinkedIn, Reddit, X).
- Justify your choice based on:
    - Audience demographics
    - Engagement level
    - Platform culture and norms

Step 3: Design Your Recruitment Message

- Write **two recruitment posts** tailored to each platform:
    - Post format (e.g., text + image, hashtag use)
    - Tone (professional, casual, academic)
    - Call to action (e.g., link to a screening survey or sign-up form)

Step 4: Ethical Considerations (10 min)

- Address how you will handle:
    - Consent
    - Data privacy
    - Authenticity of participants

Step 5: Present Your Strategy

- Prepare a **brief presentation or poster** summarizing:
    - Research topic
    - Target participants
    - Social media channels
    - Sample posts
    - Ethical considerations

Deliverables

- Social media recruitment plan (1-page summary)
- Two Draft Posts (tailored per platform)
- Short oral or visual presentation

Chapter Summary

Interview research in the digital age offers IS researchers powerful tools to explore complex, technology-driven phenomena with unprecedented flexibility and reach. By integrating digital technologies like video conferencing, online survey platforms, and social media, researchers can access diverse participants and streamline data collection. However, digital interviews require careful planning to address challenges like technical disruptions, participant engagement, and ethical concerns. Compared to traditional methods, digital interviews balance cost-efficiency and global accessibility with limitations in nonverbal cues and inclusivity. By leveraging structured protocols, robust recruitment strategies, and digital tools, IS researchers can generate rich, qualitative insights that advance theoretical and practical understanding of IS. As digital technologies evolve, interview research will continue to adapt, offering new opportunities to explore the dynamic interplay between technology and human experience.

Review Questions

1 How do the characteristics of structured, semi-structured, and unstructured interviews influence their application in IS research? Provide an example of an IS research topic where a semi-structured interview would be more appropriate than a structured one, and justify your choice.
2 Compare and contrast the advantages and limitations of face-to-face, telephone, and online interviews in the context of studying user adoption of a new enterprise system. How might the choice of interview mode impact the quality of data collected?
3 Discuss the role of digital tools like Zoom and Qualtrics in facilitating interview research in IS. What specific features of these tools enhance data collection and analysis, and what challenges might researchers face when using them?
4 Explain how online recruitment strategies, such as social media advertising or snowball sampling, can be used to access participants for an IS study on cybersecurity awareness. What ethical considerations should researchers address when recruiting through these platforms?
5 Describe the process of designing a digital interview protocol for an IS study exploring employee perceptions of AI-driven decision-making tools. How can researchers ensure participant comfort and engagement in a virtual setting, and what strategies can mitigate potential technical disruptions?

References

Charmaz, K. (2014). *Constructing Grounded Theory* (2nd ed.). SAGE Publications.
Couper, M. P. (2011). The future of modes of data collection. *Public Opinion Quarterly, 75*(5), 889–908. https://doi.org/10.1093/poq/nfr046

Deakin, H., & Wakefield, K. (2014). Skype interviewing: Reflections of two PhD researchers. *Qualitative Research, 14*(5), 603–616. https://doi.org/10.1177/1468794113488126

Kvale, S., & Brinkmann, S. (2015). *Interviews: Learning the Craft of Qualitative Research Interviewing* (3rd ed.). SAGE Publications.

Myers, M. D. (2013). *Qualitative Research in Business and Management* (2nd ed.). SAGE Publications.

Myers, M. D., & Newman, M. (2007). The qualitative interview in IS research: Examining the craft. *Information and Organization, 17*(1), 2–26. https://doi.org/10.1016/j.infoandorg.2006.11.001

Orlikowski, W. J. (1993). CASE tools as organizational change: Investigating incremental and radical changes in systems development. *MIS Quarterly, 17*(3), 309–340. https://doi.org/10.2307/249774

Salmons, J. (2015). *Qualitative Online Interviews: Strategies, Design, and Skills* (2nd ed.). SAGE Publications.

Urquhart, C. (2013). *Grounded Theory for Qualitative Research: A Practical Guide*. SAGE Publications.

Walsham, G. (1995). Interpretive case studies in IS research: Nature and method. *European Journal of Information Systems, 4*(2), 74–81. https://doi.org/10.1057/ejis.1995.9

Yin, R. K. (2018). *Case Study Research and Applications: Design and Methods* (6th ed.). SAGE Publications.

10 Content Analysis and Focus Group in IS Research

Chapter Objectives

After reading this chapter, readers should understand:

- Definition and Scope of Content Analysis and Focus Groups
- The Process of Data Analysis and the Coding Process
- The Process of Grounded Theory Coding Process
- Emerging Trends in Content Analysis and Focus Group Research

Content Analysis and Focus Group Research in Information Systems

Qualitative research in information systems (IS) employs diverse methodologies to uncover nuanced insights into technology-related phenomena, user behaviors, and organizational dynamics. Content analysis and focus group research are two powerful approaches that enable researchers to systematically analyze textual data and capture collective perspectives, respectively. Content analysis involves examining communication artifacts, such as documents or social media, to identify patterns and meanings, while focus groups facilitate interactive discussions to explore shared experiences and attitudes (Myers, 2013). The Coding Process is integral to qualitative research; however, grounded theory takes it beyond in generating a grounded theory based on the data. Both methods are particularly suited to IS, where understanding user interactions, system impacts, and digital communication is critical. This chapter examines the definitions, applications, and processes of content analysis and focus groups in IS research, addressing their strengths, limitations, and emerging trends driven by digital technologies and artificial intelligence (AI).

Definition and Scope of Content Analysis

Content analysis is a systematic, replicable method for analyzing the content of communication – such as texts, images, or multimedia – to identify patterns, themes, or meanings (Krippendorff, 2018). In IS, it involves

DOI: 10.4324/9781003545521-12

examining data sources like user manuals, software documentation, social media posts, or system logs to uncover insights about technology use, user perceptions, or organizational processes. The scope of content analysis ranges from descriptive (e.g., counting keyword frequencies) to interpretive (e.g., identifying latent themes), making it versatile for both positivist and interpretive IS studies (Neuendorf, 2017). Unlike grounded theory's inductive theory-building approach (Charmaz, 2014), content analysis can be deductive, testing predefined categories, or inductive, allowing themes to emerge, offering flexibility for IS researchers studying diverse phenomena.

Types of Content Analysis

Content analysis is categorized into three main types:

1. **Quantitative Content Analysis**: Focuses on counting and measuring occurrences of specific elements, such as the frequency of terms like "usability" in user reviews, to produce numerical data (Krippendorff, 2018). This is often used in IS to analyze large datasets, such as social media sentiment about a new system.
2. **Qualitative Content Analysis**: Emphasizes interpretive analysis of themes or meanings, such as exploring user perceptions of privacy in app reviews (Hsieh & Shannon, 2005). It aligns with interpretive IS research, prioritizing contextual depth.
3. **Mixed-Methods Content Analysis**: Combines quantitative and qualitative approaches, for instance, counting keywords and interpreting their contextual meanings (Neuendorf, 2017). This is useful in IS for triangulating findings, such as analyzing both the frequency and tone of information technology (IT) policy discussions.

Applications of Content Analysis in Information Systems Studies

Content analysis is widely applied in IS to study diverse phenomena. For example, it can analyze user-generated content on platforms like Twitter to understand public sentiment toward new technologies, such as AI adoption (Saldanha & Sahay, 2013). It is also used to examine system documentation to identify usability issues or to analyze organizational communications for insights into digital transformation strategies (Myers, 2013). In exploratory IS research, content analysis supports studies of emerging areas like blockchain or cybersecurity by uncovering stakeholder perspectives from online forums or whitepapers. Its flexibility complements methods like grounded theory, enabling researchers to build or test theories based on textual data (Urquhart, 2013).

Conducting Content Analysis

Planning a content analysis study in IS begins with defining research objectives, such as exploring user perceptions of a system or evaluating IT policy impacts (Krippendorff, 2018). Researchers must specify whether the study is descriptive, relational, or interpretive and select an appropriate type of content analysis (quantitative, qualitative, or mixed-methods). A clear research question, such as "How do users describe security concerns in mobile banking apps?" guides the design. The study should also outline the unit of analysis (e.g., sentences, paragraphs) and address ethical considerations, such as anonymizing user-generated data to protect privacy (Neuendorf, 2017).

Selecting Data Sources and Sampling Techniques

Data sources in IS content analysis may include online reviews, social media posts, system logs, or organizational reports, selected based on the research question and accessibility (Krippendorff, 2018). Sampling techniques include purposive sampling, such as selecting tweets mentioning a specific software, or random sampling for large datasets to ensure representativeness (Hsieh & Shannon, 2005). In IS, theoretical sampling, inspired by grounded theory, may be used to select data iteratively based on emerging themes (Charmaz, 2014). Researchers must ensure data relevance and manage volume, particularly with big data sources like social media, to avoid overwhelming analysis.

Coding Procedures and Coding Schemes

Coding in content analysis involves categorizing data into meaningful units using a coding scheme, which can be deductive (predefined categories) or inductive (emergent categories) (Neuendorf, 2017). For example, a deductive scheme might analyze system logs for predefined error types, while an inductive scheme, similar to grounded theory's open coding, allows themes like "user frustration" to emerge from app reviews (Charmaz, 2014). Coding schemes should be clear, with explicit definitions and examples to ensure reliability. Inter-coder reliability tests, where multiple coders independently analyze data, enhance objectivity, particularly in quantitative content analysis (Krippendorff, 2018).

Analyzing Content Data

Data analysis in content analysis involves synthesizing coded data to identify patterns, relationships, or themes. Quantitative analysis may use statistical tools to report frequencies or correlations, such as the prevalence of positive vs. negative sentiments in user feedback (Neuendorf, 2017). Qualitative analysis interprets meanings, such as how users articulate trust in IS security features, often using thematic analysis (Hsieh & Shannon, 2005).

Mixed-methods approaches combine these to provide comprehensive insights, such as quantifying complaint frequency and exploring their qualitative context. In IS, software like NVivo or MAXQDA can support coding and analysis, though researchers must ensure tools do not drive the process (Myers, 2013).

The Coding Process

Qualitative coding is a systematic process used to analyze qualitative data (non-numerical data, like interviews, focus group interviews, observations) by identifying patterns, themes, or categories. The researcher should begin with preparing the data. Gather the qualitative raw data (transcripts, notes, audio, video, memos, or even social media posts and other artifacts). Ensure the interviews and audio are transcribed. The researcher should familiarize themselves with the data by immersing themselves in the data by reading and ingesting the data multiple times or listening to the audio to get a deeper understanding. Take additional notes, if needed on recurring ideas, emotions, and concepts without any coding at this point. Start developing initial codes with a process called Open Coding by reading through the data line and assigning labels (codes) to sections that stand out. The researcher should be looking for codes that are related to the research question. These codes should reflect the content, for example, "frustration," "stress," and "team collaboration." Use descripted words or short phrases. You can code manually by using different colored highlighters on paper for different codes, or you can use qualitative data analysis software (QDAS) tools like Nvivo, Atlas.ti, Quirkos, or your choice. Next, group the codes into categories looking for patterns among your codes into broader categories. For example, the code "frustration," "anger," and "disappointment" may be listed under a category called "negative emotions." Next, identify the Themes by taking your categories and refining them into overarching themes. A theme may be called "factors or barriers to effective communication." If there are several categories, list them as well. Themes should answer your research questions or highlight the key insights. Lastly, review and refine by reviewing the data again to ensure your codes, categories, and themes align with the content, adjusting along the way by overlapping codes, splitting vague ones, or redefining the themes to better fit the data. Next, interpret and report your findings by analyzing the themes, asking the questions: What story do they tell? Write up your findings, using quotes from participants or the data to illustrate each of the themes and to support your interpretations. It's important to stay flexible, coding is iterative, so review the data constantly and adjust as you go. Be consistent with the code definitions to ensure reliability (create a code book), and if working in teams, discuss the coding and themes to reduce bias.

Coding Examples for Qualitative Methodology and Grounded Theory

Below is an example of a fictional interview transcript followed by a brief demonstration of how to apply qualitative coding methods. The data is a mock interview study exploring employees' experiences in a fictional IT company, AI Technologies.

Participant: Ashley, 32, AI Software Developer at AI Technologies

Interviewer: Hi Ashley, can you tell me how you would describe your experience working at AI Technologies?

Participant: Honestly, it's been a mixed bag. I love to create, love the creative freedom we get – I can experiment with the new coding techniques which is exciting (1), but the workload is insane. I'm often staying late hours and it's exhausting (2). My supervisor is supportive; however, he is always checking in and tries to help (3). But the team communication is not there, there's not a clear direction, and we are always rushing at the last minute (4). I feel like I'm growing as a developer, but I'm also really stressed out (5).

Applying Qualitative Coding to the Data

Step 1: Open Coding

Read through the transcript and assign initial codes to meaningful statements (the numbers reflect the codes from the transcript):

1. "Love the creative freedom" ... "experiment with new coding techniques" >Code: Creative Freedom; "Which is exciting" > Code: Positive Emotion
2. "Workload is insane.... staying late." "exhausting": > Code: Heavy workload; "exhausting" > Code: Negative Emotion
3. "Supervisor is supportive," "always check in," "tries to help"> Code: Supportive Management
4. "Team communication is not there," "no clear direction," "rushing Code: Poor Team Communication
5. Growing as a developer > Code: Professional Growth; "Really stressed out" > Code: Stress

Step 2: Group Codes into Categories

Cluster the codes into broader categories.

- *Work Environment*: Creative freedom, Heavy workload, Poor Team Communication
- *Emotional Impact*: Positive Emotion, Negative Emotion, Stress

- *Support Systems*: Supportive Management
- *Career Development*: Professional Growth

Step 3: Identify the Themes

Refine categories into overarching themes.

- ***Theme 1****: Opportunities and Challenges in the Work Environment*

Combines Creative Freedom and Professional Growth (positive factors) with heavy workload and poor team communication (negative factors)

- ***Theme 2****: Emotional Duality of the Job*

Captures the mix of positive emotion and negative emotion (stress), reflecting Ashley's conflicting feelings.

- ***Theme 3****: Role of Management in Mitigating Challenges*

Highlights supportive management as a buffer against the negative factors of the work environment.

Step 4: Interpretation

Ashley's experience at AI Technologies reveals a workplace with significant growth opportunities but also challenges like poor communication and heavy workloads, leading to a mix of excitement and stress. Supportive management helps, but there exist broader systemic issues that will need to be addressed.

This example illustrates how qualitative coding can break down raw data into meaningful insights.

Grounded Theory Coding Example

Grounded theory aims to generate a theory that is grounded in the data. Coding is completed in the same manner as illustrated in the prior example. However, the theory is directly acquired from the data and is an iterative, inductive process as well. It focuses on discovering the patterns and concepts that emerge from the data rather than testing a pre-existing hypothesis. From the same fictional data (Ashley's interview data), we will illustrate generating a theory from the grounded theory perspective.

Using the same transcript, the ***initial codes*** are:

- Creative Freedom, Positive Emotion
- Heavy Workload, Negative Emotion
- Supportive Management
- Poor Team Communication
- Professional Growth, Stress

Categories:

- Work Environment (Creative Freedom, Heavy Workload, Poor Team Communication)
- Emotional Impact (Positive Emotion, Negative Emotion, Stress)
- Support Systems (Supportive Management)
- Career Development (Professional Growth)

Themes:

- Opportunities and Challenges in the Work Environment,
- Emotional Duality of the Job
- Role of Management in Mitigating Challenges

Grounded Theory Process

Step 1: *Open Coding* (Already Completed)

We have already completed the open coding and identified the initial codes from Ashley's interview data (Creative Freedom, Heavy Workload, Supportive Management).

Step 2: Axial Coding (Identify Relationships between the categories)

In grounded theory, axial codes connect categories to understand the relationships, often using a coding paradigm like:

- Causal Conditions: What causes the phenomenon?
- Phenomenon: The core issue or process
- Context: The setting or conditions influencing the phenomenon.
- Intervening Conditions: Factors that mediate the phenomenon.
- Action/Interaction Strategies: How people respond to the phenomenon.
- Consequences: Outcomes of the strategies

In this case, the:

Phenomenon (Core Category): Emotional Duality in the Workplace. This is the central process – Ashley experiences both excitement and stress, reflecting a dual emotional state.

Causal Conditions:

- Opportunities for growth (creative freedom, professional growth) lead to excitement
- Challenges like Heavy Workload and Poor Team Communication lead to stress.
- Context: AI Technologies, a tech company with a culture of innovation but poor communication structures.

Context: AI Technologies, a culture of innovation but poor communication structure.

Intervening Conditions: Supportive Management acts as a buffer (intervening), reducing stress.

Action/Interaction Strategies: Ashley persists in her role, leveraging creative freedom to grow professionally, but she also endures late nights to manage the workload.

Consequences: Mixed outcomes: Professional growth (positive) but also exhaustion and stress (negative)

Step 3: ***Selective Coding*** – Integrate and Refine the Theory

Selective coding focuses on the core category (Emotional Duality in the workplace) and builds a story around it. We integrate the relationships in axial coding to form a cohesive theory.

Emerging Theory: The Theory of Emotional Duality in High Innovation Workplaces

In high innovation workplaces like AI Technologies, employees experience emotional duality (excitement and stress) due to tension between opportunities for creativity and systemic challenges like poor communication and heavy workloads. Supportive management acts as a critical mediator, enabling professional growth but not fully resolving stress, leading to a cycle of growth and exhaustion.

Step 4: Theoretical Sampling (Simulated)

In grounded theory, you will collect more data to refine the theory. For example, Interview other employees at AI Technologies to see if emotional duality is a shared experience or explore other companies to compare. You may ask if other employees feel the same tension between creativity and stress, or what other factors may influence this duality?

Step 5: Reach Theoretical Saturation

Saturation occurs when new data no longer adds to the theory. That means you are getting the same answers time after time. If more interviews confirm that emotional duality is driven by innovation opportunities versus systemic challenges, and management mediates the experience, the theory is solidified.

Step 6: Validate and Refine the Theory

Compare the theory to existing literature of studies on workplace stress or innovation to see where it fits or diverges. For example, this theory aligns with research on the dual nature of creative work but adds the role of management as a mediator in technical field settings.

Final Grounded Theory

Theory: In high-innovation tech workplaces, employees experience emotional duality – a cycle of excitement from creative opportunities and stress from systemic challenges like poor communication and heavy workloads. Supportive management mediates this duality, enabling professional growth but not fully alleviating stress, resulting in a persistent tension between growth and exhaustion. This theory could guide future research or interventions, like improving communication processes to reduce stress while preserving innovation.

Practice Lab 10.1: Basic Content Analysis in Information Systems Research

Lab Title

"Identifying Themes in Scholarly Research: A Content Analysis Exercise"

Learning Objectives

By the end of this lab, students will be able to:

- Conduct a basic content analysis of peer-reviewed journal articles.
- Identify recurring concepts and themes.
- Present thematic findings relevant to their research interest.

Instructions

1 **Download Three Peer-Reviewed Articles**
   - Choose three recent scholarly articles (within the last 5 years) in your specific research area (e.g., FinTech, AI in healthcare, digital transformation, cybersecurity, etc.).
   - Articles must come from reputable journals (AIS, IEEE, Elsevier, Springer, etc.).

2 **Read and Annotate**
   - Focus on the abstract, introduction, literature review, and discussion sections.
   - Highlight key terms, recurring ideas, concepts, or frameworks.

3 **Conduct a Basic Content Analysis**
   - Manually code the articles to identify **keywords** and **concepts**.
   - Group similar codes into **themes or categories**.

4 **Summarize Thematic Findings**
   - Identify 2–4 major themes that emerge across all three articles.
   - Use direct quotes or paraphrased content to support each theme.

5 **Prepare a Short Presentation (5–7 minutes)**
Include:

- Article titles and sources.
- Brief summary of each article.
- Explanation of identified themes.
- Reflection on how these themes relate to your own research interests.

Deliverables

- A 1–2 page thematic summary (bullet points or paragraph format).
- In-class or online presentation of your findings.

Focus Group Research in Information Systems

Focus groups are a qualitative research method involving moderated group discussions with 6–12 participants to explore shared perspectives, attitudes, or experiences (Krueger & Casey, 2015). In IS, focus groups are characterized by their interactive nature, allowing participants to build on each other's responses, generating rich, collective insights. They differ from individual interviews by emphasizing group dynamics and are distinct from content analysis by focusing on verbal, interactive data rather than static texts (Morgan, 1997). Focus groups are particularly effective for exploring IS topics like user acceptance, system design feedback, or organizational technology adoption.

Purpose and Objectives of Focus Group Studies in Information Systems

Focus groups in IS aim to capture collective insights into technology-related phenomena, such as user perceptions of system usability or group dynamics in IT implementation (Krueger & Casey, 2015). Objectives include exploring diverse viewpoints, identifying consensus or conflict, and generating hypotheses for further study. For example, a focus group with IT managers might explore barriers to cloud adoption, revealing shared concerns about security or costs (Myers, 2013). Focus groups are often used in exploratory phases of IS research or to complement methods like content analysis, providing contextual depth to textual findings (Morgan, 1997).

Advantages and Limitations of Focus Group Methodology

Advantages include the ability to capture diverse perspectives, stimulate discussion through group dynamics, and generate rich qualitative data in a short time (Krueger & Casey, 2015). In IS, focus groups are cost-effective for gathering feedback from multiple stakeholders, such as end-users and developers discussing a new system. Limitations include the risk of groupthink, where dominant voices suppress others, and challenges in managing diverse opinions (Morgan, 1997). Logistical issues, such as coordinating schedules or ensuring digital access in virtual focus groups, can also arise, particularly in global IS studies (Myers & Newman, 2007) (Table 10.1).

Table 10.1 Focus Group Methodology: Advantages and Limitations

Aspect	*Advantages*	*Limitations*
Data Richness	Enables in-depth discussion and exploration of complex IS topics through dynamic interaction (Kruger & Casey, 2015; Morgan, 1997; Myers & Newman (2007)	Risk of shallow insights if group dynamics hinder open sharing or if dominant participants steer the conversation (Morgan, 1997)
Efficiency	Gathers multiple perspectives quickly in a single session, making it more time- and cost-efficient than one-on-one interviews.(Morgan, 1997)	Logistical challenges in scheduling participants and moderating the session effectively (Myers & Newman, 2007)
Idea Generation	Promotes brainstorming and uncovering of unexpected themes through participant interaction (Morgan, 1997)	Groupthink can suppress unique or minority viewpoints.(Morgan, 1997)
Contextual Understanding	Provides contextual insights into user behavior, system adoption, or organizational processes.(Myers & Newman, 2007)	Findings are not statistically generalizable due to small, non-random samples. (Morgan, 1997)
Exploratory Power	Useful for hypothesis generation and early-stage exploration in IS studies (e.g., tech adoption, UX design).(Morgan, 1997)	Limited ability to test hypotheses or provide conclusive evidence. (Morgan, 1997)
Flexibility	Can be adapted for different stakeholders (e.g., users, IT staff, managers) and platforms (e.g., in-person, online) (Myers & Newman, 2007)	Virtual focus groups may reduce non-verbal cue interpretation and participant engagement. (Myers & Newman, 2007)
Participant Validation	Participants can confirm, reject, or refine each other's views, improving the credibility of findings. (Gibbs, 1997)	Sensitive topics may be avoided in a group setting due to social desirability bias. (Gibbs, 1997)
Complementarity	Can complement quantitative studies by explaining trends or survey results. (Morgan, 1997; Myers & Newman, 2007)	Data analysis is time-consuming and may be subject to researcher bias. (Myers & Newman, 2007)

Planning, Designing, and Conducting Focus Groups

Designing focus group sessions involves determining the structure, duration, and facilitation approach. Sessions typically last 1–2 hours to maintain engagement and cover 5–10 open-ended questions to spark discussion (Krueger & Casey, 2015). For example, an IS study on user experiences with a collaboration tool might ask, "What challenges do you face when using this tool in team projects?" The structure should include an introduction, warm-up questions, core discussion topics, and a closing summary. In digital settings, platforms like Zoom require additional planning, such as ensuring clear audio and breakout rooms for smaller discussions (Salmons, 2015).

Conducting Focus Groups

Conducting focus groups requires a skilled moderator to guide discussions, encourage participation, and manage group dynamics (Morgan, 1997). In IS, moderators should be familiar with the technology context to probe relevant issues, such as asking follow-ups about specific system features. Sessions should be recorded (with consent) and transcribed for analysis, using thematic or grounded theory-inspired coding to identify patterns (Charmaz, 2014). Virtual focus groups demand additional attention to technical reliability and participant comfort, such as providing clear instructions for joining (Salmons, 2015).

Future Trends and Innovations in Content Analysis and Focus Group Research

Advances in Text Analysis Software and Tools

Advancements in text analysis software, such as NVivo, MAXQDA, and Atlas.ti, have transformed content analysis and focus group research in IS by automating coding, visualizing patterns, and handling large datasets (Myers, 2013). These tools support quantitative content analysis by calculating word frequencies or sentiment scores and qualitative analysis by organizing themes. For focus groups, software can transcribe and analyze discussions, reducing manual effort. However, researchers must ensure tools complement, rather than drive, the interpretive process (Krippendorff, 2018).

Integration of AI and Machine Learning in Content Analysis

AI and machine learning (ML) are revolutionizing content analysis by enabling automated topic modeling, sentiment analysis, and natural language processing (NLP) (Saldanha & Sahay, 2013). In IS, tools like Python's NLTK or Google's Cloud Natural Language can analyze massive datasets, such as social media posts about a new software release, to identify trends or emotions. ML algorithms can also support coding by suggesting categories, though human oversight is critical to ensure contextual accuracy (Neuendorf, 2017). For focus groups, AI-driven transcription tools (e.g., Otter.ai) enhance efficiency but raise privacy concerns, requiring secure data handling (Salmons, 2015).

Emerging Applications and Methodological Innovations

Emerging applications in IS include using content analysis to study real-time data streams, such as live tweets during a product launch, or analyzing multimodal data (e.g., videos, emojis) for richer insights (Krippendorff, 2018). Focus groups are increasingly conducted in virtual reality (VR) environments to simulate collaborative IS settings, such as virtual team meetings, enhancing immersion (Saldanha & Sahay, 2013). Methodological innovations include integrating content.

Chapter Summary

This chapter introduced content analysis and focus groups as key qualitative methods used in IS research. Both methods enable researchers to explore complex phenomena related to technology, user experiences, and organizational contexts. Content Analysis is described as a systematic approach for examining communication artifacts such as social media posts, documents, and system logs to uncover patterns, themes, and meanings. The chapter distinguishes between three types of content analysis:

- Quantitative (e.g., keyword frequency),
- Qualitative (e.g., interpretation of user sentiment), and
- Mixed-methods, which blends both approaches for more comprehensive insights.

Steps in conducting content analysis are outlined, including planning, selecting data sources, choosing sampling techniques, applying coding schemes, and analyzing data. A detailed explanation of the coding process is provided, covering open coding, category formation, and theme identification. A fictional example illustrates how raw data can be transformed into meaningful insights through qualitative coding and grounded theory. Grounded Theory, as an inductive approach, is emphasized for its capacity to develop theory from data. Through axial and selective coding, researchers connect concepts and categories to form a theoretical model. The chapter showcases how grounded theory differs from traditional content analysis by focusing on theory generation rather than testing pre-existing hypotheses.

Focus Groups are presented as a complementary qualitative technique. By fostering interactive group discussions, focus groups offer collective perspectives on IS topics such as system usability and technology adoption. The chapter discusses how to design and manage focus group research – including virtual formats – and how to analyze the group data thematically. The chapter concludes by exploring emerging trends, including AI-driven content analysis and the use of VR for focus group facilitation. These advancements promise to extend the reach and analytical power of IS research. Through definitions, examples, and methodological guidance, this chapter equips IS scholars with practical tools to apply content analysis and focus groups effectively in their research.

Review Questions

1 Explain the differences between quantitative, qualitative, and mixed-methods content analysis in the context of IS research. Provide an example of an IS research topic (e.g., user sentiment toward a new software) where a mixed-methods content analysis would be more appropriate than a purely quantitative or qualitative approach, and justify your choice.
2 How can content analysis be applied to study user-generated content in IS, such as social media posts about a new technology? Discuss the steps involved in designing and conducting a content analysis study for this purpose, including data source selection and coding procedures.
3 Compare the advantages and limitations of focus group research with content analysis in IS studies. For an IS research topic, such as exploring team dynamics in agile software development, when might a focus group be more suitable than content analysis, and why?
4 Discuss the role of AI and ML in enhancing content analysis in IS research. What are the benefits and potential challenges of using tools like NLP to analyze large datasets, such as system logs or online reviews, and how can researchers ensure contextual accuracy?
5 Describe the process of designing and conducting a virtual focus group session to explore employee perceptions of a new collaboration tool in an IS context. How can researchers manage group dynamics and technical challenges in a digital setting, and what strategies can ensure participant engagement?

References

Charmaz, K. (2014). *Constructing Grounded Theory* (2nd ed.). SAGE Publications.
Hsieh, H.-F., & Shannon, S. E. (2005). Three approaches to qualitative content analysis. *Qualitative Health Research, 15*(9), 1277–1288. https://doi.org/10.1177/1049732305276687
Krippendorff, K. (2018). *Content Analysis: An Introduction to Its Methodology* (4th ed.). SAGE Publications.
Krueger, R. A., & Casey, M. A. (2015). *Focus Groups: A Practical Guide for Applied Research* (5th ed.). SAGE Publications.
Morgan, D. L. (1997). *Focus Groups as Qualitative Research* (2nd ed.). SAGE Publications.
Myers, M. D. (2013). *Qualitative Research in Business and Management* (2nd ed.). SAGE Publications.
Myers, M. D., & Newman, M. (2007). The qualitative interview in IS research. *Examining the craft. Information and Organization, 17*(1), 2–26. https://doi.org/10.1016/j.infoandorg.2006.11.001
Neuendorf, K. A. (2017). *The Content Analysis Guidebook* (2nd ed.). SAGE Publications.
Saldanha, G., & Sahay, S. (2013). Social media as a research environment: The rise of the digital agora. *European Journal of Information Systems, 22*(6), 671–684. https://doi.org/10.1057/ejis.2013.25
Salmons, J. (2015). *Qualitative Online Interviews: Strategies, Design, and Skills* (2nd ed.). SAGE Publications.
Urquhart, C. (2013). *Grounded Theory for Qualitative Research: A Practical Guide*. SAGE Publications.

11 Impact of Emerging Technologies on Qualitative Research in Information Systems Domain

Chapter Objectives

After reading this chapter, readers should understand:

- Digital Transformation in Qualitative Research
- Digital Tools for Qualitative Research
- Emerging Technologies in Qualitative Methods
- Advanced Tools for Qualitative Research

Digital Transformation in Qualitative Research

The rapid evolution of digital technologies has profoundly transformed qualitative research in information systems (IS), enabling researchers to collect, analyze, and interpret data in innovative ways. Digital tools and platforms have expanded the scope, scale, and accessibility of qualitative methods, offering new opportunities to explore complex IS phenomena such as user behavior, technology adoption, and organizational dynamics (Myers, 2013). From social media analysis to virtual reality (VR)-based ethnographies, digital transformation has reshaped traditional approaches like interviews, content analysis, and focus groups, while introducing novel methodologies like mobile ethnography. This chapter examines how digital tools enhance qualitative data collection, explores emerging methods such as digital ethnography, social media analysis, and virtual focus groups, and discusses the integration of AI, multimedia, VR, augmented reality (AR), and mobile technologies in IS research. It also addresses opportunities and challenges, providing a roadmap for leveraging digital transformation to advance qualitative IS scholarship.

Leveraging Digital Tools for Data Collection in Qualitative Studies

Digital tools have revolutionized qualitative data collection in IS by enabling remote, scalable, and efficient methods. Platforms like Zoom, Microsoft Teams, and Qualtrics facilitate interviews and surveys, while social media and

DOI: 10.4324/9781003545521-13

messaging apps (e.g., Twitter, WhatsApp) support participant recruitment and asynchronous data collection (Salmons, 2015). Software such as NVivo and MAXQDA streamlines coding and thematic analysis, enhancing rigor and transparency (Myers, 2013). These tools allow researchers to access diverse, global populations, such as remote workers or online communities, and capture real-time data from system logs or user interactions. For example, a study on cloud computing adoption might use Qualtrics to collect user feedback across organizations, complementing grounded theory's iterative approach (Charmaz, 2014). However, challenges include ensuring data security, managing technical disruptions, and addressing digital literacy disparities, which require careful ethical and methodological planning (Kvale & Brinkmann, 2015).

Digital Ethnography: Exploring Virtual Communities and Online Environments

Digital ethnography, also known as netnography, involves immersive observation of virtual communities and online environments to understand social and technological interactions (Kozinets, 2015). In IS, it is used to study online platforms, such as open-source software communities on GitHub or user forums on Reddit, capturing naturalistic behaviors in digital spaces. Researchers engage through participant observation, analyzing posts, comments, or interactions to identify cultural patterns or user sentiments (Hine, 2015). For instance, a digital ethnography of a cybersecurity forum might reveal user concerns about data breaches, informing IS security strategies. Unlike traditional ethnography, digital ethnography leverages digital traces (e.g., forum threads) for analysis, aligning with content analysis methods (Krippendorff, 2018). Challenges include navigating ethical issues like consent in public online spaces and managing large, unstructured datasets (Kozinets, 2015).

Social Media Analysis: Mining Insights from User-generated Content

Social media analysis involves extracting insights from user-generated content on platforms like Twitter, LinkedIn, or YouTube, using techniques like content analysis or sentiment analysis (Saldanha & Sahay, 2013). In IS, it is used to study public perceptions of technologies, such as AI ethics or software usability, by analyzing posts, comments, or hashtags. Quantitative approaches count frequencies (e.g., mentions of "privacy" in tweets about a new app), while qualitative approaches explore themes, such as user trust in system updates (Neuendorf, 2017). Tools like Python's NLTK or Hootsuite Insights automate data collection and analysis, enhancing scalability. For example, analyzing Twitter discussions about blockchain adoption can reveal stakeholder priorities, complementing focus group findings (Myers, 2013). Challenges include data noise, sampling biases, and ethical concerns like user privacy, requiring transparent data handling practices (Saldanha & Sahay, 2013).

Virtual Focus Groups: Engaging Participants in Remote Settings

Virtual focus groups, conducted via platforms like Zoom or Microsoft Teams, enable interactive discussions with geographically dispersed participants, making them ideal for IS research on global or remote teams (Krueger & Casey, 2015). They retain the interactive nature of traditional focus groups, capturing group dynamics and collective perspectives on topics like user acceptance of collaboration tools. For example, a virtual focus group with information technology professionals might explore barriers to cloud migration, generating hypotheses for further study (Salmons, 2015). Designing virtual sessions requires structured protocols, clear technical instructions, and skilled moderation to manage dynamics and ensure engagement (Morgan, 1997). Advantages include cost-efficiency and accessibility, while limitations include technical disruptions and reduced nonverbal cues, necessitating strategies like breakout rooms or pre-session tech checks (Krueger & Casey, 2015).

AI and Machine Learning in Qualitative Analysis: Opportunities and Challenges

AI and machine learning (ML) are transforming qualitative analysis in IS by automating tasks like coding, sentiment analysis, and topic modeling. Tools like Google's Cloud Natural Language or IBM Watson can analyze large datasets, such as user reviews or system logs, to identify themes or emotions, reducing manual effort (Saldanha & Sahay, 2013). In IS, artificial intelligence (AI) supports content analysis by suggesting codes or clustering similar responses, complementing grounded theory's inductive approach (Charmaz, 2014). For example, ML algorithms can analyze employee feedback on a new ERP system to identify adoption barriers. Opportunities include scalability and efficiency, but challenges include ensuring contextual accuracy, as AI may misinterpret nuanced meanings, and ethical concerns like data privacy (Neuendorf, 2017). Human oversight remains critical to validate AI-generated insights and maintain rigor (Krippendorff, 2018).

Multimedia Data Analysis: Incorporating Audio, Video, and Images in Research

Multimedia data analysis involves examining audio, video, or images to uncover insights in IS research, such as user interactions with interfaces or organizational communication patterns. For instance, analyzing video tutorials on a software platform can reveal usability issues, while images from social media may reflect user sentiments about a product launch (Krippendorff, 2018). Tools like Adobe Premiere for video analysis or NVivo for multimedia coding support this process, enabling researchers to integrate multimodal data with textual analysis (Myers, 2013). This approach extends content analysis by capturing nonverbal cues, such as tone or visual context, but requires specialized skills and raises ethical issues like consent for multimedia use (Hine, 2015). In IS, multimedia analysis enriches studies of digital experiences, such as user engagement with virtual assistants.

Virtual Reality (VR) and Augmented Reality (AR) in Immersive Qualitative Research

VR and AR technologies create immersive environments for qualitative IS research, simulating real-world or digital settings to study user behavior. VR can replicate a virtual office to observe team interactions with collaboration tools, while AR overlays digital information to study mobile app usage in physical contexts (Saldanha & Sahay, 2013). For example, a VR-based study might explore how developers interact in a simulated agile development environment, capturing naturalistic data. These methods extend digital ethnography by offering controlled, immersive settings, but they require significant resources and technical expertise (Hine, 2015). Ethical challenges include ensuring participant comfort in immersive spaces and managing data privacy, particularly with biometric data collected in VR (Salmons, 2015).

Mobile Ethnography: Studying Digital Behavior in Real-time Contexts

Mobile ethnography involves using smartphones or wearable devices to collect real-time data on user behavior in natural settings, such as app usage or location-based interactions (Kozinets, 2015). In IS, it is used to study mobile banking, fitness apps, or IoT device interactions, capturing in-the-moment experiences via diaries, photos, or GPS data. For example, a mobile ethnography study might ask users to log their interactions with a payment app, revealing usability challenges (Hine, 2015). This method aligns with grounded theory's iterative data collection, allowing emergent themes to guide further study (Charmaz, 2014). Advantages include real-time, contextual insights, but challenges include participant burden, data overload, and ethical concerns like geolocation privacy (Kozinets, 2015).

Advances in Qualitative Data Analysis Software

In recent years, qualitative data analysis (QDA) software has evolved significantly, reflecting broader technological shifts, researcher needs, and methodological innovations. Modern QDA tools are far more than basic coding platforms; they now offer features that streamline data preparation, enhance analysis, foster collaboration, and integrate advanced analytics. Key advances include:

1. **AI-Assisted Coding and Thematic Discovery:**
   Many platforms now incorporate ML and natural language processing (NLP) algorithms.

- **Automated Coding Suggestions:** The software can scan transcripts and suggest potential codes or themes, speeding up early analysis and reducing the time spent on manual coding.
- **Topic Modeling and Semantic Analysis:** Built-in algorithms identify clusters of related concepts and patterns in large text corpora, helping researchers notice emergent themes that might otherwise be overlooked.

2 **Enhanced Multimodal Analysis:**
As qualitative data increasingly include images, videos, social media content, and audio recordings, QDA tools have expanded beyond text-based analysis.

- **Integrated Transcription:** Automated, high-accuracy transcription services are now commonly embedded, allowing researchers to quickly convert audio or video content into searchable text.
- **Image and Video Coding:** Some software supports direct coding of visual elements, linking notes or codes to specific frames or image segments.
- **Integration with Social Media and Online Data:** Direct import and analysis of tweets, forum posts, or other web-based data streams are increasingly supported.

3 **Cloud-Based and Collaborative Environments:**
Cloud computing has transformed how researchers work with QDA software.

- **Real-Time Collaboration:** Teams can work simultaneously on shared projects, coding data, refining themes, and generating reports together, even when geographically dispersed.
- **Version Control and Audit Trails:** Cloud platforms maintain detailed histories of coding and analytic decisions, improving transparency and trustworthiness.
- **Data Security and Scalability:** Secure cloud infrastructures enable handling of large, complex data sets while ensuring data integrity and privacy.

4 **User-Friendly Interfaces and Customization:**
Advances in UX (User Experience) design have made QDA software more intuitive and adaptive.

- **Drag-and-Drop Functionalities:** More user-friendly dashboards and drag-and-drop coding features streamline the learning curve for new users.
- **Flexible Coding Schemes and Visualizations:** Enhanced data visualization tools (e.g., word clouds, conceptual maps, cluster diagrams) help researchers see connections between codes and themes at a glance.
- **Custom Queries and Smart Filters:** Researchers can easily craft complex queries to explore relationships among themes, demographic variables, or time-based events.

5 **Integration with Other Research Tools and Data Sources:**
Modern QDA software often works seamlessly with other platforms that researchers use.

- **Reference Manager Integration:** Direct connections to tools like Zotero, Mendeley, or EndNote allow quick import of relevant literature for context building.
- **Export to Statistical Packages:** For mixed-methods projects, qualitative findings can be exported to tools like SPSS, R, or Excel for further quantitative examination.
- **APIs and Custom Scripting:** Some platforms provide application programming interfaces (APIs) or options to use Python or R, enabling advanced customization and analysis workflows.

6 **Support for Longitudinal and Big Qualitative Data:**
As research projects span longer time frames and incorporate larger data sets, software vendors have responded by improving performance and features for big qualitative data.

- **Efficient Data Handling:** Improved indexing and search capabilities speed up navigation and retrieval even in massive projects.
- **Longitudinal Tracking:** Enhanced time-based coding and annotation features help researchers compare how themes evolve across different phases of the study.

7 **Training, Community, and Support:**
Tool developers increasingly offer robust support ecosystems.

- **Online Learning Resources:** Video tutorials, webinars, and community forums aid researchers in mastering advanced features.
- **Methodological Guidance:** Some platforms include built-in guides or templates for specific qualitative approaches (e.g., grounded theory, narrative analysis), helping researchers maintain methodological rigor.

Current advances in qualitative data analysis software (QDAS) reflect a convergence of methodological flexibility, technological sophistication, and user-centered design. AI-driven coding assistance, multimodal data handling, real-time collaboration, richer visualization tools, and seamless integration with other research platforms empower qualitative researchers to work more efficiently, creatively, and transparently. As qualitative inquiry grows in complexity and scale, QDA software will continue to evolve, offering even more powerful capabilities to help researchers derive meaningful insights from diverse, rapidly expanding data sources.

Qualitative Data Analysis Software (QDAS)

QDAS refers to specialized tools that assist researchers in organizing, coding, analyzing, and interpreting qualitative data – such as interview transcripts, field notes, images, and video recordings. While these tools do not replace the researcher's interpretive expertise, they streamline the data management process, facilitate systematic analysis, and offer features like search, retrieval, visualization, and reporting. Below are some well-known QDA software options and their key characteristics.

NVivo

Overview: NVivo is one of the most widely used qualitative data analysis programs. Developed by Lumivero (formerly QSR International), it supports a broad range of data types, including text, images, audio, video, and even social media and web content.

Key Features:

- **Automated Coding Assistance:** NLP-driven auto-coding features suggest initial themes.
- **Advanced Queries and Visualizations:** Tools for exploring relationships between codes, running matrix queries, and visualizing data in charts, maps, and word clouds.
- **Team Collaboration:** NVivo Teams or NVivo Collaboration Cloud support distributed teams working on the same dataset.

ATLAS.ti

Overview: ATLAS.ti is a comprehensive qualitative analysis platform known for its versatile and user-friendly interface. It handles various data formats and is suitable for both large and small projects.

Key Features:

- **Flexible Coding:** Easily organize and link codes, memos, and quotations.
- **Network Views:** Powerful visualization tools let you create conceptual maps to show relationships between concepts.
- **Mixed Methods Integration:** Support for quantifying code occurrences and integrating basic statistical insights.

MAXQDA

Overview: MAXQDA by VERBI Software is a robust, versatile tool that supports multiple languages and is known for its intuitive interface and strong visualization capabilities.

Key Features:

- **Multimodal Support:** Handle text, PDF, images, video, surveys, social media data, and more.

- **Document Comparison:** Easily compare documents, track coding frequencies, and visualize overlaps.
- **Built-In Mixed Methods Tools:** Incorporate simple quantitative analyses, code frequencies, and statistical tables.

Dedoose

Overview: Dedoose is a cloud-based, subscription-based QDA platform that appeals to researchers looking for accessibility and collaborative features.

Key Features:

- **Web-Based:** Access the platform from any internet-connected device without installing software.
- **Team-Friendly Environment:** Real-time collaboration for multiple researchers working simultaneously.
- **Mixed Methods Emphasis:** Offers integrated tools for linking qualitative codes to quantitative data (e.g., demographic variables).

QDA Miner

Overview: QDA Miner, developed by Provalis Research, focuses on powerful text analysis and content analysis capabilities. It can be combined with WordStat, a quantitative content analysis module, to handle large datasets.

Key Features:

- **Advanced Text Analysis:** Integrate with WordStat for text mining, keyword extraction, and topic modeling.
- **Customizable Coding Schemes:** Flexible coding structures and easy retrieval of coded segments.
- **Statistical Integration:** Supports basic statistical techniques for quantitative-qualitative integration.

HyperRESEARCH

Overview: HyperRESEARCH has been a longstanding tool in QDA, offering a straightforward interface and core qualitative analysis features.

Key Features:

- **Straightforward Coding Interface:** Ideal for researchers who need essential coding, memoing, and retrieval functions.
- **Cross-Platform Compatibility:** Runs on Windows, macOS, and Linux.
- **Simple Interoperability:** Export and import options for integrating with other software or sharing data.

Quirkos

Overview: Quirkos is a more recent entrant focused on simplicity, accessibility, and data visualization. Its colorful, bubble-based interface appeals to novice users and small projects. Quirkos includes help tutorials and user friendly with low learning curve.

Key Features:

- **Interactive Visual Interface**: Codes appear as interactive "bubbles" that grow in size as data is coded, providing immediate visual feedback.
- **Easy Learning Curve**: Designed for researchers new to QDA software.
- **Cross-Platform and Cloud Options**: Works on multiple operating systems and offers cloud-based access.

Choosing the Right Tool

Considerations:

- **Data Types**: Some tools handle diverse data (audio, video, social media) more smoothly than others.
- **Project Complexity**: Large, multi-researcher projects might benefit from advanced collaboration features.
- **Analysis Depth**: Researchers aiming for sophisticated text analytics or integration with quantitative data might lean towards tools with advanced queries, NLP capabilities, or mixed methods features.
- **User-Friendliness and Support**: Ease of use, the availability of tutorials, customer support, and community forums can influence choice.

The landscape of QDAS has expanded and matured, offering tools that not only streamline the coding process but also integrate advanced analytics, artificial intelligence, visualization, and collaborative functionality. By selecting the tool that best aligns with their project's scope, data format, methodological approach, and team structure, qualitative researchers can substantially enhance the efficiency, rigor, and creativity of their analytic process.

Chapter Summary

Digital transformation has revolutionized qualitative research in IS, offering innovative tools and methods to explore technology-driven phenomena. Digital ethnography, social media analysis, and virtual focus groups leverage online platforms to capture diverse, real-world insights, while AI, multimedia analysis, VR, AR, and mobile ethnography push methodological boundaries.

These approaches enhance the flexibility, scalability, and depth of qualitative IS research, complementing traditional methods like grounded theory and content analysis. However, challenges such as data privacy, technical disruptions, and the need for human oversight require careful consideration. By embracing these digital advancements while maintaining methodological rigor and ethical standards, IS researchers can generate robust, contextually rich theories that advance our understanding of technology's role in human and organizational contexts.

Review Questions

- How has digital transformation influenced the methodologies used in qualitative IS research?
- What are the advantages and limitations of using digital ethnography in virtual communities?
- In what ways can social media analysis contribute to understanding user behavior in IS contexts?
- Describe the benefits and challenges of conducting virtual focus groups in qualitative research.
- How do AI and ML support qualitative data analysis, and what ethical concerns arise?
- What role does multimedia data play in enriching qualitative insights in IS research?
- How can VR and AR be used to simulate immersive qualitative research environments?
- Explain the concept of mobile ethnography and its application in studying real-time user behavior.
- What are the key features of modern QDAS (e.g., NVivo, MAXQDA)?
- Discuss the ethical and methodological considerations researchers must address when using digital tools for qualitative IS studies

References

Charmaz, K. (2014). *Constructing Grounded Theory* (2nd ed.). SAGE Publications.

Hine, C. (2015). *Ethnography for the Internet: Embedded, Embodied and Everyday*. Bloomsbury Academic.

Kozinets, R. V. (2015). *Netnography: Redefined* (2nd ed.). SAGE Publications.

Krippendorff, K. (2018). *Content Analysis: An Introduction to Its Methodology* (4th ed.). SAGE Publications.

Krueger, R. A., & Casey, M. A. (2015). *Focus Groups: A Practical Guide for Applied Research* (5th ed.). SAGE Publications.

Kvale, S., & Brinkmann, S. (2015). *Interviews: Learning the Craft of Qualitative Research Interviewing* (3rd ed.). SAGE Publications.

Morgan, D. L. (1997). *Focus Groups as Qualitative Research* (2nd ed.). SAGE Publications.

Myers, M. D. (2013). *Qualitative Research in Business and Management* (2nd ed.). SAGE Publications.
Neuendorf, K. A. (2017). *The Content Analysis Guidebook* (2nd ed.). SAGE Publications.
Saldanha, G., & Sahay, S. (2013). Social media as a research environment: The rise of the digital agora. *European Journal of Information Systems, 22*(6), 671–684. https://doi.org/10.1057/ejis.2013.25
Salmons, J. (2015). *Qualitative Online Interviews: Strategies, Design, and Skills* (2nd ed.). SAGE Publications.

12 Publication Process and Strategies in Qualitative Information Systems Research

Chapter Objectives

After reading this chapter, readers should understand:

- Publishing Qualitative Research in Information Systems
- Selecting Journals, Conferences, and the Publication Research Process
- Preparing Manuscript
- Ethics & Peer Review Processes

Publishing Qualitative Research in Information Systems

Introduction

Publishing qualitative research in information systems (IS) is a critical step in disseminating knowledge about complex, technology-driven phenomena, such as user behavior, system adoption, and organizational dynamics. The publication process involves navigating journal selection, manuscript preparation, peer review, and ethical considerations, all while ensuring the research's impact and visibility. Qualitative IS research, often employing methods like grounded theory, content analysis, or focus groups, requires distinct strategies to meet rigorous academic standards and appeal to diverse audiences (Myers, 2013). This chapter provides a comprehensive guide to the publication process, offering practical strategies for selecting journals, preparing manuscripts, addressing reviewer feedback, and leveraging open access (OA) and interdisciplinary outlets. It also explores future trends, such as digital publishing innovations, to equip IS researchers with tools to enhance the reach and influence of their qualitative work.

DOI: 10.4324/9781003545521-14

Overview of the Publication Process in Qualitative Information Systems Research

The publication process in qualitative IS research involves several stages: conceptualizing the study, conducting research, writing the manuscript, selecting a journal, submitting the paper, navigating peer review, revising as needed, and publishing the final article (Davison & Martinsons, 2011). Qualitative research, with its emphasis on rich, contextual insights, requires careful alignment with journal expectations, as IS journals often prioritize methodological rigor and theoretical contributions (Myers, 2013). For example, a grounded theory study on cloud computing adoption must articulate its emergent theory clearly to meet the standards of journals like *MIS Quarterly*. The process is iterative, involving multiple revisions to refine arguments and address feedback. Researchers must also consider ethical transparency and the potential impact of their work, ensuring findings resonate with academic and practitioner audiences (Walsham, 1995) (Table 12.1).

Table 12.1 Qualitative Research Publication Process and Strategies for Success

Step	*Explanation*	*Strategies for Success*
1. Conceptualizing the Study (Myers, 2013)	Defining the research problem, theoretical framing, and methodology appropriate for qualitative inquiry.	• Identify a compelling and underexplored IS phenomenon. • Conduct a literature gap analysis. • Choose a qualitative approach that aligns with your research question (e.g., case study, grounded theory).
2. Conducting the Research (Myers, 2013; Walsham, 1995)	Collecting and analyzing qualitative data through interviews, observations, or document analysis.	• Ensure data saturation and triangulation. • Maintain detailed field notes and memos. • Use qualitative software (e.g., NVivo, ATLAS.ti) to manage data systematically.
3. Writing the Manuscript (Myers, 2013)	Crafting the paper with clear sections: introduction, literature review, methodology, findings, discussion, and conclusion.	• Emphasize theoretical contribution and methodological rigor. • Include rich, contextual narratives. • Follow journal-specific style guides.
4. Selecting a Journal (Davison & Martinsons, 2011)	Choosing an academic journal that aligns with your topic, methodology, and contribution.	• Review journal scopes and recent publications. • Target journals known for publishing qualitative IS research (e.g., MISQ, JAIS, EJIS). • Assess the impact factor and audience.

(Continued)

Table 12.1 (Continued)

Step	*Explanation*	*Strategies for Success*
5. Submitting the Paper (Davison & Martinsons, 2011)	Uploading the manuscript and supplementary materials to the journal's submission portal.	• Follow submission guidelines exactly. • Include a strong cover letter highlighting contribution and fit. • Use ethical disclosure statements where required.
6. Navigating Peer Review (Myers, 2013)	Receiving feedback from reviewers and editors; addressing critiques related to theoretical clarity, methodological validity, or contribution.	• Read feedback carefully and unemotionally. • Identify common concerns across reviewers. • Acknowledge limitations transparently in your revision.
7. Revising the Manuscript (Davison & Martinsons, 2011; Myers, 2013)	Making changes based on reviewer feedback and preparing a detailed response document.	• Prepare a point-by-point response letter. • Justify changes with references where appropriate. • Maintain a professional tone in rebuttal.
8. Publishing the Article (Walsham, 1995)	Final acceptance, copyediting, and online publication.	• Review proofs carefully for errors. • Promote your publication via academic networks and social media. • Consider translating insights for practitioner outlets.

Selecting the Right Journal: Strategies for Identifying Suitable Outlets

Choosing an appropriate journal is a critical decision that shapes a study's visibility and impact. Researchers should consider the journal's scope, audience, and methodological preferences (Davison & Martinsons, 2011). Strategies include:

- **Review Journal Aims and Scope:** Examine journals like *Information Systems Research* or *Journal of Information Technology* to ensure alignment with qualitative IS topics, such as user experience or digital transformation (Myers, 2013).
- **Assess Methodological Fit:** Some journals, like *European Journal of Information Systems*, are receptive to qualitative methods, including grounded theory or ethnography, while others may favor quantitative approaches (Walsham, 1995).
- **Evaluate Impact and Reach:** Use metrics like Journal Impact Factor or SCImago Journal Rank, but prioritize journals with strong IS readership, such as *MIS Quarterly* or *Information & Organization* (Davison & Martinsons, 2011).

- **Consult Recent Issues:** Analyze recent articles to confirm the journal publishes qualitative IS research, such as case studies or focus group studies, and to identify relevant editors or reviewers (Myers, 2013).

  For example, a study on social media analytics might target *Information Systems Journal* for its qualitative focus and IS relevance. Tools like Elsevier's Journal Finder or Springer's Journal Suggester can assist in identifying suitable outlets.

Manuscript Preparation: Writing Techniques and Formatting Guidelines

Effective manuscript preparation is essential to communicate qualitative IS research clearly and persuasively. Writing techniques include:

- **Craft a Compelling Narrative:** Structure the manuscript to tell a coherent story, integrating rich qualitative data (e.g., interview quotes, focus group excerpts) with theoretical insights, as seen in grounded theory studies (Charmaz, 2014).
- **Emphasize Methodological Rigor:** Detail the research process, including data collection (e.g., interviews, social media analysis) and analysis (e.g., coding, constant comparison), to demonstrate transparency and trustworthiness (Myers & Newman, 2007).
- **Align with Journal Guidelines:** Follow the journal's formatting requirements, such as word limits, citation style (often APA in IS), and section structure (e.g., introduction, methods, findings, discussion) (Davison & Martinsons, 2011).
- **Highlight Contributions:** Clearly articulate the study's theoretical, practical, or methodological contributions, such as extending IS adoption theories or informing system design (Walsham, 1995). For instance, a manuscript on digital ethnography of online communities should use vivid data excerpts and a clear theoretical framework to engage readers. Tools like EndNote or Zotero can streamline citation management, while templates from journals ensure formatting compliance.

Navigating the Peer Review Process: Tips for Authors

The peer review process evaluates a manuscript's quality, rigor, and contribution, often involving multiple rounds of feedback. Tips for navigating this process include:

- **Understand Reviewer Expectations:** IS reviewers prioritize methodological clarity, theoretical novelty, and practical relevance. Ensure the manuscript addresses these, particularly for qualitative methods like content analysis or focus groups (Davison & Martinsons, 2011).
- **Prepare for Diverse Feedback:** Qualitative research may face scrutiny over generalizability or subjectivity; pre-empt this by justifying the study's context-specific insights, as in grounded theory's substantive theories (Charmaz, 2014).

- **Engage Constructively:** View reviewer comments as opportunities to strengthen the manuscript. Respond politely and systematically, addressing each point with evidence or revisions (Myers, 2013).
- **Seek Peer Input Pre-submission:** Share drafts with colleagues to identify weaknesses, enhancing clarity and robustness before submission (Walsham, 1995).

  For example, a study on virtual focus groups might receive feedback on participant diversity; authors should revise to clarify sampling rationale or acknowledge limitations. Patience and resilience are key, as reviews can take months and require significant revisions.

Ethical Considerations in Publishing Qualitative Research: Ensuring Integrity and Transparency

Ethical considerations are paramount in qualitative IS research to maintain integrity and trust. Key principles include:

- **Informed Consent and Anonymity:** Obtain consent from participants (e.g., interviewees, online community members) and anonymize data to protect privacy, especially in digital ethnography or social media analysis (Kozinets, 2015).
- **Transparency in Methods:** Clearly document data collection and analysis processes, such as coding schemes or focus group moderation, to ensure replicability and credibility (Myers & Newman, 2007).
- **Avoiding Plagiarism and Fabrication:** Use proper citations and original data, avoiding self-plagiarism or falsified findings, which undermine trust (Davison & Martinsons, 2011).
- **Ethical Use of Digital Data:** Address privacy concerns in social media or system log analysis, adhering to platform policies and ethical guidelines (Saldanha & Sahay, 2013). For instance, a study analyzing X (Twitter) data should disclose how user anonymity was preserved and obtain institutional review board (IRB) approval if required. Ethical lapses can lead to retractions or reputational damage, underscoring the need for rigorous standards.

Enhancing the Visibility and Impact of Qualitative Research Outputs

Maximizing the visibility and impact of qualitative IS research ensures it reaches academic, practitioner, and policy audiences. Strategies include:

- **Leverage Digital Platforms:** Share articles on platforms like ResearchGate, Academia.edu, or Twitter to reach broader audiences, particularly for studies on trending IS topics like artificial intelligence (AI) adoption (Myers, 2013).
- **Engage with Practitioners:** Translate findings into accessible formats, such as blogs or whitepapers, to inform IS professionals, as seen in case studies on system implementation (Walsham, 1995).

- **Present at Conferences:** Submit to IS conferences like ICIS or ECIS to gain feedback, network, and increase citations, enhancing the study's academic reach (Davison & Martinsons, 2011).
- **Use Altmetrics:** Monitor social media mentions or downloads to gauge impact beyond traditional citations, especially for OA articles (Saldanha & Sahay, 2013). For example, a focus group study on user trust in mobile apps could be shared via LinkedIn to engage developers, amplifying its practical impact. Visibility enhances the study's contribution to IS scholarship and practice.

Strategies for Addressing Reviewer Feedback and Revisions

Addressing reviewer feedback effectively is crucial for publication success. Strategies include:

- **Organize Feedback Systematically:** Categorize comments into major (e.g., methodological concerns) and minor (e.g., formatting issues) to prioritize revisions (Davison & Martinsons, 2011).
- **Respond with Clarity:** Provide a detailed response letter, mapping each comment to specific changes or justifying why changes were not made, maintaining a respectful tone (Myers, 2013).
- **Strengthen Weak Areas:** If reviewers question qualitative rigor, enhance sections on data triangulation or theoretical saturation, drawing on grounded theory principles (Charmaz, 2014).
- **Iterate with Care:** Revise thoughtfully to maintain the manuscript's coherence, avoiding over-revision that dilutes the original contribution (Walsham, 1995).

For instance, if reviewers critique a content analysis study's coding scheme, authors might include an inter-coder reliability test or clarify category definitions. Persistence and attention to detail improve acceptance chances.

Open Access Publishing: Benefits and Considerations for Qualitative Researchers

OA publishing, where articles are freely accessible online, is gaining traction in IS research. **Benefits** include:

- **Increased Visibility:** OA articles, published in journals like *Journal of Open Research Software*, reach wider audiences, boosting citations and impact (Suber, 2012).
- **Broader Accessibility:** Practitioners and policymakers can access findings without paywalls, enhancing practical relevance, as seen in studies on digital inclusion (Myers, 2013).
- **Funding Support:** Many institutions and funders, like the European Research Council, support OA through article processing charge (APC) waivers or grants (Suber, 2012).

Considerations include:

- **Cost:** APCs can be high, posing barriers for unfunded researchers, though waivers or institutional support may mitigate this (Davison & Martinsons, 2011).
- **Journal Quality:** Some OA journals lack rigorous peer review; researchers should prioritize reputable outlets like *PLOS ONE* or established IS journals with OA options (Suber, 2012).
- **Copyright and Licensing:** Understand Creative Commons licenses to ensure appropriate use and sharing of qualitative data (Saldanha & Sahay, 2013).

  For example, an OA article on virtual reality in IS training could attract global educators, but authors must verify the journal's credibility.

Publishing Qualitative Research in Interdisciplinary Journals: Challenges and Opportunities

Publishing in interdisciplinary journals, such as *Organization Science* or *Big Data & Society*, offers opportunities to bridge IS with fields like management, sociology, or data science. **Opportunities** include:

- **Broader Impact:** Interdisciplinary journals reach diverse audiences, amplifying the relevance of IS topics like AI ethics or digital transformation (Walsham, 1995).
- **Theoretical Enrichment:** Engaging with multiple disciplines, as in a study combining IS and organizational behavior, can strengthen theoretical contributions (Myers, 2013).

  Challenges include:
- **Methodological Misalignment:** Interdisciplinary reviewers may be unfamiliar with qualitative IS methods like digital ethnography, requiring clear justification (Kozinets, 2015).
- **Balancing Audiences:** Manuscripts must appeal to diverse readers, which may dilute IS-specific focus, such as technical system details (Davison & Martinsons, 2011).
- **Increased Competition:** Interdisciplinary journals attract submissions from multiple fields, raising acceptance thresholds (Walsham, 1995).

  For example, a study on social media's role in IS innovation might target *Big Data & Society* but needs to frame findings for sociologists and data scientists, balancing technical and social insights.

Future Trends and Innovations in Publishing Qualitative Research in Information Systems

The future of publishing qualitative IS research is shaped by technological and cultural shifts:

- **Digital Publishing Platforms:** Platforms like PubPub or Figshare enable interactive, multimedia publications, such as embedding focus group videos or coding visualizations, enhancing engagement (Suber, 2012).

- **AI-Assisted Publishing:** AI tools can assist in manuscript preparation, such as generating abstracts or suggesting keywords, but require human oversight to preserve qualitative nuance (Saldanha & Sahay, 2013).
- **Preprint Repositories:** Sharing preprints on arXiv or SSRN accelerates dissemination and feedback, particularly for emerging IS topics like blockchain (Myers, 2013).
- **Collaborative and Transparent Peer Review:** Open peer review models, adopted by some OA journals, increase transparency but may deter candid feedback (Davison & Martinsons, 2011).
- **Focus on Reproducibility:** Qualitative IS research is adopting standards like COREQ to document methods, enhancing credibility and aligning with grounded theory's auditability (Charmaz, 2014).

These trends promise greater accessibility and innovation but require researchers to adapt to new tools and ethical frameworks, ensuring qualitative depth is maintained.

Chapter Summary

Publishing qualitative research in IS is a multifaceted process that demands strategic planning, rigorous writing, and ethical integrity to achieve academic and practical impact. By selecting appropriate journals, crafting compelling manuscripts, and navigating peer review with resilience, researchers can effectively disseminate insights from methods like grounded theory, content analysis, or digital ethnography. Ethical considerations, such as transparency and data privacy, underpin trust in qualitative IS scholarship, while strategies like OA and interdisciplinary publishing enhance visibility and relevance. Future trends, including AI-assisted publishing and interactive platforms, offer exciting opportunities to innovate, but researchers must balance technological advancements with qualitative rigor. By mastering these elements, IS researchers can contribute robust, impactful theories that advance our understanding of technology's role in human and organizational contexts.

Review Questions

1 What strategies can qualitative IS researchers use to select an appropriate journal for a study on digital transformation? Discuss how factors like journal scope, methodological fit, and impact metrics influence the decision, and provide an example of a suitable journal.
2 How can qualitative IS researchers ensure methodological rigor and transparency in their manuscripts, particularly for methods like grounded theory or digital ethnography? Explain the role of detailed documentation and data presentation in meeting reviewer expectations.
3 Discuss the ethical considerations involved in publishing qualitative IS research that uses social media data. How can researchers balance

transparency and participant privacy, and what steps should they take to address potential ethical concerns?

4 Describe the process of addressing reviewer feedback for a qualitative IS manuscript, such as a focus group study on user acceptance of a new system. What strategies can authors use to respond constructively to major and minor comments while maintaining the manuscript's coherence?

5 Explore the benefits and challenges of OA publishing for qualitative IS research. How might publishing a study on AI ethics in an OA journal impact its visibility and accessibility, and what considerations should researchers keep in mind regarding costs and journal quality?

References

Charmaz, K. (2014). *Constructing Grounded Theory* (2nd ed.). SAGE Publications.

Davison, R. M., & Martinsons, M. G. (2011). Methodological practice and policy for organisationally and socially relevant IS research: An inclusive–exclusive perspective. *Journal of Information Technology, 26*(4), 288–293. https://doi.org/10.1057/jit.2011.18

Kozinets, R. V. (2015). *Netnography: Redefined* (2nd ed.). SAGE Publications.

Myers, M. D. (2013). *Qualitative Research in Business and Management* (2nd ed.). SAGE Publications.

Myers, M. D., & Newman, M. (2007). The qualitative interview in IS research: Examining the craft. *Information and Organization, 17*(1), 2–26. https://doi.org/10.1016/j.infoandorg.2006.11.001

Saldanha, G., & Sahay, S. (2013). Social media as a research environment: The rise of the digital agora. *European Journal of Information Systems, 22*(6), 671–684. https://doi.org/10.1057/ejis.2013.25

Suber, P. (2012). *Open Access*. MIT Press.

Walsham, G. (1995). Interpretive case studies in IS research: Nature and method. *European Journal of Information Systems, 4*(2), 74–81. https://doi.org/10.1057/ejis.1995.9

Index

Note: *Italicized* and **bold** pages refer to figures and tables respectively.